Praise from Britain for *George and Sam*

"Any parent will come away from the book with unqualified awe for [Moore's] reserves of love, patience, and the capacity to rewrite all expectations of family relationships." —*The Observer*

"Intelligent, admirably dispassionate. An unhysterical, thought-provoking portrait shot through with moments of unexpected humor." —Lucasta Miller, *The Daily Telegraph*

"What makes this book stand out from others along similar lines is that it is outstandingly well written . . . powerful and deeply affecting. Moore has written a vivid appreciation of her children, conveying her enjoyment of life with them as well as telling us about the more hair-raising aspects of her family life. This is a love story as well as a case history." —*The Guardian*

"Sparkling clarity, plenty of good advice, outstandingly well written. Powerful and deeply affecting." —*Mail on Sunday*

"[Moore] is wonderfully upbeat, funny, and completely without self-pity, and her work will be an inspiration to all those people—parents and professionals—who are brought face-to-face with the tragic and puzzling phenomenon of autism." —*Daily Mail*

"Wonderful . . . a remarkable book. It is compassionate, luminously intelligent, and wise. Charlotte Moore observes that the very marginal benefits of treatment cannot be extrapolated from George and Sam, never mind from n=1 to everyone. And this skepticism, along with her humanity and humor, may be the most important contribution to her brilliant book, which takes the currently fashionable genre of philosophy to new heights." —Raymond Tallis, *The Times Literary Supplement*

"Wonderful . . . [Moore's] account is always uncompromising, fantastically lucid, and wry. You finish her remarkable book enriched." —Alstaire Sooke, *The Telegraph*

"Extraordinary . . . For the parents of an autistic child, the author's observations, assessment of treatments, and practical advice should be essential reading. For those unaffected, it will be simply inspiring." —Julian Barnes, *Country Life*

"*George and Sam* . . . does a great public service by demystifying this most complex of disabilities. . . . She covers everything. One of Moore's great strengths is to provide a lucid analysis of the trials that an autistic child and his parents face while simultaneously telling her own story. [She] describes with great intelligence and necessary dark wit what it's like to enter the world of autism. Though she worries toward the end of the book that she has made life in an autistic family sound like hell, the fact is that she shows how the abnormalities of autism become a normal part of a family's everyday life, and how parental love knows no bounds." —Douglas Kennedy, *Mail on Sunday*

"The truly distinctive feature of *George and Sam* is its author's lack of self-pity. . . . Finely observed, well-researched, and elegantly written, *George and Sam* is full of insights into the mysteries of autism. 'Acceptance is all,' wrote Charlotte Moore in one of the newspaper columns from which this book originated. This simple yet profound message is what makes *George and Sam* such a valuable contribution to families affected by autism."

—*British Medical Journal*

George & Sam

Also by Charlotte Moore

George & Sam

TWO BOYS, ONE FAMILY,

AND AUTISM

Charlotte Moore

St. Martin's Press

New York

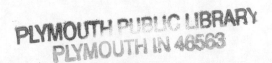

www.stmartins.com

Library of Congress Cataloging-in-Publication Data

Moore, Charlotte, 1959–
    George and Sam : two boys, one family, and autism / Charlotte Moore ; with a foreword by Nick Hornby.—1st St. Martin's Press ed.
        p. cm.
    Originally published: United States : Viking, 2004.
    ISBN-13: 978-0-312-35893-8
    ISBN-10: 0-312-35893-8
    1. Moore, Charlotte, 1959—Family. 2. Autism in children—Popular works.
3. Autistic children—Care. 4. Autistic children—Family relationships. I. Title.

RJ506.A9M665 2006
618.92'85882—dc22   2006012810

First published in Great Britain by Viking, an imprint of Penguin Books

First U.S. Edition: December 2006

10   9   8   7   6   5   4   3   2   1

For Jake
and
in memory of
Ruby Cruse
and
Mary Oliver,
who both loved the boys

Contents

Acknowledgments

As I hope this book makes clear, the quality of our family life depends on the goodwill of a large number of people, and I'm deeply grateful to them all.

This book came into being as a result of the "Mind the Gap" columns I wrote for the *Guardian*. Thanks to Alan Rusbridger for taking me on, and to Ian Katz and Matt Seaton for their help and encouragement. Thank you also to the many *Guardian* readers who wrote to me; their messages were invariably supportive and interesting. The idea for the book was shaped by my agent, David Godwin, and my editor, Tony Lacey. Many thanks to them and to everyone else at Viking who was involved. Thank you, too, to fellow parent Nick Hornby for his generous foreword, and to Thérèse Jolliffe for allowing me to quote from "Autism: A Personal Account" (Thérèse Jolliffe, Richard Lansdown, and Clive Robinson, *Communication* 26, National Autistic Society, December 1992).

Thank you to Saskia Baron for her patience and care when working with us on *The Autism Puzzle*. Making the documentary was integral to the book's progress. Thanks, also, to Kate Lithgow for her kindness in letting me use Crear, her beautiful Scottish retreat, to get some of the writing done.

The ASD (Autism Spectrum Disorder) staff at Torfield and Saxon Mount schools are too numerous to thank individually, but I'm grateful to them all. Thank you to Pat and the rest of the boys' taxi team. The generosity of the Paragon Trust has enabled me to run the boys' therapy programs; many thanks to them and to all the tutors past and present—at time of writing, they are Sue Lynch, Vikki Kindell, Mark Lovegrove, Andie Lawler, Jan Relf, Ian Bailey, and Delia Langham. Special thanks to Ian for keeping us all happy, and to Delia for years of incredible commitment and understanding.

Eva Littna did an enormous amount of work on the manuscript as well as putting in lots of time with the boys. Many thanks to her, and to Hilary Smith for babysitting above and beyond the call of duty. The boys and I have received a great deal of support from both sides of the family; warm thanks to all their grandparents, uncles, aunts, and cousins. Our friends, too, have been wonderfully tolerant and helpful. Thank you, all of you, and most especially Em, Chris, Sophie, and Iggy Clarke, and to Simon White for raising morale.

I'm grateful to all those who have shared their experiences of autism with me and in some cases allowed me to quote them. So many people have contributed to the boys' lives over the years—a big thank-you to all the neighbors, shopkeepers, doctors and dentists and their assistants, teaching staff, policemen, and members of the public who have had dealings with us. I hope you know who you are. Finally, thank you to Deirdre Hazell and Freda Catt for cleaning up after us!

Foreword

I'm guessing—I can't know for sure, of course, but this seems a reasonable supposition—that you have picked this book up, if not with a heavy heart, then with an oppressive sense of duty. Perhaps you have an autistic grandson or nephew—most autistic kids are boys—and you feel that the least you can do is to find out more about his condition, especially since you don't know him as well as you'd like to. (How can you, when he won't speak to you, or play with you, or possibly even be in the same room as you?) So maybe reading a book will help, somehow—will show that, even though you feel excluded from his world, you do care.

Or perhaps you are more directly affected; perhaps your own child is autistic, as mine is, in which case your need to read a book on the subject might feel more urgent. If the diagnosis has been recent, then you will almost certainly be desperate to know more. Maybe something in these pages will help to alleviate the panic you feel when you're told that your child has a condition for which there is no cure; indeed, maybe you're hoping that

George and Sam will tell you that there *is* a cure, contrary to all the information you've been given by health professionals. Books tend to need narratives, after all, and the most popular kind of narrative for books about disability is the kind that takes us from the darkness into the light, from despair to hope, from disaster to triumph.

It would be nice to think that there might be a third category of reader, too: some of you might want to read *George and Sam* in the same way that we all read *Wild Swans,* even though many of us had no burning interest in the history of China; or Claire Tomalin's book about Samuel Pepys, despite a long-held suspicion that Pepys's diaries might be on the dull side. Perhaps you read Charlotte Moore's brilliant columns about her autistic sons in the *Guardian;* if you did, then you'll already know that in the right hands, this subject, like all subjects, can be made to entertain, as well as educate and move. The nonfiction best-seller lists frequently prove that we all want to know more about everything, even if we didn't know that we wanted to know—we're just waiting for the right person to come along and tell us about it.

I have an autistic son, but even so, I would place myself in this last category of readers. Like a lot of people, I sense within me a reluctance to read books about disability. I think I'll end up feeling guilty, or hopeless, or manipulated, or just *bad.* (And there are so many disabilities—where does one start? Where, more to the point, does one *stop?*) And I particularly don't want to be made to feel bad precisely because I have an autistic son. As any parent in my situation will tell you, energy and optimism are precious commodities, not to be squandered, and certainly not on a book that describes a condition with which you are wearyingly familiar. So I hope you, and the author, will understand when I say that this is not the sort of book I would normally have chosen to read.

If you belong in the second category, I should tell you right now that Charlotte Moore offers no cure for autism, nor does she attempt to make you feel better about the huge chunk of bad luck that has fallen from a clear blue sky, like a chunk of frozen 747 urine, and landed right on your head. This is a clear-eyed observation of her sons and their behavior; she makes no attempt to sentimentalize them, and she certainly doesn't attempt to tell us that they are now, as she speaks, embarked on a program or a diet that will eventually take them to Cambridge or the Royal Academy of Dramatic Arts or 10 Downing Street. She knows that her sons are autistic, and will stay autistic, for the rest of their lives, unless there is some currently unimaginable scientific breakthrough. And as a consequence, I would say that this might be the only book you need to read about your child's condition. It tells you the things you will need to know—about education, and diet, and behavior modification, and sleep—but the advice is sensible and practical, rather than evangelical, and in any case it is not the point of the book. The point of *George and Sam* is to inform, yes, but also to entertain us and engross us and, like all the best books, to resonate.

I'm not sure I would have found it quite so entertaining a few years ago, when my son was first diagnosed. Nowadays, I'm used to glancing out of the kitchen window on a freezing November night and seeing a naked boy bouncing on a trampoline in the dark. It makes me laugh. (I don't *just* laugh, by the way, before anyone contacts Social Services. I go outside and get him in, too.) Back then, when I didn't understand Danny so well, and didn't really want to think about how his disability might affect me beyond the next few days, the naked trampolining would have alarmed and depressed me; it would have been yet another indication that my life as a parent was not the one I had anticipated.

This process of letting go is long and difficult, and I feel as though I'm right at the beginning of it. Charlotte Moore is, I suspect, right at the end, and there are very, very few parents who ever get there. And this is what makes *George and Sam* a great book: Moore's willingness (perhaps "ability" is the more appropriate word, because none of us is *willing* to give up the life we had planned for ourselves) to see her boys for what they are provides her with a unique perspective. Writing is as much about character as it is about talent, and Moore's character—her wryness and flexibility, her intelligence and her lack of judgmentalism, her lack of both self-pity and of self-aggrandizement—mean that she is ideally qualified to tell us this story in a way that hasn't been told before. She also has the advantage of having two autistic sons, rather than one. The word "advantage" can only really be applied to this particular project, the one you are holding in your hands; those of us who have one autistic child, and just about manage to keep our heads above the water (and even then not every day of the week), cannot really imagine life with two, even after Charlotte Moore has explained it to us. But what it does mean is that she resists extrapolation, because experience has taught her that you cannot really extrapolate with autistic children. No two autists are alike, and this is as true of their response to therapies and medication as it is of their behavior and abilities. Moore writes here of the improvement in George's behavior and language after receiving Auditory Integration Therapy; when Sam was given the same treatment, however, there was no discernible improvement. Lucky for us, in a way. Moore is much too sharp to write a whole book about AIT, but she might have been tempted had there been spectacular results in Sam's case, too. Plenty of other people have written whole books about diets and such like, and though they might help a minority of children, they will not help all, and they will be of absolutely no interest to a general reader. If no two autists are alike, then in George and Sam, Moore has access to a microcosmic world of autism.

George and Sam is painfully funny, in a way that is only possible because Moore has learned to appreciate and recognize what she's got in her three boys. (This book is about George and Sam, mostly, but Jake, her youngest, who is not autistic, provides her with all sorts of usefully contrasting material.) I once heard her describe George and Sam as "autistic through and through," meaning that, contrary to some fondly nurtured parental beliefs, there is no normal child trapped inside, waiting for release. That recognition enables her to look at her children with love and joy, rather than love and regret, to observe their behavior with a winning delight in its eccentricity. Where else will you read about a child so obsessed with white goods that visits to the launderette constitute a treat? Or a child who, for reasons best known to himself, wants everyone to pretend that he doesn't eat, even though he does? The weirdness, the sheer otherworldliness, of autistic thinking is a never-ending source of wonder and fascination—what does it say about them, and what does it say about us?—and Moore's laconic, unshowy narration provides the perfect setting.

I began by saying that the most popular books about disability take us from darkness into the light, and that this book didn't really follow that pattern. On reflection, this isn't strictly true, because *George and Sam* is luminous. True, it doesn't provide us with the kind of redemption that allows us to weep sentimental tears and then forget all about it (which, after all, is the unwitting function of many against-all-odds books). But it does ask—and, more impressively, answer—important questions, questions that apply to all of us: To what extent are we really prepared to accommodate our children? Are we properly equipped to love them the way they are? If our lives do not turn out the way we had hoped, what is the best way of living them? Do six After Eights constitute a decent breakfast? Charlotte Moore knows, but I'm not telling. You'll have to read this wonderful book to find out.

—Nick Hornby

George & Sam

Prologue

Monday morning. We're in a hurry—of course we are. Every working mother with three school-aged sons is in a hurry on a Monday morning.

George is nearly thirteen. The physical process of puberty is beginning, but he seems unaware of this, just as he's always been unaware of the effect his exceptional good looks have on people. He wanders into the kitchen, naked. He climbs on to the Aga and sits there twiddling a piece of cardboard. I send him to get dressed; his skin is red and mottled from the heat. He returns with all his clothes on the wrong way around. I fill a lunch box for eleven-year-old Sam. Plain crisps, gluten-free biscuits, marzipan, an apple that I know he won't eat, but I suppose I live in hope. George doesn't have a lunch box, because George maintains the fiction that he doesn't eat anything at all, and a lunch box is too blatant a reminder that this cannot be the case. I smuggle his food supplies—mainly Twiglets and chocolate—into his school taxi, underneath his swimming things.

I make George's breakfast—but I have to pretend it's not his breakfast. "I'm making this for Sam," I announce, pointedly. I toast two slices of rice bread; Sam's diet excludes wheat, oats, barley, rye, and all dairy products. I place them on two plates, which George has selected by sniffing. I spread Marmite in an even layer right up to the edge of the crusts, cut them into quarters, then busy myself elsewhere. George slips down from the Aga; as long as my back's turned, he'll risk the toast. "These are for Sam," he states as he starts to eat.

"Yes, they're for Sam," I confirm, without looking around.

Sam's always the last up. He's awake, but he's under his duvet, murmuring; his vocalization is somewhere between a hum and a chant, and is almost completely incomprehensible. He fingers the toy owl he's had since babyhood. The owl has no name, no character; Sam has never played with him, but then he's rarely played with any toy. The owl is a tactile comforter, not a friend.

Sam won't get up and dress until the taxi driver rings the doorbell. I did try ringing it myself, to get him moving, but Sam's not daft. He only fell for that once. And the dressing process can be infuriatingly slow. Pants on—pants off again. Shirt inside out—outside in—inside out once more. Six pairs of identical tracksuit trousers rejected—the seventh finally, mysteriously, acceptable. Socks stuffed down into the toes of his trainers, pulled out, stuffed in again. One step forward, two steps back—and endless little rituals about touching things and moving things in his bedroom. If I try to intervene, the whole process starts all over again.

At last he's dressed—no time for niceties like washing or brushing teeth. Now Sam has to get down the stairs all in one go. If anything blocks his way, or if he has a crisis of confidence halfway down, he'll freeze. He takes the stairs at a gallop, gets as far as the front door. I open the door for him. Mistake! Sam has to do

everything for himself. He opens and shuts the door six times before he can bring himself to leave the house. George's taxi arrives.
I note with pleasure that the toast has been eaten—but where is
George? In the lavatory of course, where he spends about a quarter of his waking hours. He emerges, and makes for the front
door—but wait, there's something odd about his gait. He's pulled
up his trousers, but forgotten about his pants. I ignore his protests,
hoick up his pants, waft a brush over his uncut hair, and propel him
toward the taxi. "Don't wave! Don't say goodbye!" he commands,
and hands me a fragment of candy wrapper to add to the collection that already covers the kitchen table. Two empty Fanta bottles, eight yellow lollipop sticks, silver foil, Softmint wrappers . . .
hoarding litter is George's latest obsession.

A call from the playroom reminds me of the existence of my
youngest child. *Blue Peter* has finished; Jake, four, wants his Ready
Brek. He chats as he eats; he'd like to meet Gareth Gates, he'd like
to be Young Sportsman of the Year. Have I found his reading book?
Can he have three kinds of sugar on his cereal?

I take Jake to the local primary school, where he is in kindergarten. He greets his friends on the way in, dismisses me with a
hug and a kiss. Neither George nor Sam ever embrace me in
greeting or salute.

As I leave, I peep through the window. Jake is cross-legged in
the middle of the group; he is listening to what the teacher has
to say. His hand shoots up. He's right in there, a proper schoolboy,
a social animal. He couldn't be more different from his older
brothers—but then, Jake's not autistic.

Eight o'clock. The day ought to be drawing to a close, but the
boys have several hours to go. I take Jake up to bed, leaving George
and Sam rampaging downstairs. I wonder what I'll find when I

return. Once, Sam emptied a gallon can of olive oil all over the kitchen floor. I have locks on all the cupboards now, but Sam is cunning, and good at finding keys. Will he eat a hundred vitamin pills, or put packets of butter into the oven, or throw plates into the trash, or fill the dollhouse bath with honey? All these have been done. Jake takes a good half hour to settle. His brothers make him nervous; he has to fall asleep with the light on and an adult beside him. Once he's truly asleep, I lock his door. That way, I know Sam can't leap on him if my vigilance slips for a moment.

As I leave Jake's room, I hear a familiar squeaking. It's Sam, barefoot, trampolining by moonlight. He throws his whole being into it; his intricate hand movements make it look as though he's casting spells; his habitual vocalization has become a throaty chuckle. This free, uninhibited, physical response is an aspect of autism I really like.

The boys still share a bath without a shred of self-consciousness. They have a close physical relationship. There's a deep bruise on George's arm, surrounded by a ring of tooth marks. I ask George about it. "It was Sam," he confirms without rancor. I notice some reciprocal pinches and scratches on Sam's thigh. Like most brothers, they fight, apparently to their mutual satisfaction.

The long evening progresses. George watches videos—*Bob the Builder, Bananas in Pyjamas,* things aimed at children a quarter of his age. Sam flits in and out, uttering incantations. I eat my supper and flick through the paper, thinking wistfully of the television I inevitably miss.

Bedtime at last. I read stories to George while Sam hums and whirrs. George wants the same stories he's liked since toddlerhood—Dr. Seuss, Beatrix Potter, "The Gingerbread Man." There's an unshakeable innocence about George that is attractive, but he'll soon be a teenager. Should I really still be reading him *Rumples and Tumbles Go to the Country*?

I switch off the light and lie down on the sofa between their two beds. I doze off with them—this is the best way of convincing them that the day really is over. I wake with a start at midnight, take a last look at their perfect sleeping faces, and go to unlock Jake. Then to my own bed, where I'll have about three hours before one or the other joins me there.

Does It Run in the Family?

I suppose every child regards its family life as normal. It's only in adulthood that we reassess the things we took for granted. Certainly, nothing in my stable, effortless childhood prefigured the position I would find myself in as an adult—a single mother of three sons, two of them autistic.

I live in the house where I grew up. It's an overgrown Sussex farmhouse with a large untidy garden. When my grandfather died, my parents moved in, on April 1, 1960—my first birthday. Thirty years later, I moved back there with my husband, Min, and George, then six months old.

The house hasn't changed much since the 1960s; the externals of George and Sam's childhood experiences are similar to mine. They sleep in the room I once shared with my brothers, and the dragons, sea lions, and goldfish painted on the walls by my aunts look down on them as they once looked down on us. The kitchen is still dominated by an inefficient Aga; the crumbling garden walls are still there for them to risk their necks, as my brothers and I used to. We walk through the same fields, splash in the same streams. As the boys lie in bed they hear the sounds I always heard, the creaks and rustlings of an old and drafty house, the train rumbling through the valley, the crooning of wood pigeons in the big yew tree outside.

Yet internally, their childhoods could hardly be more different from mine. George and Sam's experiences are disparate, unconnected, a series of sensory impressions that don't add up to make a pattern. When I lay in bed and listened to the train, I imagined dragons. I knew that dragons didn't exist, but I chose to tell myself stories about dragons; I involved the painted dragons on the wall in these stories. I knew that the noise was the London train, the one my father took to work each day. There was no confusion in my mind between the real and the pretend worlds, and to me, both made sense. I'll never know, because they can't tell me, but I believe that, for George and Sam, neither makes sense. When you're autistic, *everything* is experienced differently. The assumptions and explanations of the people around you are of very little help.

There were three of us children. Charles is two years older than me and Rowan two years younger. We were bookish and unsporty; Charles was quite tough and adventurous; Rowan and I were rather weedy. We went to the village primary school and brought friends home to play. We kept a great many animals. We made dens in the woods behind our house. We quarreled fiercely over Racing Demon, Pit, and Monopoly. When we weren't fighting, we played elaborate imaginative games based on invented worlds. Rowan and I ruled jointly over the whimsically named Land of Nursery. Rowan's responsibility was primarily for organizing building programs, controlling civil wars, and colonizing outlying regions with his Hornby train set, while I concerned myself with social and domestic dramas. Charles's country, the United Moore Republic, was more austere. It was a military dictatorship with no female inhabitants.

These invented worlds were not retreats for us. They were shared. They were not a substitute for real life but an extension of life, a rehearsal for what would concern us as adults. We moved freely in and out of one another's games, though we bickered as we did so. None of us, in other words, exhibited the autistic "triad of impairments"—of imagination, communication, and social interaction.

Play of this kind hardly exists for George and Sam. They have many toys, but few of them are put to their intended use. Their play is limited, end-stopped, and—above all—unshared. George, aged thirteen, went off to school this morning clutching three toy tank engines. He likes these engines, will move them about a bit and give them a few snatches of dialogue—lifted from his Thomas the Tank Engine videos—but he has no intention of inviting other children to join him in playing with them. If another child initiated a game, George wouldn't know how to reciprocate. If anyone suggested that he was too old to be playing with tank engines, he wouldn't know what that person meant. Sam's play, such as it is, is even more private, because it's largely nonverbal. It's hard to tell, even, whether he is actually playing in an imaginative sense at all, or whether he's just making movements and noises for their own sake.

For me, the life of the playground was by far the most important and interesting part of school; for George and Sam, outside "play" is just existing in fresh air. I was deeply involved in an ever-shifting network of friendships and alliances; my sons have no independent social life, nor do they appear to want one. Each day, they go to an autistic unit attached to a special-needs school in

Hastings. George is interested in the other children, probably regards them as his friends, and has occasionally asked me to invite
them home, but it would never occur to him to ring them up or
invite them himself. Sam seems barely aware that the other children exist. As far as I can tell, neither of them imagines that they
will not be at school forever. They have no ambition, no thoughts
about their adult selves, no perspective on anything except the
here and now. The contrast between my experience of being a
child and theirs could hardly be greater.

When, after George and Sam had been diagnosed, Min and I
needed to decide whether to risk having another baby, we went to
the Maudsley Hospital for "genetic counseling." It's now generally accepted that autism has genetic causes, that it does "run in
families." The picture is somewhat obscured by the fact that, due
to the antisocial nature of the condition, full-blown autists are
much less likely than almost any other group to become parents
themselves. In preparation for the consultation we were asked to
note down any family members who were eccentric, depressive,
obsessive-compulsive, schizophrenic, even dyslexic—and of course,
any who were actually autistic.

My family has lived in the same place for a long time. They have
always been great letter-writers and recorders of information, they
have been socially stable, their lives have not been hugely disrupted
by war or disaster, and none of them ever throw anything away.
All this means that I can tell you a very great deal about my family for several generations. Don't worry, I won't—not much. But
my report for the Maudsley was pretty comprehensive. I came up
with some cases of mild depression, one obsessive-compulsive, no
dyslexia. Lots and lots of left-handers—I'm not sure if that's relevant. No schizophrenics, and no confirmed autists—and absolutely

no one who wasn't able to lead a normal life, if by that one means marrying, holding down a job, maintaining friendships, bringing up children.

There are eccentricities, as there probably are in most families. In my case, they cluster most markedly around my paternal grandfather, the one who died when I was a baby. Grandfather had extreme food fads. He abhorred fat of any kind and couldn't bear people to eat butter or cheese anywhere near him. Although he was a kind man, he imposed his fussiness on his forbearing wife— family meals were utterly plain and monotonous. He made up his mind about something, and never changed it. "In 1898," he remarked, "I ate an apple that I *almost* liked."

Grandfather took comfort in familiar objects. When he went to boarding school, in 1894, he had a dressing gown—"the New Dressing Gown." In 1959, during his final illness, the hired nurse threw the New Dressing Gown away. My mother is convinced this hastened his end.

Grandfather kept a diary for every day of his adult life. It is a startlingly un-intimate record. If you want to know about Welsh miners' strikes in 1919, or the times of trains from London to Chatham, then Grandfather's your man. He recorded the weather every single day. This is not so odd, given that his great love was the sea and sailing ships, but less easy to explain is his habit of recording the life span of each of his razor blades. It is hard to come up with a better example of "autistic" information: "12 February 1932. This morning I discarded my razor blade, after 86 days of use." The fact is recorded purely for its own sake. It has no resonance, no wider context.

Grandfather was a literal-minded man. He argued against the existence of angels, because in order to support their wings they would have to have a breastbone twelve feet deep. Going to the cinema with him was agony, says my aunt, because inaccuracies enraged him. "That's not a man-of-war. Where are the puttock shrouds?" he would demand of the luckless usherette. "How can you show such nonsense in your cinema?" He talked to everyone in the same way, making no allowances for education, age, class, or show of interest. The local policeman once called in, to inquire about a shotgun license, and was found in the drawing room, imprisoned by politeness, while my grandfather read him extracts from Swift's *Journal to Stella*.

This last characteristic was admired. He was a polite man, except when exasperated by inaccuracies of rigging, and most people felt flattered by the way he discoursed with them. My grandfather's eccentricities were generally seen as harmless and endearing, though for his children irritation and embarrassment also played a part. His Pavlovian response to the sound of the hornpipe caused my poor aunt acute distress—when he heard it played by Battle Town Band, he danced the length of the High Street. At the theater, once, he was in a box, and wanted to make contact with his companions who were seated below, so he turned his program into a paper airplane and threw it down to them midperformance. He had no fear of heights (a common autistic trait) and loved walking round the tops of factory chimneys or the battlements of Bodiam Castle. He delighted in disregarding the sign at the railway station that said "Passengers must not cross the line." "I'm not a passenger," he would proclaim with autistic pedantry as he skipped across the tracks.

All this makes him sound like a classic case of undiagnosed Asperger's syndrome. And yet there is plenty of evidence in the opposite direction. His marriage was happy and stable, though perhaps this says more about my grandmother, who was by all accounts a particularly loving, humorous, and tolerant woman, than it says about him. He was an affectionate and interested father; he wrote "baby books" about each of his four children, recording funny remarks and charming habits as well as statistics about teeth and weight. He maintained several lifelong friendships, and seems to have enjoyed socializing. Following his father's wishes, he became a doctor. For himself, he would have preferred a maritime career. He became the medical officer of health to Battle Rural District Council and wrote detailed and sympathetic notes about the diseases—rickets, TB, scarlet fever, diphtheria—that he encountered in the cottages of the poor. But at times his sense of medical priorities was not all it might have been. During the Second World War, he was asked to give lectures on first aid to volunteer nurses. My aunt popped in on the fourth of eight lectures to see how things were progressing. The young trainees were earnestly taking notes on the causes and spread of the Black Death.

Though Grandfather seems to have been closer to autism than other members of my family, he was far from being a diagnosable case. What of my sons' father's family? Are there any genetic clues to be found?

The Smiths—Min's father's family—came from Birmingham, and hadn't moved about very much, so we know a fair amount about the last three generations. But Min's mother, Eva, didn't know her father. He was a Czech architect who died of cancer, and we don't know much more than that. Eva's mother, Elvira, came from a highly educated Hungarian family—Jewish, but they'd given up practicing. There were mental health problems—Elvira's older sister committed suicide—but, with most of the family in concentration camps, there were mitigating circumstances.

It's hard to disentangle Elvira's innate psychological makeup from the historical circumstances in which she found herself. She was a great survivor. She escaped to England before the beginning of the war, and because she was pregnant with Eva she was able to remain here. She had a second child, Marina, and she left the girls in a series of boarding schools and orphanages while she struggled to make a living. She was a single mother; she married three times, but the marriages were all short-lived. It would be interesting to know whether she felt guilt about leaving the children, because guilt is a very nonautistic emotion. I wonder, too, whether she experienced the less rational guilt at being one of the family members to avoid the camps.

By the time I knew Nana, as we always called Elvira, she was an active old woman, furiously resisting old age, and very, very preoccupied with herself. As with my grandfather, it would be stretching a point to place Nana on the autistic spectrum, but there were certain characteristics . . . like my grandfather, she talked in exactly the same way about exactly the same things to whoever she met. She had a fund of interesting stories—she had friends who were well-known artists and writers—but because she never paid attention to anyone else, she rarely added new ones, and she didn't attempt to remember whether she'd told them to you before. She was always pleased to see me, but I never got the impression that she knew me at all.

Nana was academically able. She had trained as a lawyer, spoke seven languages, and became the successful headmistress of an approved school. But when she read, or talked, she seemed interested only in finding evidence to confirm what she already thought about things. She never modified anything—her opinions, her manner, her appearance—to suit her circumstances. Her liveliness and force of character gave the impression that she was a sociable person, a "party animal," but the impression was a false one. She was, I think, very much alone.

George couldn't bear Nana. She died just a month or so before his autism was diagnosed, and I regret that I was never able to explain away his tearful, clinging behavior when she came to visit. Nana had a deep, resonant, heavily accented voice. She had been a very good-looking woman; in her seventies, she still wore plunging necklines, high heels, and masses of clanky jewelry. She would pick her way across our muddy garden in sling-back stilettos and mink coat, utterly failing, as an autist would, to adapt to circumstances. We told her, as politely as we could, that her dramatic gestures, overinsistent hugs, and elaborately presented gifts were all frightening for George, but she could not take this in.

Could Nana possibly have been autistic? She had many eccentricities. She would remove food from the table and take it home in her handbag, and she was incapable of buying anything new— for Christmas I once received a box of bath salts with a pre-decimal price tag. She rarely—as far as I could see—ate a proper meal, but created strange concoctions; I remember broken-up Ryvita mixed with quantities of neat tomato purée, and bags and bags of raw carrots. It would be feasible, however, to attribute this behavior to the trauma of her experiences as a refugee. Other peculiarities, like the fact that she was unsure which part of the ear to attach clip-on earrings to, are more obviously reminiscent of the syndrome. There was something false about Nana, but not false as in scheming. It was as if she had constructed a whole persona to carry her through life, because despite her apparent sophistication, she didn't really seem to understand the way the world worked.

I'm sure other members of the family, reading this, will protest vigorously. "Nana autistic? What nonsense!" And certainly I would never have come up with such a theory if George and Sam's condition hadn't encouraged me to subject their forbears to intense scrutiny. On the Smith side, their father's father's family, there seems at first sight to be nothing. The Smiths were a straightforward bunch who worked hard, moved up in the world, married and had children, enjoyed participating in sport, and were reasonably socially active. Several of them were successful salesmen, which suggests a nonautistic ability to observe and predict human behavior. But then there was Cousin Artie. Cousin Artie was a pretty remote connection—Grandfather Clive's second cousin. He died a long time ago. But it is significant that, despite his remoteness, stories are still remembered about him. Artie was very intelligent, with an amazing memory for facts, but he never made the success of himself that people expected. He never married; he lived alone, sweeping up dust and storing it in jars, doing without crockery—he used an old sardine can as a dish—and burying his money in the garden. Cousin Artie had an even less accessible brother, Cousin Victor, who committed suicide. Depression and suicide are common among high-functioning autists and people with Asperger's syndrome, particularly when their condition is undiagnosed.

Our trawl through family history threw up poor long-dead Artie as the closest thing to a full-blown autist. Arguably the examination of any family could reveal such a character. Why did Min and I produce George and Sam? Did the eccentricities in both our gene pools combine to produce exactly the right ingredients for autism? People have often asked me, why have you got two? And the only accurate reply is, I don't know. In a way, it doesn't really matter. I've never raged against fate, or cast about much for explanations. Nothing in my own childhood experience led me to expect that anything would be "wrong" with my children, but then there they were, and—well, you just get on with it.

The Maudsley estimated our chances of having a third autistic child as one in twenty. There was a much higher chance—one in six—of the child having a minor learning problem—being a slow reader was the kind of example they cited. If the child was male, the "danger" was much greater, so of course we hoped Jake would be a girl. I found out that he wasn't halfway through the pregnancy. There was a little scare—the midwife couldn't find the heartbeat—and I was rushed off to hospital for an extra scan. The heartbeat was swiftly located, and so were the genitals. "Do you want to know?" asked the nurse. I hadn't thought I did, but suddenly it made sense to get the disappointment of the new baby's gender out of the way before the birth itself. So the anxiously waiting extended family had several months to get used to the idea that I would have a third boy.

Five years later, the worry seems extraordinary. Jake is not only not autistic, he's the least disappointing child it's possible to imagine.

TWO

The Wonderbaby

George wasn't my first baby. There was another, who would now be fourteen. Min and I married in 1987, and in the autumn of 1988 we were living in a rented flat in Maida Vale. Min worked at home, writing children's books. I was an English teacher. We both very much wanted a baby, but I don't think we imagined that having one would make an enormous difference to our lives. I certainly intended to carry on working full-time. Min would look after it, supplemented by some kind of au pair, or perhaps a day nursery. That was the idea. It seems that we didn't think about it very hard.

I was twenty-nine, healthy and energetic. I became pregnant the minute I wanted to, and felt fine—the odd surge of nausea, nothing more. I sailed through the first three months, eating well, cutting alcohol down to the occasional glass of wine. I was entirely confident about this pregnancy. The first ultrasound scan was booked for the eighteenth week of pregnancy in the middle of January. We went to the old Westminster Hospital, dingy and old-fashioned, with people shuffling along the corridors and smoking and coughing their guts out. Min and I waited with other parents-to-be for the first exciting glimpse of our baby. I drank cup after polystyrene cup of water; a full bladder makes the scan easier to read.

Neither of us had seen an ultrasound image before. I lay on my back, staring at the screen, unable to interpret the swirls and loops that met and parted like oil on water. The nurse doing the scanning passed the monitor back and forth, back and forth over my stomach, not looking at me, intent on the image. "I'm afraid I can't see all of it. Could you wait outside, to give Baby a chance to turn round?" I had no misgivings. We sat on the bench outside, cracking jokes. Perhaps I hadn't drunk enough water? I refilled my polystyrene cup.

We were called back in. Now, there were several more white-coated people in the room. A more senior-looking woman took over the scanning. Nobody said much, and it seemed to me that they were avoiding my eyes. I began to feel alarmed, but still I couldn't make much sense of what I saw on the screen.

The doctor sighed, and turned to me. My baby had no legs, and only half an arm. The head and torso looked normal, but the scanner wasn't sufficiently accurate to rule out further damage. She pointed out the relevant detail on the screen. Suddenly I saw it all. There was the baby, round-headed, jaunty, its half-arm raised like a little flag.

The hospital staff were kind and helpful. They introduced the idea of termination as an option. But they put no pressure on us. They wouldn't let us make any decision right away. It was a Thursday—we were to come back on Monday for a consultation.

Min was sure that termination was best. I wasn't. I had lots of experience with disabled people; I had friends in wheelchairs due to spina bifida or cerebral palsy. They were all opposed to abortion—well, you would be, wouldn't you? Who would wish themselves undone?

Disability had no horror for me. Before the scan, I would have said, "Oh, I'll keep any child, whatever it's like." But when I saw that baby twirling around in the only environment in which it would ever be wholly comfortable, I thought, if you keep this child, you're asking it to be a hero, and is that fair?

Min's certainty helped me to decide. Ironically, in view of our eventual separation, I worried that keeping the baby would put our marriage under pressure. We settled for termination. In my childhood I had kept a great many cats. If a kitten was born with any kind of deformity, the mother cat would quickly destroy it. I do know that humans are not the same as cats, but I found the memory helpful.

The pregnancy had passed the stage where a simple evacuation could be carried out, so labor had to be induced. It was expected to take twelve hours. After forty-eight hours of fruitless labor I was given a general anesthetic and the baby was removed while I was unconscious.

Throughout the labor I was given shots of Demerol, which made me feel most unlike myself; I always refused it during my subsequent labors. Every now and then I would be lifted up and told to push, but nothing happened. I dreaded seeing the baby, but at the same time I wanted to; it is a great regret to me that I never did. When I came around from the anesthetic I asked to see him (the baby was almost certainly a boy), but the kind nurse said, "Baby's not looking his best, dear." Later I discovered what she meant; the baby had gotten stuck, and had to be cut up to be removed.

The hospital was fairly grotty, but the nurses were excellent. The sister canceled her day off so she could see me through to the end. Another very young nurse sat with me talking in the early hours, after the baby had gone. "Everyone deserves to have a baby," she said. That struck me as profoundly true. I think it still does.

One reason I had wanted to see the baby was to convince myself of the reality of what had happened. I've been appalled, since, to read about the widespread use of general anesthetic during childbirth in North America in the 1950s and 1960s. If you're unconscious when you give birth, how much harder it must be to accept the child as really, truly yours. I was given a scan photo to keep, which was helpful. In irrational moments, when I began to worry that I had ended the life of a perfectly healthy child, I could look at the photo, which showed clearly that there were absolutely no legs. I was young and fit, and I recovered quickly. By April, I was ready to conceive again. George was soon on his way, due exactly a year after the date of the termination.

The limbless baby hadn't shaken my confidence. It felt like a random piece of bad luck. No one came up with a reason for it. "We don't keep data on this kind of thing," said the consultant, "because it's so extremely rare. Actually, we had a lady in here a few weeks ago with something similar . . ." If anything, that disaster made me feel all the more certain that my next baby would be absolutely fine.

Again, the pregnancy was straightforward, almost symptomless. I had more ultrasound scans than usual—five or six in all, the first at only eight weeks. They reassured me that this baby was physically complete, but in later years I worried—could ultrasound possibly trigger autism? The incidence of autism was rising; ultrasound was a newish procedure to which the entire neonatal population was subjected. Could there be a link? I've never come across any scientific support for this idea, though ultrasound has been blamed for other problems. I still don't feel happy about bombarding tiny fetuses with rays, and tried, unsuccessfully, to prevent Jake from being scanned more than once. But this was a long way in the future. At the time, I just enjoyed watching the prawnlike George shifting the four white dots that were his limbs in miniature boxing movements.

We didn't want to know George's gender and were not clever enough at reading scans to detect it. I felt sure that I was going to have a girl—a girl with hair. I felt confident that I would have an easy, natural birth. I was remarkably unworried about the whole business, though I do remember being given a little romper suit early on in the pregnancy, and really not wanting it. It seemed to be tempting fate, to possess clothes for a baby who was so very far off being born.

On January 25, 1990—ten days after my due date—I was seized by a great restlessness, a manifestation of that same impulse that drives pregnant cats to turn circles inside laundry baskets and unfeasibly small cardboard boxes. Cold winds were twisting dry leaves into whirlpools on the pavements of Maida Vale; I'd invited a friend—just one—to supper, so I waddled to the shops and saw fit to buy five pounds of stewing steak, five pounds of potatoes, and a quantity of suet. On the return journey, the wind blew into a gale; the carrier bags cut into my hands; my bump was vast. Every few steps I had to stop and realign my various burdens. Back at home, I unpacked the meat and felt sick. I lowered myself into a hot bath and felt even sicker.

I paced the flat, leaning on the backs of chairs, and punctuating the day with mugs of tea. I've yet to see a convincing portrayal of a woman in labor on television or at the cinema. In my experience there's no sudden stab of pain, no rolling of eyes and clutching of bed rails. For me, it's a slow buildup of pressure, like being squeezed by a giant elastic band.

By late afternoon I was throwing up. That's a feature of labor that Hollywood doesn't dwell on—I vomited constantly throughout all mine. I rang my friend Richard and said perhaps he shouldn't come to supper after all. I never did find out what happened to all that meat.

At about seven in the evening we set off for Saint Mary's, Paddington. It was a short drive, but the stormy weather meant that the traffic crawled along. I was of course convinced that my baby would be born in the car. I needn't have worried; I still had fifteen hours to go.

Saint Mary's is a famous hospital, but I was unimpressed. There was no attempt at continuity of care. I was examined by several different people (and, during labor, internal examinations are THE most painful thing). None of them seemed to pass on any information to the others, and all of them failed to realize that George was in the posterior position—lying spine to spine with me, and "presenting" with his face rather than the crown of his head, which usually means a longer and more difficult labor. The delivery room was cramped and lightless, and the sound-proofing poor. I could hear a woman screaming and wailing, heartbroken. I longed to ask what had happened to her baby, but I didn't dare.

I'd written a long "birth plan"; I didn't want an epidural, De-merol, or my waters broken—I didn't want any intervention at all. I was extraordinarily confident that I wouldn't need any. And when, at first examination, they told me I was already five centimeters dilated, I was jubilant. "You'll have your baby by midnight," I was told. But midnight came and went, and George was well and truly stuck. Yes, I was fully dilated, but nothing was happening. They attached me to a drip, to speed things up. They broke my waters with one of those horrible crochet hooks. They clipped a monitor to George's unborn scalp to measure his distress. A midwife with sweaty armpits and a heavy cold flumped clumsily down on my bed; the jolt was agony. Because of the drip and monitor, I wasn't allowed to get off the bed. This was the worst thing; never in my life have I so much wanted to move about.

The night wore on—high winds and screaming women. My birth plan was looking increasingly like an elaborate fantasy. Still, no one had realized that George was in the wrong position. Dawn broke. A resident appeared and ordered an epidural. He wanted to do a cesarean, but George was too far down. If he'd suggested cutting me open with a rusty saw, I'd have welcomed it. I didn't care about anything, certainly not the baby. I just wanted the whole process to come to an end.

The epidural was set up. The pain vanished; I was laughing and joking. They tried to suck George out with the ventouse, but it kept popping off his head, sending the resident reeling backward across the floor. They made a huge cut and inserted the forceps—the giant salad servers. I was flat on my back, with my legs in stirrups; I couldn't see what was going on, but I could see that Min was looking a bit green. The storm was over. The small window was full of bright sunlight. At ten in the morning of January 26, George was hauled out. He was small and thin—only six pounds five ounces, despite being ten days late. He was streaked with meconium, the blackish green tarry stuff that new babies have in their bowels, and which they void all over the place if they are distressed. George was very distressed. He was held up to me, cord still attached—bloody, muddy, with a furious bald head and the most enormous ears. This was not the dainty prewashed girl with hair I'd been envisaging for nine months. They laid him on my stomach; he was writhing and slippery, and I squealed, not with delight. His Apgar scores—a series of checks on the newborn's pulse, heartbeat, breathing, skin tone, and so on—weren't great, so they put him on a machine to clear out his tubes. I mistook the whine of the machine for his newborn voice. They wiped him a bit, wrapped him up, and gave him to me to be put to the breast. "He's beautiful," said the nurse. I looked at her in astonishment. "Well," she said, "you should see the one next door."

The top of poor little George's head was a tender purple cap, from the suction of the ventouse. Red looping marks from the forceps were clearly visible on his cheeks. He had scaly skin, a large nose covered in tiny white spots, white-and-purple fists, and large, bright, widely spaced eyes. Those eyes, as I was soon to discover, rarely closed. Right from the start George was vigilant, alert.

He suckled eagerly. I lay there nursing him while the resident tidied me up. Then we were wheeled off to the ward. Both George and Sam were born in subterranean delivery rooms; with both of them, the journey upward to the ward felt like another kind of deliverance. With Sam, I remember my mother walking beside the trolley, telling me that Terry Waite had just been released, and the news seemed appropriate.

I was lifted into bed, because the epidural hadn't worn off and I couldn't stand. George was put in a crib by my side, maddeningly out of reach. I could hardly move. I'd had dozens of stitches and felt extremely weak. One of the other mothers, a tall Jamaican woman with a tiny dry-skinned baby for whom she'd provided a giant tub of Vaseline, astonished me by lifting her large suitcase onto her bed herself. She saw how feeble I was, and walked the crying George up and down for me. Then she tucked him into bed with me. I was very grateful. I didn't want George in the crib. A baby—a little girl called, I think, Alexandra—had been snatched from a hospital by a woman posing as a social worker or something similar. We new mothers followed the story with anxious attention. Alexandra was found, alive and well, after a few days. There have been several similar stories since; I always like to keep my newborns in bed with me.

I have often heard autistic people described, sometimes by themselves, as aliens, visitors from another planet. That's certainly how

George felt to me for the first few days of his life. Was that because I sensed his otherness, or was it just a pretty normal reaction to the shock of a new baby and a difficult birth? I looked at George with wonder and deep, deep interest, but it wasn't, immediately, love.

Research suggests that babies who later turn out to be autistic have often had a difficult birth. The first assumption would be that the child has been damaged by the process; perhaps the supply of oxygen to the brain was interrupted. But then, what of the countless normal children who have also endured difficult births, and who seem unaffected? And though my labors with George and Sam weren't straightforward, neither were they emergencies. I've heard of far, far worse.

There's another theory about "autistic" births, which sounds quite plausible to me. This theory suggests that the autism is already active, as it were, prenatally. The difficult delivery is the result of the baby's failure to cooperate with the birthing process. Already, the baby's instincts are somehow awry. This idea made much more sense to me after I'd had Jake. With George and Sam, nothing that happened during labor made much sense. They were both in the wrong position with the cord wrapped around their neck, and neither of them was going to get born on his own. With nonautistic Jake, it was all quite, quite different. His labor took four hours and was utterly straightforward. I had no pain relief at all, not even a whiff of gas and air. I had no stitches, and very little bleeding. Of course it hurt, but it was the kind of pain that made sense. Giving birth to Jake was an active process, not a passive one; it really did feel as if both he and I knew what we were doing. I actually enjoyed it.

George stayed awake all of that first day. A crowd of visitors arrived. He was passed around, and he stared at them all with his big thunder-colored eyes. When night fell and the visitors left, I thought perhaps he'd sleep, but I was wrong. He cried all night. I suckled

him and cuddled him, but he went on crying. I rang the bell for the
night nurse. She was grumpy. "Change his nappy," she ordered. She
didn't offer to do it herself. I couldn't possibly change his nappy—I
could hardly sit up. And besides, I felt that George's woe was for
something far more profound than the need for a new nappy.

Things improved, as they always do. I stayed in hospital for five
days—quite a long time, but I had been fairly knocked about—and
by the end of it George and I were both a lot more cheerful. We
were surrounded by a wall of flowers and cards, and George had
plenty of admirers. The need to have people admire your baby is
strong, especially with your first. The girl in the bed opposite was
only about sixteen. She had no flowers, just one pink balloon, saying, "It's a girl," tied to the foot of her bed. Her shaven-headed
boyfriend came to visit her; they had nothing to say to each other.
The baby was called Stephanie. When they left hospital, they
were going to live in a B and B.

I knew I was lucky, and soon I began to feel lucky. George was
healthy and gained weight fast. The scars and bruises faded. He
was obviously very bright—everyone said so. He fixed his attention on faces and objects for long periods; he focused very well.
He was excited by anything red—and, thirteen years later, he still
is. He would vibrate with pleasure at the sight of a teddy with a
red bow. I don't know why the experts insist that new babies can't
see color, when they so clearly can.

George was breast-fed. It never crossed my mind that he
wouldn't be. Nor had it occurred to me that breast-feeding would
be anything other than a completely easy process, like turning on a
tap. It was quite a blow to discover that I found it difficult, uncomfortable, boring, and not hugely rewarding. There are pleasures—
the tiny face guzzling away is a very sweet sight, and the steady
weight gain, all your own work, is satisfying. But though I remained

a committed breast-feeder—I fed Jake until he was twenty months, by which time he was saying things on crowded commuter trains like "Other side now, please, Mummy"—I can't say it was ever my favorite aspect of motherhood.

The midwives and health visitors encouraged demand feeding. The idea is that the baby takes what he needs, and the mother's supply adjusts accordingly. You are meant to achieve a perfect balance. It's a far cry from the only-every-four-hours-and-don't-you-dare-touch-him-in-between-times rule imposed on my mother's generation.

Demand feeding makes sense to me—in fact it's the only option for me, since I find it impossible to ignore a crying baby. But in those early weeks a "perfect balance" did not seem to be what George and I were achieving. George wanted to feed *all* the time. He would feed for ages, fixing me all the while with his gimlet eye. If I did anything other than return his gaze, he would stop sucking and cry. Other mothers have told me how breast-feeding allowed them to read the whole of Proust, or George Eliot, or at least watch lots of telly, but I could do none of these things. George was, and is, a very controlling child.

Poor eye contact is one of the distinguishing features of autism, yet in those days George couldn't get enough of it. Not just with me, either—his father, friends and relations, people in shops . . . George has large, bright eyes, beautifully shaped—gray-blue, with long curling black lashes. They have a Slavic slant in the corners; it is hard to deny the impression they give of sensitivity and intelligence. Nowadays he finds prolonged eye contact difficult—"Don't look at me! Look at Sam! Look at that cupboard!" But as a baby he went to the other extreme. His desire for eye contact seemed to go with his need to be held upright—he hated lying flat. He wanted to know what was going on; he sought stimuli of all kinds, particu-

larly visual stimuli. A psychologist later described him as "overvigilant," and I think that's about right.

For the first three weeks of his life he never slept for more than
an hour and a half at a stretch. That meant that I didn't, either—
George seemed to thrive on this regime, or nonregime, but I did
not. The health visitor called. "Get him a pacifier," she ordered;
"otherwise, you will die." Health visitors can be very useful people. With that pronouncement she cut away all my middle-class
disdain. "He's a sucky baby," she said. "Some of them just are. He's
using you as a dummy, so you may as well get him one." Min raced
to the chemists round the corner and came back with a fistful of
pacifiers. He inserted one. Silence, and rest. I fell asleep at once.
George didn't wake for three hours. When I woke, I felt as if I had
been on a Caribbean cruise.

Why do people persist in believing Locke's idea that a baby is
a blank slate? Surely only a man could have come up with that.
As every mother knows, a baby is a slate with a great many things
already written on it. In George's case, most of them were inde-
cipherable, but "I like putting things in my mouth" was up there
in large, clear letters. It has never been rubbed off. All babies
explore objects with their mouths; the lips and tongue are even
more useful than the fingers for examining the peculiar properties
of something new. With most babies, mouthing peaks at about
ten months and fades out during toddlerhood, as the child finds
a variety of other ways to find out about his environment. With
both George and Sam the habit began early and has never truly
ended. They would both put absolutely anything into their mouths,
except, of course, food of any significant nutritional value. They
moved on from rattles and rubber ducks to earth, paint, stone, cardboard, ring pulls, drinking straws, slugs, spiders . . . Sam, at eleven,
still loves chewing modeling clay and biting the tips off felt pens.

When his class planted daffodil bulbs he pulled them up and bit chunks out of them.

George gave up his pacifier on the day the newborn Sam came back from hospital, which was also—alas—the day he gave up his afternoon nap. It was as if he was saying, "Don't think you can fob me off with this anymore, and don't think I'm ever going to let you out of my sight again." Sam kept his pacifiers for years and years. I'm ashamed to say that when, finally, I furtively binned them, like the monster mother in Jill Murphy's excellent *The Last Noo-Noo,* Sam may have been as old as eight. I do remember asking the dentist whether the pacifier would make Sam's adult teeth stick out, and the dentist looking at Sam trashing his surgery, and saying, "Well, possibly, but it's a question of priorities, isn't it? I mean, if it helps . . ."

So, at three weeks old, George was plugged, and the pacifier gave a little more order and sanity to our lives. He slept more, though not much. In any twenty-four hours, George was awake for fourteen, which is an awful lot for a newborn. I now know that sleep problems are extremely common among autists. During George's insomniac babyhood I took comfort from the reassurances of everyone who met him—"Oh, he doesn't sleep because he's so bright!"

George did everything early. I noted it all in his baby book with pride. He smiled at three weeks, laughed at one month. He soon reached out for toys, and at two months could handle things quite competently. He sat at five months, crawled at six, stood alone at seven, and took his first unaided steps on the day he was nine months old. He was an ambitious baby; I remember him dragging a huge pack of nappies, three times his size, across the living-room floor. He had one of those wheeled baby walkers that are now thought to be so dangerous; he loved it, and at six months would scoot around the kitchen in it, grabbing things. I remember him seizing a cauliflower from the vegetable rack and careering away with it, chuckling with glee.

His fascination with color, which I had first noticed in hospital, continued, as it does to this day. He had a musical mobile of four rotating plastic bears; he would lie on his mat watching this intently, reserving his energy for the reappearance of the red bear. When this tinkled into sight he would throw himself into a frenzy, waving his arms and legs and gurgling. He was about a month old.

He found certain visual details hugely exciting—the honeycomb grid on the front of a radio, for example. I remembered this when, a couple of years later, he pored endlessly over the picture of a honeycomb in a nature book. He loved music, and the sound of running water—if he was crying, I used to turn on a tap to soothe him. All his senses seemed to be on red alert—he hated being dressed or undressed, but his bath was a great joy. He didn't reject physical contact, which is often the first sign of autism in babies, but he was never relaxed. When my mother held him she said he felt stiff, though I, who hadn't handled many babies, didn't notice. It wasn't until I had Jake, eight years later, that I realized what a "normal" baby felt like. Jake, a neat little parcel, nestled into the crook of my arm as if he'd grown there. George wanted to be held, but he wasn't truly cuddly. He accepted hugs but didn't return them; he did stretch out his arms to reach things, and that "thing" might be a person. George wanted to be held *up*, so that he could see things—people were useful pieces of furniture rather than comfort givers. And he *never* kept still. From the moment he could wriggle, wriggling was what he did. I remember holding my cousin Helena's twin girls, who are exactly the same age as George, when they were about ten months. They sat in my lap, snug and plump. I thought, George never sits like this. He squirmed in my lap like a puppy. But the difference didn't worry me. I just assumed it was the difference between boys and girls.

It wasn't possible to think of the infant George as anything other than highly intelligent. Baby books rightly warn us against interpreting the early reaching of milestones as significant, but we can't help it. If a child is showing enthusiasm for picture books at three months, or sitting confidently astride ride-on toys at six months, as George was, adults just do say "Isn't he bright?" I am not sure, now, how to interpret George's precocity, which continued until the age of precisely two and a quarter. Was it just that, being awake for more hours than other babies, he had more time to learn new skills? Or does it mean that he really does have great intelligence, which with time has become shrouded in the mists of autism? As I write, thirteen years later, George's academic skills are scant. He has basic numeracy and literacy, no more. There is no area in which he overtakes or even matches his peer group, except that he still learns songs quickly, has a good memory for both the words and the melody, and can sing well when he tries.

There's a popular belief that inside every autistic child is a genius struggling to get out. I don't subscribe to this. It's probably true that most autists have more ability than they can or will display. It's also true that they have "islets" of ability, a few areas in which they are disproportionately skillful. Sam, who is academically much less able than George, is relatively good at jigsaw puzzles. He's not *very* good at them—all normal eleven-year-olds would be better. But he's much better at jigsaws than he is at, say, reading. IQ profiles are not a satisfactory way of assessing autists, but they do usually illustrate this intellectual profile of peaks and troughs.

My own feeling is that George, as a baby, could not rest. He sought stimulus all the time, and at that stage new knowledge and new skills provided stimulus. It doesn't now. George crammed himself with knowledge for two and a quarter years, he over-loaded, and he shut down.

Min and I became boastful about our prodigious baby. I forgive us—new parents simply cannot get into perspective the impor-tance of their offspring in the greater scheme of things. We would make him perform his party pieces, doubtless to the dismay of our friends—grandparents can take any amount of this kind of thing, but friends shouldn't have to. Did our boasting mask a faint anxiety that all was not quite well with our little star? It's possible. I couldn't help noticing that compared to other babies George was exhaust-ing, demanding, and disobedient, though I chose not to see this as a problem.

The baby book I followed most closely was Penelope Leach's *Your Baby and Child*. I found most of her advice sympathetic, but every now and then I would simply fail to recognize what she was talking about. She describes the time when the baby changes from being "a totally unpredictable and therefore rather alarming novelty" and becomes "settled into life . . . whether he's settled at two weeks or at two months, that moment will come." Having experienced Jake, I know exactly what she means. But I remember reading this when George was tiny, and thinking, no, she's look-ing through rose-tinted spectacles. George didn't "settle into life." He didn't know night from day; he was up, laughing and larking about, at any time. The gaps between his feeds were of wildly varying length. There was no guarantee, even, of what would com-fort or amuse him. What worked one day would often fail the next.

No one suggested anything was wrong. The doctor who gave him his six-week check thought he was wonderful. "There's a baby who's in love with his mother," she remarked, as George's gaze followed me around the room, and his little limbs waved with ex-citement whenever I came near. Like normal babies, George was fascinated by the human face. He became hugely enthusiastic about a photograph of Paloma Picasso on the back cover of a magazine, all black eyebrows and big red lips, when he was only a few days old. My mother and I look quite alike, and when George was a baby our haircuts were similar. George would turn from one of us to the other, puzzled, trying to work it out.

Recent research, using gaze-tracking devices, has established that autistic people focus on the lower half of the face, particularly the mouth. The "neurotypical" gaze roves from background to foreground, from eyes to mouth to hands, taking in a whole range of clues about the intentions and state of mind of the watched person. The autist, by concentrating almost exclusively on the lower face, misses nearly all of these clues. Ironically, given that many use little speech themselves, autists are heavily dependent on the spoken word for their understanding of a social situation, and, as most of us know, what is said and what is meant are often quite different. It would be interesting to know whether, when baby George was scrutinizing faces so intently, he was autistically only truly looking at the lower half, or whether scanning the whole face was a skill he once had but has now lost.

Three features of early infant development were absent in both George and Sam, although I realized this only when I had Jake. Babies of three to four months are supposed to play, first with their fingers, then with their toes. They spread their hands in front of their faces and wiggle their fingers; they lie on their backs, catch their feet, and bring them up to their mouths. Jake did this at the right time, just as he did everything else. George and Sam didn't. I do vaguely remember noticing that George's feet weren't going into his mouth, and thinking, oh well, perhaps he's not very flexible. It seems possible to me now that this was an early sign of autism. Adult autists report a peculiar, disjointed sense of their own bodies. Donna Williams, for instance, writes that she thinks some-body has touched her arm, looks down, and realizes that it is her own hand. Perhaps the baby who fails to establish the boundaries of his own body through playing with hands and feet is likely to experience this disconnectedness in later life.

The second possibly significant omission is about faces again. Babies usually look doubtful or even cry when they see their mother in a hat, sunglasses, with a new hairstyle, and so on. Neither George nor Sam ever had this reaction. Jake couldn't bear to see me even with wet hair, for months. Some mothers of deeply autistic children believe that their child doesn't even recognize them. I think this unlikely; I'm sure George and Sam have both always recognized me, but they may not feel the need or the inclination to display that recognition. My guess is that George and Sam didn't react to seeing me with a towel around my head, or whatever, because though they know me and, after a fashion, love me, they don't have normal expectations of what a mother should be or do. Most babies' emotional instincts conform to a pattern; those of autistic babies do not.

Their reaction, or lack of reaction, on switching from breast to bottle may fit in here. It's something that every nursing mother dreads, particularly if—as in my case—the switch is necessary be-cause she's going back to work. One feels guilt for exchanging the baby's birthright for cold, unloving, rubber-insulated feeding, to coin a phrase. Some babies can't bear it—my cousin's baby daugh-ter was so cross about it that Caroline found herself rushing back from the City to Wandsworth (a forty-minute trip on a good day) every four hours to give Mary another suckle.

Well, neither George nor Sam turned a hair. They guzzled down their first bottles of formula with indifferent greed. They really didn't seem to notice. I'd planned to keep the breast-feeds going night and morning for some time, but in the face of their nonchalance there didn't seem to be much point. Jake, by contrast, never had a bottle at all. His desire to be fed by me and me alone was ferocious. When he was twenty months old, my friend Clare took matters out of his and my hands. "Go away for a weekend," she ordered. "You need to get your life back. I'll look after him. It doesn't matter if he hates me." I spent a weekend in Barcelona. Jake was angry, but it worked.

Though George was a "difficult" baby, he was also great fun. He loved peekaboo and tickling games; he loved to be rocked, bounced, sung to. This meant that it was easy to leave him to be looked after by other people—they found him very engaging. And, strong though his interest in me was, he didn't seem to mind my absence much. Penelope Leach tells us about "eight-month anxiety," and I recall friends' babies crawling desperately after them, weeping, if they had the temerity to go to the lavatory on their own. Neither George nor Sam did this, and this is the third of my significant developmental differences. At the time I concluded, smugly, that my babies were so emotionally secure that they didn't need to cry. I was wrong about that. Their lack of reaction was a sign of autism, not of security. As in so many other ways, they didn't fit the pattern. Jake, who had the least "reason" to be anxious, as I didn't go back to work after his birth and was rarely out of his sight, exhibited classic eight-month anxiety. Now, aged five, he has strong relationships with several adults and confidently spends time away from me. His emotional development keeps pace with his growing maturity and understanding; he spread his wings once he was ready to do so. For his brothers, despite appearances, babyhood was full of gaps. We're trying hard to fill them now.

THREE

Please Replace the Handset
and Try Again

All autists have abnormal language. Some have no spoken language at all but can be taught to use signs. A very few never achieve any means of communication, spoken or signed. This complete absence is rare—most will tug an adult by the sleeve or guide a hand toward a desired object, and this, although basic, is communication of a sort. Others speak with extreme, almost preposterous, fluency. "Talking like a dictionary" can be a symptom of high-functioning autism. This may not sound like too much of a problem, but on closer examination the speech patterns will be found to lack flexibility. Slang and idiom will be poorly understood; metaphor and simile may be taken literally. And the super-fluent speech will take no account of the listener's level of understanding; the autist will probably be unable to modify his elaborate vocabulary for the benefit of a child or a foreigner. It's highly likely, also, that the autist will talk almost entirely about things that interest or concern himself. He may have been trained to ask polite questions but will rarely take in the answers. Even the highest-functioning autist will have difficulties with the give-and-take of normal conversation.

Echolalia is a very common feature of autistic speech. The autist mimics words or phrases, or even whole chunks of dialogue. He may perfectly capture the voice and intonation of the person he's imitating, but unlike a true mimic he won't be able to improvise for satiric or comic effect. He won't be able to think, this is the sort of thing Mum might say—he'll simply imitate what Mum actually has said. Echolalia is particularly common in young autistic children just learning to speak. It's usually a relatively good sign—any speech is better than no speech, in terms of future development. Some echolalic children—George included—build on their "echoes" and learn to produce speech of their own. Nor should the echoes be regarded as empty of meaning. They may be—but not necessarily. Many children don't echo any old phrase. They choose phrases that are in some way interesting or useful to them, though their value may be obscure to their neurotypical listeners.

All echolalic behavior in young children should be investigated, unless you're very sure that a joke is intended. Parrot talk is not a normal part of language development. Of course, all children imitate—that's how they acquire speech. But very quickly, the normal child will put words together in her own way. She may pick up adult expressions and put them into her sentences, often with precocious effect, but she won't simply bounce your phrases back at you, unadorned, unless she is autistic.

Some autists invent words and phrases. These may be "stims" (sounds that give them some kind of sensory stimulus or satisfaction) or they may be genuine coinages. Sam's invented words include "stonkers," "splockiator," "splainiator," "mushroom hands," and "Chenta and Gleed." I don't know what these mean, but I think stonkers and mushroom hands are something to do with clocks, and splockiators and splainiators are machines. When we visited the science museum Sam seemed to think there were splockiators and splainiators in it. "Chenta and Gleed" would be a good name for a Disney film, and indeed I think that Sam has a pair of characters in mind, possibly based on himself and George. But I'm really not sure.

It's unusual to find an autist with normal use of grammar. The ability to follow grammatical rules seems to be something innate—even deaf communities, using only signing, develop their own grammatical systems with ease and speed. But this doesn't seem to be true of autists. Perhaps their problems with grammar are something to do with their lack of "central coherence"—they can focus on details but cannot see an overall pattern.

Nearly all of them have difficulties with personal pronouns. George couldn't use "I," "me," and "my" until he was six and a half; Sam still hardly uses them. George used the second or third person. "Do you want a drink?" meant that he wanted a drink. I remember him saying, nervously, at a party, "Everybody here likes George." He was really asking me a question—"Does everybody like me?"

A psychologist might interpret this pronoun problem as the manifestation of a defective sense of self, and this could be true. I think, though, that it's more likely to be a mechanical thing, connected to the way the autistic child acquires language, through echolalia. The parent says, "Do you want a drink?" The autistic child, who wants the drink, but has difficulty with an "abstract" word like "yes," repeats the phrase. The child's lack of grammatical connectedness makes it difficult to swap "you" for "I." Grammar can be learned, but for the autist it's not instinctive. High-functioning autists may use "perfect" grammar, but like their elaborate vocabularies, it will have the quality of being learned by rote. Past and future tenses seem to cause particular problems, perhaps because sequencing is a typical autistic difficulty.

It seems to me that most autistic children (I don't know many adults yet) use language in two distinct ways. The first is to get what they want. They have learned that saying "Biscuit" to an adult is a more effective way of getting a biscuit than screaming, arm tugging, or rolling on the floor, though it takes many of them years to reach this realization. So they use our language to us, to fulfill their most pressing needs. But they don't use our language to find out more about us as people—they don't want to hear stories about what Mummy did when she was a little girl; they're not interested in what Daddy saw when he went away on that business trip. Autists live in the moment, and the functional, concrete nature of much of their language reflects this.

Then they have a second kind of language. This kind they use for their own private satisfaction. They murmur phrases to themselves, they repeat snatches of video dialogue, they reduce words to odd, elided syllables to be yelled out or whispered. It's hard to tell whether language used in this way has any meaning in the conventional sense or is being relished purely for its sound effects. I'm inclined to think there is some meaning. George weaves phrases from different videos together to produce some kind of story of his own, or that's what it feels like. Sam's far less coherent vocalizations are often based on things that once interested him—"The TUMble the DRYer eeeeoooaaah!" he'll chant at ever-increasing volume. This kind of language is private and has nothing to do with communication. George now distinguishes clearly between his two modes of speech—"I'm not talking to you, Mummy. I'm talking to myself."

George acquired language early. By his first birthday he had several words, of the usual "duck," "ball," and "brm-brm" variety, and he could show that he understood many more by directing his gaze or pointing. Yes, pointing. Lack of pointing in a baby (from about ten months) is, at time of writing, held to be the earliest indication of autism, but this needs to be assessed very carefully. Both George and Sam did point, and at the right age, too. I'm relying on memory here, because for obvious reasons I didn't take detailed data at the time, but I think the difference is that they mainly pointed on request. "Where's the moon?" Point— "Well done, darling!" They also pointed to get their needs met. Biscuit tin—point—result. But what they didn't use, or used only to a limited extent, was the shared-attention point. They didn't call my attention to things in order to make me see, enthuse, inform, or share. I have a clear memory of George at about eighteen months, squatting, studying a ladybird. He was fascinated, and I remember thinking, fleetingly, shouldn't he want to show me that? But he didn't. He observed it for a long time, and then he stomped off.

As with so many developmental details, I didn't fully appreciate the difference until I had Jake. By ten months, Jake had his arm permanently extended in a point. If he spotted something interesting, he had to make sure that everyone else in the room had spotted it too. At the same age, Jake constantly brought things to show me, which the other two never did. I remember remarking on that to a friend. "George never offers me his toys," I said. "Maybe he's selfish." And I laughed, and thought no more about it. For Jake, pointing and sharing toys was all about communication. Jake is a great communicator. Like George, he learned to talk early; unlike George, communication was his motivation. It's only now that I realize that George didn't acquire language primarily to communicate. He acquired language because he enjoyed language; words were a major stimulus. They still are. Like many autists, George has extremely acute hearing. His imitations of accent or tone of voice are exact. When he was attending the village school, aged about five, I wanted to know whether gym was called gym, PE, PT, or whatever. "George," I asked, "when you put on your shorts and sneakers and go into the hall, do you call it gym?" "No," said George, "you call it George." I began again, elaborating on my question. "Do you call it gym or PE?" "No," said George, in immaculate estuary English, "you call it pay-ay."

There seemed to be nothing unusual about the early stages of the baby George's language development except that it was pretty fast. If I'd been very alert, I'd have noticed the absence of babble and gobbledegook. George had made the usual coos and gurgles, but he'd never gone in for the long nonsense sentences, the strings of syllables that imitate the pattern, though not the meaning, of adult speech. Right from the start, George spoke clearly and precisely, in a melodious voice. He still has this—when he's not shrill and agitated, his voice is musical and attractive. I'd like to make a bit of a point about this lack of infant babble, but my point is undermined by that fact that Sam babbled and burbled away with the best of them. Directing a flow of nonsensical speech-pattern babble toward a listening adult was one of Sam's specialties.

George's baby book records that at fifteen months he knew forty-three words, and that there were many more he had repeated two or three times and then seemed to forget. This is a lot for his age, but it is not astonishing. I also note that he will follow instructions to jump, dance, wave bye-bye, clap hands, and so on. It is perhaps significant that gestures are supplied on request, rather than produced spontaneously. However, George at that age didn't lack spontaneity. There was nothing passive or robotic about him. In the same entry I mention that "he has become very tyrannical with his stories, fishing them out and bashing people with them to imply they should read them to him." I also remember him following me around the kitchen, holding out a book and pleading "In-a-minute," because that was a phrase he'd associated with adults and story reading. His appetite for stories was the most unusual aspect of his early language acquisition. When he was sixteen months old I discovered that if I paused when reading a familiar story, he could supply the missing word. He could do this with any word (including "and," "the," etc.) at any point in at least fifty stories. The same applied to songs and nursery rhymes. By eighteen months, George could sing really well. By Christmas, a month before his second birthday, he could sing several carols, including long ones like "Good King Wenceslas," note- and word-perfect, though I do remember him getting stuck on the "Glorias" in "Ding Dong Merrily"—a bit like not knowing when to step out of a revolving door.

This prodigious memory is fairly common in autists. Of course at the time we interpreted it as yet another manifestation of his amazing intelligence. George still has a retentive memory, though he's less interested in using it. He still learns new songs quickly, and knows the dialogue of his videos by heart. It's the closest either of my sons gets to the "savant" skills possessed by a small minority of autists. Savant skills feature disproportionately in the public consciousness. This isn't surprising, because it is fascinating to come across someone who can do calendar calculation in the blink of an eye, or someone who has only to glance at a complicated architectural structure in order to reproduce it on paper with accuracy and panache. But it should be reiterated that most autists have no such skills.

And even if they do, their talents may be of limited value. With autism, one skill doesn't lead on to another in the way one might assume. The boy who can tell you the day of the week for any date you care to fire at him doesn't necessarily have ability in any other mathematical area. I knew a child who at five could reproduce sections of road maps; this hasn't led to any wider interest in cartography or town planning. It was just a knack. George's early love of language didn't encourage him to learn to read or write. The basic literacy skills he now has are the result of the efforts of determined teachers who have gone on and on at him and plied him with candies. It's still very, very unusual for George to use reading or writing for his own pleasure or information. A phrase comes back to me from one of the boys' school reports—"All new skills must be built on the back of existing ones." Excellent educational theory, but extremely difficult to apply to autistic children, whose skills resemble an archipelago of islands scattered across a sea of confusion. Most of the islands aren't even within hailing distance of one another. Just sometimes, autistic skills come together and cohere to excellent effect. Temple Grandin's ability to think in three dimensions has combined with her instinctive understanding of the link between physical pressure and the control of anxiety to make her one of the world's leading designers of cattle-handling equipment. This is excellent for all concerned, not least for the destressed cattle. But Temple Grandin is an unusually productive autistic adult. More often, the talent just sits there, a source—arguably—of some pleasure to the autist, and of pride giving way to frustration to the parent, who slowly comes to realize that her child's perfect pitch or gift for calculus or ability to memorize the number stamped on every manhole cover they pass on their daily walk to school is a discrete, isolated skill, not the key to unlocking a "normal" intelligence.

There was nothing mechanical about George's early language,

despite his amazing capacity to learn by rote. He relished language. He loved poetry—R. L. Stevenson's *A Child's Garden of Verses* was one of the books he frequently bashed me with, and this was before Sam was born, so George was considerably less than two. He would stand on a chair to recite: "Dark brown is the river, Golden is the sand, It flows along forever, With trees on either hand." This was cute, and unselfconscious. His poetic tastes were catholic. He memorized the greeting inside all the cards he got for his second birthday and carried them around, intoning, "Hello there lickle two-year-old, Your happy day is here, And that's the time for wishing you, Fun throughout the year, Lots of love from Aunty Gill."

He used the phrases he'd learned from stories and deployed them in conversation. This was George's version of echolalia, and he used his echoes so cleverly that we were slow to perceive it as a problem. His twin cousins, William and Katharine, are just a little younger than him; they were scuttling about the kitchen, getting into everything. George, regarding them from his high chair, looked doubtful. "These Things will not bite you," he said. "They want to have fun." This is a line from *The Cat in the Hat,* and indeed the twins were very like Dr. Seuss's anarchic Thing One and Thing Two.

George's echolalic fluency masked a serious deficit. He could point to the sky and say, "There were fluffy white clouds in the pale blue sky" (*Ant and Bee and the Rainbow*), but he couldn't say, "Look, Mummy—clouds!" He could look at our cleaning lady and say, "There in the doorway was a huge green alligator," but he couldn't say "Jane's got a green dress." When he picked up a toy telephone, he didn't say, "Hello, Daddy," or improvise any kind of imaginary conversation. Instead he said, in a perfect computerized voice, "Please replace the handset and try again."

In short, he had real difficulty constructing sentences of his own. He was like a foreigner with a phrase book; he stored memorized sentences and pulled out whichever seemed best fitted to the occasion. He did sometimes put his own words together. I remember him seeing a photograph of the recently deceased Robert Maxwell with his mouth open, and saying, "Man done a yawn." But his ability to create his own sentences and inflection was limited, especially when compared to his huge vocabulary. And his tremendous enjoyment of fairly "advanced" stories and poems led us to overlook the inadequacies of his comprehension. He had a book about Labrador puppies, a factual book with quite a difficult text, aimed at eight- or nine-year-olds. George loved this book as much as any, and listened to it again and again.

One day I paused during the reading and pointed to a picture of the puppies. "What are these, George?" I asked. "Two pigs," he replied. He'd heard *The Puppy Book* read a hundred times, but he hadn't realized it was about puppies.

By his second birthday, George could recognize all the letters of the alphabet and could form a few short words with magnetic letters on the fridge. Sam, though much less precocious, could also identify letters early on. In the only home movie we have from their early days, Sam, aged twenty months, is poring over *Dr. Seuss's ABC*, and, interestingly, calling my attention to his favorite letters. He finds *w* particularly amusing. I had good reason to assume I had a pair of early readers on my hands. How wrong I was. At thirteen, George has a reading age of maybe six or seven. Sam, now eleven, after long hours of labor and many candies, can identify a handful of words—"Sam," "pig," "sun," "hot," "cat."

Watching Jake learn to read was completely different. Jake is an effortless reader. He could read a bit by three and a half; now, at just five, he's quite fluent. Words like "laughed," "excited," and "through" cause him no problems. For Jake, everything is connected. His intellectual world is all joined up. He uses reading without noticing he's doing so—for computer games, in shops, for filling in the puzzles in children's magazines. He reads recipes aloud to me while I cook. He can see that reading tells us what we need to know.

George learned letters quickly because he has sharp eyes and a good memory. He learned to recognize words as discrete shapes; he still finds it difficult to break words down phonetically. But it never occurred to George to put his "reading" to any use. Even at the height of his passion for stories, George never showed curiosity about a new book. During his third and fourth years, as his autism closed him in, he became resistant to any new books at all. He would sit on the floor, surrounded by his old favorites, each one open at a particular page; he would turn from one to another, mixing extracts like a DJ mixing tracks. For George the language of the books was moving farther and farther away from its meaning.

Our scrap of video footage shows George at three and a half. Like most children of that age, he is talking all the time. He's talking to me, as well, or at least with reference to me—he frequently looks in my direction, requiring a response. But if I give the "wrong" response, he overrules me. He's looking at *The Mixed-Up Chameleon* by Eric Carle. He is "reading"—reciting—it, with considerable expression. But he doesn't think that the illustration of a seal is a seal. He thinks it's a pigeon. "It's a purple pigeon," he repeats. He looks to me for confirmation. I point out that textual evidence suggests it is, in fact, a seal. George denies this. "It's a purple pigeon," he reiterates several times, firmly and without rancor.

George's voice is clear, rather singsong. By this stage, there are quite a lot of his own constructions as well as some echolalia. An untrained observer would probably not suspect a problem. What is most autistic about George's speech is its omissions. I'm his mother; I'm holding a camcorder for the first time. He doesn't ask a single question. If it had been Jake, there'd have been a stream of them—"What's that?" "What's it for?" "Why are you doing that?" "Can I have a go?" George doesn't even seem to notice.

Three-year-olds are often described as being "like sponges," soaking up enormous amounts of information about the world around them. They ask endless questions (and don't always seem to listen to the answers) because they are powerfully driven to find out as much as they can. Knowledge is power. George—bright, vocal, bookish George—asked no questions, beyond the most basic— "Where's Sam?" Sam didn't even reach that level. Now, George does ask questions, on the lines of "Where's X?" "What's that?" "What day is it today?" Sam only uses questions that he has learned by rote—"Can I have a sweet?" (He's only learned "I" by rote, as well.) Neither of my autistic boys has ever used the word "why?"* Curiosity is unsettling; it feels as if, beyond the boundaries of the here and now, they sense an immense bewilderment. They don't want to venture into that territory. Instead, they annex only small pieces of information, fence themselves in with concrete certainties. "That's a purple pigeon!"

On March 23, 1993, I recorded everything George said during a fifteen-minute period. George was three years and two months—still ten months before his diagnosis. We were alone in the kitchen; Sam was asleep upstairs. I said nothing to George during the fifteen minutes, so all his remarks were self-generated. I reproduce this monologue in full, because it illustrates several of the key characteristics of autistic language, though of course

---

*Stop press: April 2003: George asked me, "Why is Tom [the cat] sneezing?" and since then has asked several more "why?" questions. Progress does happen!

I didn't realize that at the time. My commentary is in square brackets:

Yellow and blue mixed together make green. [Playing with Play-Doh.]

(Sings own "song"—incomprehensible.)

What shall we do now? [Not directly addressed to me.]

(noises)

Look—they're doing painting. [Pointing into space.]

Look!

They're doing painting.

Are they in Sam's room?

No they're not in Sam's room.

Are they in George's room?

No they're not in George's room. [I didn't know who or what "they" were.]

What shall we do now? [Imitation of adult voice.]

Mummy, I can't see you. [Repeated five times, in singsong. He could see me. This was a line from one of his books, about a little hippo.]

Mmm mmm mmm mmm.

There—that's enough. [Referring to Play-Doh.]

Beetles! [Looking at scrapbook with insects on the cover.]

(laughter)

That says Mummy!

That says George!

Granny! [The words "Mummy," "George," "Granny" are written in the scrapbook.]

A comb for Granny. [Quote from *Lucy and Tom's Christmas* by Shirley Hughes.]

A handkerchief for Grandpa. [Quote from same source.]

Oh no!

(squeal)

Oooh.

There—go and play.

(laughter)

A calendar for Granny.

A packet of seeds for Grandpa to grow flowers from when springtime comes. [More *Lucy and Tom*.]

[Goes to Aga, points behind it. Addresses me directly for the first time.]

We go that way? [There's not much space behind the Aga!]

That way?

This way! This way! This way!

George—I'm going to get your nose. [Reference to a chasing game played by Delia, his nanny.]

George!

Sam—I'm going to get your nose. [Repeated five times, running up and down the kitchen. Sam is still upstairs in bed.]

Sam!

Boo!

I got Sam's nose!

Aaaah . . .

Got George's nose!

Got your nose.

George—I'm going to get your nose. [Repeated twice.]

(noises)

Here I come . . . aaah . . . got it!

George—I'm going to get your nose. [Repeated twice.]

Yes I mam—no—yes I *am*. [All this section imitating Delia's intonation.]

Go up! [To me, meaning, upstairs. I don't respond.]

We go up?

Put Mummy's slipper back on. [My slipper wasn't off.]

Each Peach Pear Plum. [Referring to Each Peach Pear Plum by Janet and Allan Ahlberg.]

I spy Tom Thumb.

(something incomprehensible)

I think . . . oh no, Teddy, we take you back. [No teddy in sight.]

Another . . . yes . . . there. [Arranging Play-Doh pots on the edge of the playpen.]

[Long silence.]

Some orange perhaps.

Right. Right. Blue time. [Picks up blue lid.]

No, put them away.

Now put them away. [Stacking pots.]

There. There.

Put them away. [To me.]

We go to toilet? [Fills nappy.]

I spy the three bears. [Quoted from Each Peach Pear Plum by Janet and Allan Ahlberg.]

There's a marked difference between the relative sophistication of the quoted material ("A packet of seeds for Grandpa . . .") and the rather awkward, unpracticed quality of George's own phrases ("We go that way?"). There's a certain inconsequentiality—seeing "Granny" within the scrapbook is enough to send George off into Lucy-and-Tom land. There's little symbolic play; the most extended piece of play is the nose-catching game, and here George is simply rehearsing the way Delia played with him and Sam, without any improvisation. The speech is very clear, and he corrects his one mistake ("mam" for "am"), but it lacks the organic connectedness of "normal" language.

And, perhaps above all, George seems to have so little need of an audience. Most small children will talk to themselves as they play, but they'll frequently call an adult's attention to their activities if an adult's available. And I was very available, just standing there, writing things in my notebook, but George, though fully aware of my presence, hardly drew on this human resource at all. Just as neither George nor Sam has ever asked "Why?," so neither of them has ever said, "Look at me"—that defining request of neurotypical childhood.

FOUR

Two in the Family

George's autism was diagnosed just before his fourth birthday. At that time, as the doctor's notes record, we had "no worries" about two-year-old Sam—indeed, we used some of Sam's abilities, such as pedaling a trike, to highlight George's deficits. It may seem odd, having one autistic child, that we failed to spot the symptoms in our second, but right from the start Sam was very, very different from his brother. We got used to the idea that one set of characteristics—George's—amounted to autism, but there seemed to be little overlap between these characteristics and Sam's behavior, eccentric though that often was. And besides, I'd never heard of more than one autistic child in a family. It didn't occur to me that it could happen. I've since discovered that it isn't even particularly rare.

Sam's apparently cheerful nature also delayed the need to worry about him. George was such a bundle of nervous energy—volatile, ethereal, powerfully attractive. Sam, from birth, was the opposite—placid, quiet, a creature of habit, the kind of baby you have to remember to notice. He wasn't a model baby. He did wake at night, though not as often as George, but at least he seemed to know night from day. Unlike George, he would lie quietly in his cradle, not asking for anything. Like George, he smiled early, but he didn't have the same passionate attachment to me. Sam quite liked people, but it was a long time before he seemed to distinguish between them.

I expect I attributed Sam's early placidity to a combination of my greater experience and his easier birth. The labor was longish— thirteen hours, and unpleasant for me, but not, I think, especially stressful for Sam. Like George, he was in the posterior position, which prolonged the early stages, but the midwives massaged me hard to avoid another forceps delivery; Sam turned just in time, and was actually born quickly, without intervention. I could sit up and watch. I have a clear memory of his head coming out, like a tortoise poking out of its shell.

Sam's Apgar score was good, and he fed easily and immediately. He weighed six pounds fifteen ounces and put on weight very fast. George had looked like his father at birth; Sam resembled no one, except, my mother claimed, jockey Lester Piggott. He was born at lunchtime on November 18, 1991—Monday's child, but no one at that stage could claim that he was fair of face.

Later that day, he turned deep purple and choked on his mucus. The nurses kept him with them for much of the night, to keep an eye on him. There didn't appear to be any lasting damage, but he was inclined to snuffle for much of his babyhood and beyond. Sam passed a number of milestones early, but with nothing like George's accelerated development. He was strong and muscular, and could sit up early, but there was nothing remarkable about his progress. If anything, there seemed to be a subtle lack of—what was it? Spark? Engagement? Curiosity? Sam smiled, handled toys, looked at pictures, but he didn't truly explore the world. At this early stage he showed no distinct tastes or preferences, for people or for things, unless it was for his soft owl, who shares his bed to this day.

And he was very quiet. Rereading his baby book, I find I have written that Sam at seven months is "still very quiet and makes no consonant sounds at all—he just says 'Ah ah ah,' and that not very often. However he is not deaf as he always turns his head to his name, and enjoys certain tunes very much." Later this was to change, and Sam, as mentioned in the previous chapter, became a great babbler, producing long inflected nonsense sentences accompanied by earnest hand gestures.

It is common for an autistic child to be suspected of deafness before the correct diagnosis has been made. Mothers are often puzzled by the child who ignores all their remarks but comes running from the bottom of the garden at the sound of a bag of crisps being opened. Sam didn't ignore us; he could follow instructions and was soon responding to "Wave bye-bye," "Clap hands," and so on. But he didn't seem alert to adult speech in the way that, later, Jake was, and I now realize that he never turned his head from one speaker to another to follow conversation.

Sam acquired language slowly but surely, until his second birthday. He had a couple of words by his first birthday; at eighteen months I list twenty, the usual mixture of animal noises and useful commands—"up," "no," "gain." I comment, "He has many fewer words than George had, but he uses them more effectively." In a funny way, this remained true. Even though Sam has never achieved verbal fluency, and at one point almost gave up talking altogether, the few words he did retain were those that would get his needs met.

Sam didn't echo, except in the way that babies always repeat new words. His voice was, and is, unusually deep and husky, not musical like George's. He often speaks much too loudly. He didn't pronounce words clearly; when he was three, this revived the idea that he might have some hearing loss, and he was checked for glue ear. I now realize that his lack of interest in and cooperation with his hearing tests were the most significant part of the exercise. In the test room were a number of toys that would entice most three-year-olds—wooden men in a boat, trains, that kind of thing. There were also three black boxes that magically lit up to reveal three toys—a pig, a penguin, and a helicopter. The pig and the penguin danced, the helicopter's propellers rotated. The idea was to see if the child turned his head in the right direction in response to sound. Sam didn't, not because he couldn't hear, but because he wasn't interested, except, mildly, in the helicopter. His response to these lovely toys was, to say the least, muted. And he didn't want to fit the wooden men into their boat when the doctor asked him to, either. At the time I didn't attach much significance to his lack of interest, but having had Jake I now know that a normal three-year-old, unless he's ill or very tired, *will* be attracted by toys, *should* cooperate, *should* want to show the doctor what he can do. It's a bit like those notices people put up at college, which said SEX in big red letters, and then underneath gave you some information about something like the Debating Society. If you're normal, you just can't help paying attention to certain things.

The question of Sam's glue ear dragged on throughout his fourth and fifth years. Perhaps he did have it—he certainly produced excessive amounts of mucus. It was obvious, though, that he had no serious hearing loss. Though not echolalic, he was very good at imitating certain sounds. At sixteen months, I write that "he does an accurate imitation of the sound of the water draining out of the bath," and he soon extended his repertoire to include imitations of washing machines, drills, microwaves (even though we didn't have one), food processors, and the like. The idea of hearing loss was finally laid to rest when, aged five, some time after his autism diagnosis, he was given a general anesthetic and had his hearing tested by a computer. His hearing was perfect.

Would it have been possible to detect Sam's autism during infancy? I wrote a full account of him at twenty months:

Sam is very solid, with thick muscular arms and legs and a large tummy. He has thick fairish hair with more than a hint of red in it, and light brown eyes. He is extremely sturdy, walks for miles, runs, jumps, kicks and throws balls, climbs all over the place. He jumped out of the bath yesterday, and has escaped from his crib. It is no longer possible to write a list of the words he knows as he now copies such a lot . . . He joins in several nursery rhymes, supplying the end words. He does not pronounce words clearly, for instance his word for mummy is "nen" and baby is "de-dun" or something like. He likes books, though again not as much as George did—he favours those with photographs and is not interested in stories so much as naming objects. He tries to eat the picture of a biscuit in one of them. He plays very independently and never minds being on his own. His favourite activities include grubbing in muddy puddles, etc. He shows no especial preference for any type of toy—except soft toys which he loves, especially Owl—but will play with whatever comes to hand. He loves music, and dances with vigour. He eats very heartily; mainly jars of baby food. He is not interested in what adults eat. He feeds himself entirely and is good with a spoon. His especial love is salty snacks like Pringles. If given a chance he will push up a chair and climb up and raid the biscuit tin ("kikkit").

He is better with his hands than George was and enjoys filling containers, sorting shapes, etc. He has been known to take his T-shirt off. [George was extremely slow to make the slightest attempt at dressing or undressing.] He is quietly sociable and enjoys meeting other children. Most of the time he is easy and sunny but if thwarted (e.g., not allowed to open the fridge) he will roar for several minutes at incredible volume. He wakes at about 8:30 and always has to carry everything that was in his crib—Owl, Teddy, pacifier, empty milk bottle, etc. He has one long nap 2:30–5:00 but will forgo this if we are out. We put him to bed about 7:30 but he is often awake until about 9—he will lie burbling to himself. He usually wakes once during the night and has a bottle of milk. Not brilliant, but better than George at that age—or indeed than George now.

Does this make Sam sound like a child with a profound lifelong disability? I think not. Even bearing in mind that the writer is me, his mother, biased, and doubtless casting a rosy glow, it is hard on a first reading to see this as anything other than the description of a robust, happy, normal toddler. Our little bit of video coincides with this time. With George, yes, you can see . . . he's a gorgeous golden-haired three-year-old, but his movements are unusual. There's lots of flapping and jumping, and he's going on and on about that purple pigeon.

But Sam—Sam just looks like a healthy toddler enjoying himself. He's very, very bouncy—he's jumping and tumbling on an old mattress that I've put out for the purpose. He cuddles his soft toys. He points to things—the clock, for instance—names them, and *draws my attention to them.* He turns over the pages of *Dr. Seuss's ABC,* showing delight in naming a few letters—and, again, looks at me for confirmation. He climbs up to the window and looks out, interested in the world outside. It's nap time; I tuck him into his crib. He smiles, snuggles down with Owly and a bottle of milk. I leave; he doesn't object. What a contented, well-adjusted child!

Does this mean that at twenty months Sam was not autistic? Did he become autistic later, as a result of the MMR vaccine or some other insult or trauma? There's been a tenfold increase in the number of children diagnosed with autism over the last two decades. Opinion is divided as to whether this is a "real" increase, or an increase due to a more accurate diagnostic process, a greater understanding of the condition among doctors and psychologists. In the past, autism was often called "infantile schizophrenia" or "infant psychosis." This was at the severe end of the spectrum. At the more able end, children who would now be recognized as having Asperger's syndrome might have been called lazy, disturbed, eccentric, or just plain awkward. So, yes, a large part of this apparent increase in incidence must be attributed to a broadening of the diagnostic criteria. Most experts subscribe to this view. But like many parents, I can't shake off the feeling that there's been a "real" increase as well. If the number of autists has remained constant, where were they when I was growing up? Some were inappropriately locked up in mental hospitals and children's homes, and some were floundering undetected in mainstream schools, as is probably still the case; I suspect the condition is still underdiagnosed. But in all my childhood, even my early adulthood, I never came across a child who I can identify retrospectively as an undiagnosed autist. When I visited my friends' houses, there was never a little brother twirling and flapping in the corner. On buses, in shops, in parks, I don't remember normal-looking children shrieking or hooting or picking up the used bus tickets. I often see such children now. When I was young, I never heard any talk of children who had been "put away." I don't even remember any markedly eccentric children. We often saw visibly handicapped children, with Down's syndrome ("Mongols," as they used to be called), or "spastics" in wheelchairs, their heads lolling to one side. But if the incidence of autism was really one in a hundred, as it's now said to be, it seems strange to me that I never came across even one. I'm no scientist, and I have no convincing hypothesis to put forward to account for the increase, but my instinct tells me that better diagnosis doesn't account for all of it.

Many theories for the "epidemic" (a term I dislike, as it suggests a catchable illness) have been put forward. The MMR vaccine is the most notorious, but heavy metals and other pollutants, food intolerances triggered by changing diet patterns, and modern methods of food production have all come under scrutiny. I simply don't feel that I know enough to nail all my colors to a single mast. But, thinking about cheery twenty-month-old Sam, it's easy to see why so many parents believe that they have "lost" a normal child to autism, and why they devote so much time and effort in trying to find that sunny baby again. I don't wish to contradict such parents. I can't rule out the possibility that, in some cases, autism was triggered by some external disaster. But I feel certain that this is not what happened to either George or Sam.

George and Sam were born autistic. It's just that nobody noticed. And nobody can be blamed for not noticing, because the signs were so subtle. I have an idea that the regression often observed in autistic children of two or three years is something to do with what's expected of them; their brains are struggling and failing to cope. The parent, who nearly always believes he has a normal child, pushes the child in directions that would be wholly appropriate for a neurotypical, but that the autist simply cannot follow. Take language development. Many autists can manage nouns with ease.

"Car," "cup," "shoe"; these come in different shapes, colors, and sizes, but they are recognizably themselves, in or out of context. Concepts, or abstract words, are much less reliable, and therefore threatening. Verbs like "eating" or "walking" aren't so bad, but adjectives and adverbs are dangerously unstable and emotive. It took George years to use words like "angry" or even "thirsty" (though he could easily ask for a drink). Sam still hardly ever does. When Sam was small, adults often asked him what his favorite color/food/game was. Sam couldn't cope with "favorite." He turned it into a noun. He just couldn't get the hang of its real meaning even though he said it often, and over time, by some association of ideas, it became more or less synonymous with "rainbow."

In babyhood one is only expected to use nouns—"teddy," "ball," "crib"—or a few unambiguous prepositions like "up." Adjectives are limited to the most visual or tactile, the least abstract—you'd say "blue" or "hot" to a baby, but you wouldn't say "emotional" or "confusing." My theory—based, I admit, on the observation of my own sons—is that autistic babies are quite happy with "concrete" words, but when language needs to reach beyond the here and now, when language casts out nets to capture thoughts and feelings, past and future, possibilities, plans, it slips out of the autist's grasp, and so may be discarded altogether. George tried to cope by using his quotations, which fulfilled the pattern of conversational exchange and sometimes trawled in information that was useful to him. When George, at two and a quarter, asked visitors, "Do only insects have antennae?" he wasn't looking for an answer, and he certainly wasn't showing off. He was demonstrating that he knew that talking was appropriate human behavior, though he didn't really understand why. And he wasn't interested in any response the visitor might make. Whatever they said, George would supply the right answer: "No, wood lice have antennae." George wasn't interested in antennae (though he did like putting wood lice in his mouth). It was just something he'd learned by rote at Drusilla's Zoo.

George circumvented with his sophisticated form of echolalia; Sam used simple, concrete words, singly or in pairs, for as long as he could, and then he stalled. He tried babbled "sentences," into which he eventually inserted one relatively distinct word—"Aba dala loola laaa *icekeem*." He did learn to put words together, slowly. At Easter, when he was two and a half, he said, "Choc-choc egg— g'een one—Ham want it" (he called himself "Ham" for a long time). I recorded this as his longest-ever sentence. This utterance was motivated by intense desire; nothing could have motivated Sam more than a chocolate egg. But the usual motivation for a child learning to talk, which is the desire to understand the world through communication with older beings of his species, wasn't really there.

Language development, then, after the early stages, makes too many demands on the autistic brain, which can result in "overload" and "shutdown." Social interaction, similarly, can seem normal in the first year or so, before it degenerates. Perhaps this is because babies are not aware of themselves as separate entities. The world comes to them; they have not sufficient reserves of memory and experience to consider themselves objectively, as beings with relationships and social responsibilities. Autists seem to have a weak or confused sense of identity. Both my sons show indifference or aversion to photographs or films of themselves. Most children like stickers or mugs with their own name on them, are interested in what other people say about them, want to read their own school reports. Autists seem to find all this baffling, boring, or frightening. If George finds any mention of himself in, say, a letter from school, he will furiously ink it out. Some autistic babies are aloof from birth, stiffening or crying when touched, avoiding eye contact, happiest when left alone. These are the children likely to receive the earliest diagnoses. Others, like mine, are smiley and responsive. Both George and Sam nearly always responded favorably to social advances from both children and adults during their first two years. With hindsight I can see an unusual quality in their social reactions, but the reactions were certainly there. In the second and third year of life, so much more is expected of a child than that they should smile back at a smiling face. The child separates himself from the mother, learns to play and share with other children, finds his instinctual behavior directed and channeled by moral and social judgments—in short, learns to become a social being. Most children achieve this transition successfully. They are hardwired to do so. Autistic children are not. The fact that autistic behavior becomes apparent during the second and third years, that the child regresses, loses or abandons skills, cuts himself off, becomes uncontrollable, may be the result of him coming up against a set of expectations that he is not equipped to fulfill. To use a crude analogy: a dog is a pack animal; a cat is not. It is very, very difficult to train a cat to behave like a dog. It is very, very difficult to train an autistic child to behave like a social being.

To return to my rather partial account of Sam at twenty months: if you know what you're looking for, the warning signs are there. Even in the physical description, there are hints. Sam's extremely impressive musculature, for instance, was partly the result of autistic restlessness. To this day, Sam's body is like a drawing by William Blake. He no longer has an ounce of fat on him, but the muscles on his legs are the result of eleven years' incessant bouncing. His big tummy has gone now. For years he had a stomach like a beach ball. When I removed gluten and casein from his diet, it went flat, as it has remained. I discuss the autistic reaction to gluten and casein in chapters 7 and 12, but for now it suffices to suggest that Sam's round twenty-month tummy was partly due to an intolerant reaction to wheat and milk.

His escapology, here limited to jumping from bath and crib, became a huge problem later, when Sam took himself for long, unaccompanied walks, which often resulted in a 999 call. I had extra locks put on all our doors; we couldn't leave a door or window open on a warm day. Once, Sam watched yet another lock being put on the front door, thought about it, and climbed Tom Kitten-like up the chimney. I heard the fall of soot and came into the room to see a pair of sandaled feet dangling above an (unlit) fire. With the crib-jumping goes my comment that he "climbs all over the place." Autists, so full of social fears, often have little sense of physical danger. They can have exceptionally good balance (although, confusingly, the opposite can also be true) and an amazing head for heights. Both boys have had phases of being extremely physically adventurous, including, in Sam's case, a tiresome summer spent mainly on the roof of our house, pulling out tiles. I'm tempting fate to write this, but neither of them has ever had a serious accident. Once, Sam fell off our garden wall and scraped his face, and George fell downstairs at eleven months, but that's it. Most families I know have spent more time in the emergency room than we have. Could it be that autists are protected from danger by their lack of awareness of it? Sam, scrambling surefooted across a slippery roof, doesn't pause to take stock of his situation, whereas another child might stop, panic, and slip. They are protected, too, by their aloneness. Most cracked heads and greenstick fractures are caused by playground skirmishes, but an autistic child won't come near anyone else at playtime if he can avoid it.

Sam continues to prefer books of photographs over stories. Most babies start with images of familiar objects, of the dog/

apple/socks variety, and move on to stories later. Sam did learn to enjoy some stories, but usually because they referred to his special interests. He liked *The Tiger Who Came to Tea* because cakes featured prominently, *Jemima Puddleduck* because he had a thing about eggs. *Peace at Last* by Jill Murphy, about a family of bears going to bed, was a favorite for ages because it had an alarm clock, a cuckoo clock, *and* a grandfather clock. Sam used to point out a space on one page where he felt another clock should have been. But his taste for stories like these was only an extension of his early interest in books that featured photographs of biscuits. I think it's true to say that Sam has no fictive imagination. He has never identified with a fictional character, never shared their hopes and fears. He has never listened to a story and wondered what happens next? He doesn't care whether Jeremy Fisher gets swallowed by the trout or not; he just likes the bit about digging for worms because there's something about worms that intrigues him.

"He plays very independently and never minds being on his own." Isn't this every mother's dream? After George's wakeful, watchful babyhood, Sam's "independence" was a relief. But I now feel that a twenty-month-old *should* mind being on his own. The ability to amuse oneself is valuable, but a very young child should also be in constant interaction with his mother or mother substitute, showing, asking, sharing. The adult enables the infant to access the world, scale it down, bring it within his grasp. Sam, contentedly alone, was strengthening the barriers to knowledge and understanding that autism was erecting around him.

I note Sam's taste for "grubbing in muddy puddles, etc." Sam was, of course, not the only toddler to enjoy puddles, but he was—and still is—more deeply enthralled than most children by the physical properties of things. So is George, though Sam's approach is more hands-on. Paint, mud, water, soap, butter, wind, ice, Play-Doh, shit; Sam kneads and mashes and splashes and throws himself about in these things. Both he and George have an intimate relationship with the four elements, and on the whole this is an aspect of their condition I really like. It's lovely when they run and run, with the wind in their hair. It's lovely, though nerve-racking, to see them entranced by the shifts and crackles and falls of fires. It's less lovely when they rub excrement into their hair, the curtains, the cracks in the floorboards. This isn't a sign of emotional disturbance, or even deliberate naughtiness. It's just another manifestation of the desire to poke about in puddles. Lacking normal social instincts, neither of them has a sense of revulsion, or shame. It's been hard work training them to accept the difference between poo and Play-doh, but we do seem to be winning. It's been several years since smearing was a major problem, though it's still not safe to leave Sam alone in the bath . . .

Sam's twenty-month lack of preference for any particular toy could also be symptomatic. A characteristic of autism, one of the clearest signs in a toddler, is that toys are rarely put to their intended use. Babies simply explore the physical properties of toys—soft, rattly, bouncy, chewy—but by twenty months they should have moved beyond this stage. Cars should be pushed along the carpet, dolls should be fed, put to bed, and—I'm afraid—scolded. As time goes on, soldiers should fight, trains should stop for passengers, balls should be aimed toward goals. Of course, "normal" play is hugely flexible. A toy soldier can inhabit a dollhouse, a soft rabbit can become a soccer ball, cars can have characters and conversations. But at a remarkably young age normal children will pick up the toy manufacturers' intentions, even if they then decide to put the toy to rather different use.

Autistic children show a diminished interest in toys. When they do pick them up, they explore them physically, rather as a baby would. The child will often hold a toy car close to his face and spin the wheels repeatedly. Both George and Sam would run little trains quickly past their eyes. Bricks or trains will be laid out in rows, and woe betide anyone who moves them. Soft toys, like Sam's Owly, may be obsessively fingered and sniffed, but it's unlikely they'll be given a personality. Autistic play is essentially static. It's striking how very young neurotypical children will home in on toys that correspond to their own nascent interests or aptitudes. Most children will try out a range of playthings, but a particular bent for animals, vehicles, buildings, or whatever, soon manifests itself; early interests are nearly always observable in later life, even if their outward form has changed. Sam's lack of preference for any particular toy resembles his lack of discrimination between people, his failure to engage with most human activities. There is a kind of blankness.

I mention Sam's early love of music. That has never altered. George is "the musical one," with a good singing voice and an excellent musical memory; Sam has a voice like a bullfrog, but he too, in a lesser way, has a large repertoire of songs, and he shows pleasure and animation when music is played. He likes a strong beat—reggae and ska always get him moving.

It's extraordinary, now, to read that Sam once ate "very heartily." Eating problems are almost universal among autists. I'm so used to it, so out of touch with normal eating in children, that I still hold my breath when Jake happily eats fruit and vegetables—it looks miraculous to me. At twenty months, Sam's diet and eating habits seemed normal and healthy enough, but a note of warning is struck by that phrase "He is not interested in what adults eat." Penelope Leach suggests parents include the child in their meals, offer tastes of whatever's going. Sound advice, except that it depends on the natural curiosity of the neurotypical child. Most toddlers do want to know what their parents are eating, even if they then reject it. I remember Jake, the Christmas before he was two, asking for chestnut stuffing simply because he'd never had it before. This would have been unthinkable with either of his brothers. This isn't simply about fussy eating; some toddlers are fussy eaters; some are not. It's about eating as a social, shared activity, and for Sam it simply wasn't. When, years later, I decided to take gluten and casein out of his diet, people said, "Oh, but won't that be sad because he won't be able to share your meals anymore?" But he never did share our meals, so it wasn't sad.

My description of Sam as "quietly sociable" is a little rose-tinted. I don't think Sam ever sought the company of a child other than George, to whom he is genuinely close. But, unlike George, he showed no anxiety about the proximity of other children. If older children kissed him or picked him up, he would smile. If another child wanted his toy, he would hand it over without hesitation or complaint. He never, I think, offered toys to children or made overtures of any kind other than smiles. Sometimes the antics of others amused him, but apart from the most basic chasing, bouncing, and splashing games, Sam has never sought to join any group activity.

His roaring when thwarted sounds like classic toddler behavior, which indeed it was. Unlike other toddlers, he didn't grow out of it. Just last night, he and I had a fight over Chipsticks—a difference of opinion about opening a new packet before the old one was finished—that lasted on and off all evening. The roaring has been replaced by jumping up and down and biting his hand, but the single-mindedness is still there. His sleeping habits were not exceptional at twenty months—they were to become so later on. It's unusual, though not unheard of, for so young a child to lie awake for an hour and a half without calling for attention. Taken on its own, it sounds like an entirely good thing, like the independent play, but it can also be seen as a symptom of unnatural emotional detachment, a short circuit in Sam's social wiring. I well remember Sam's need to take everything out of his crib every morning. He would waddle into the kitchen, bowed under the weight, blankets trailing behind him in bridal fashion. Was this an early manifestation of obsessive tendencies, of the need to create rituals? Later, aged about five, he went to the opposite extreme and stowed objects under his duvet. I once uncovered a cache of sixty-three different items—the usual soft toys and picture books, but also things as disparate as a cheese grater, my party shoes, and a cereal-packet plastic statuette of soccer star Alan Shearer.

So, yes, with hindsight and vastly increased knowledge of the subject I can identify my account of Sam at twenty months as the unwitting profile of a child with autism. But I'm not at all surprised that I didn't spot it at the time. Nobody did. Sam and George were seen, in the usual way, by midwives, health visitors, and doctors. Until George was three and a half, none of them noticed anything wrong at all.

FIVE

Diagnosis

How does one arrive at a diagnosis of autism? There have been three important stages in reaching the current definition. In 1943, Leo Kanner was the first to describe "classic" autism, which is sometimes called "Kanner's syndrome." The two characteristics he emphasized above all others were "an extreme aloneness, from the earliest days," and an intense desire for "the preservation of sameness."

Hans Asperger, only a year later in 1944, published his own findings. Asperger's case studies tended toward the high-functioning end of what is now generally accepted as the autistic spectrum. While Kanner's children were withdrawn, aloof, locked in a limited world of their own, Asperger's had stronger social instincts but a poor and eccentric understanding of how to operate on a social level. Asperger emphasized that, despite "considerable and very typical difficulties of social integration," "his" children had "particular originality of thought and experience, which may well lead to exceptional achievements in later life."

Kanner and Asperger were working independently of each other. Kanner was in Baltimore; his account was published in English and quickly became well known. Asperger was in Vienna; his paper, written in German and published during the Second World War, received little attention. It was not until the 1990s that Asperger's work became well known in Britain and America. Now, "Asperger's syndrome" has become widely used as a description—crudely speaking—of "able" autistic people. But there is still catching up to do; for many years, due to a quirk of history, it was Kanner's definition that reigned supreme.

In the early 1970s, as a result of a London study by Lorna Wing and Judith Gould, a "triad of impairments" was established. This triad is still the main diagnostic criterion. To be counted as autistic, the child (or adult) must have impaired communication, impaired imagination, and impaired social interaction. The degree of impairment varies enormously. Wing is insistent on autism as a "spectrum disorder," ranging from extreme intellectual and behavioral disability to mild social handicap.

Then, in 1985, Simon Baron-Cohen, Alan Leslie, and Uta Frith augmented the diagnostic picture by adding the "theory of mind." The autist has no theory of mind; he is mind-blind. He does not fully understand that your experience of the world is different from his own. This applies whether his IQ level is low or high. This was demonstrated by the "Sally-Anne experiment." Autistic, normal, and Down's syndrome children were all shown a scenario enacted by dolls. Sally has a basket; Anne has a box. Sally has a marble. She puts it into her basket and leaves. While Sally is away, Anne removes Sally's marble and places it in her own box. Sally returns. The child is asked, "Where will Sally look for her marble?"

Anyone reading this book will (I assume!) know that Sally will look in her basket, because that's where she believes the marble to be. The nonautistic children gave the correct answer; so did most of the Down's children. All but a few of the autistic children gave the wrong answer. They said Sally would look in the box, because that's where the marble actually was. They could not understand that Sally didn't know this.

These three stages toward diagnosis—the 1940s papers, the "triad of impairments," and the "theory of mind" discovery—do not quarrel with one another. Wing does not contradict Kanner; Frith does not supersede Wing. They augment one another and, put together, indicate the immense complexity of this condition, which defies any simple diagnostic test.

Taking Kanner's criteria in isolation, neither George nor Sam would be classed as autistic. Neither of them is, or has ever been, "extremely alone." When George's behavior first gave me cause for anxiety, the idea of autism did enter my head, but I dismissed it, thinking, "He can't be autistic—he's too affectionate." George has always sought people out, and discriminated strongly between them. His relationships are lopsided and peculiar, but they are full of feeling. Aged thirteen, he still climbs into my bed most nights and cuddles me, and he's not just using me as a human hot water bottle. Sam, though more aloof than George, also has favorite people. He, too, enjoys physical contact on his own terms, and seeks it out. At times he has established an "in-joke" with a particular person, which is reserved for that person alone. For instance, he goes, laughing, to Ian, our nanny, and says, "One-two-three!" meaning, please pick me up and throw me in the air. On the telephone to Grandfather Clive—always a favorite person—he used to say, "Grandfather Clock—Grandfather Clive!" plainly with humorous and sociable intent.

So, my boys are not "alone" in Kanner's sense, though their human relationships are all profoundly odd. Neither do they

conform to Kanner's second criterion; they are not strongly motivated by a desire for "the preservation of sameness," though this
is observable in a diluted form. Kanner was thinking of the kind
of autists who insist on wearing exactly the same Buzz Lightyear
pajamas, day and night, or who won't tolerate the slightest re-
arrangement of the furniture, or who need to eat nine Smarties at
eleven o'clock each morning, and woe betide anyone who dis-
turbs the color order in which those nine Smarties are assembled.
The lives of many families are dominated by such insistences. I'm
lucky in that both my boys are—relatively—flexible. We've had
phases when George would only wear black or red (currently, it's
pink and tartan, but with some leeway), and both boys find some
kinds of change quite difficult—Sam was recently incensed when
I removed a fireguard, so I put it back, because it didn't matter
much. But I've been able to move things around in their bedroom,
get a new car, take them on certain kinds of holiday, and move
them from one school to another, without extraordinary fuss.

So they would have slipped through Kanner's net. What about
Asperger's? Asperger avoided concise formulations and was perhaps more cautious than Kanner in his conclusions. His emphasis
is on social integration and the uneven pattern of intellectual
achievements. My sons would have fitted on these counts, though
Sam's intellectual achievements are far, far lower than those of any of
the children Asperger studied. And neither of them has the "excellent ability of logical abstract thinking" that he describes—neither
George nor Sam remotely conform to the "nutty professor" stereo-
type. Asperger notes the "characteristic peculiarity of gaze" and
"poverty of facial expression," but in George and Sam these characteristics are subtle, easy to miss. Both can maintain eye contact, and
both have a considerable range of facial expressions, though some
are missing—pride and embarrassment, for example. But I've seen

such nonautistic expressions as guilt and mischievousness clearly shown on both their faces.

Neither George nor Sam fits neatly with Asperger's case studies, though George comes closer. What of Wing's "triad of impairments"? It's interesting that despite being so different from each other, both boys fit under this umbrella. It's important to emphasize that word "impairment." Impaired communication doesn't mean no communication. Very few autists have no communication at all, though many have no speech. The children in whom communication is most profoundly impaired are those who appear to have no desires—the state of "Nirvana" admirably described by Clara Claiborne Park in *The Siege*, her account of her successful battle to create desire, to introduce motivation, into the closed world of her daughter, Jessy.

Some autists, as mentioned in chapter 3, have clear, fluent speech, and use immense vocabularies with more than usual ease. Where, then, is the communication impairment? Look closely, and it will always be found. The autist may be literal-minded, baffled by irony and metaphor—though some use striking metaphors of their own construction. Phrases like "You'll be the death of me" or "I cried my eyes out" can cause distress and puzzlement to autists. George, sitting quietly in the kitchen with a glass of water, overheard us adults talking about George Best, the soccer star, and his drinking problems. Best had been treated with a drug that turned alcohol into an instant, deadly poison. Someone remarked, "If George Best has one more drink, he'll die." Our George began to weep, silently. It took me a long time to discover the reason. "If I have that drink I won't die!" he exclaimed at last, dolefully regarding his tumbler of blameless water.

However apparently fluent the speaker, if he is autistic, he is unlikely to use slang or colloquialisms with any ease. And, most significant of all, communication will be one-sided. The autist may want to tell you about computers or tornadoes or the Highway Code but is unlikely to listen carefully to what you say in return, unless you provide information that happens to dovetail with his particular interest. Female readers who have sat through dinner parties smiling politely while their male companions hold forth may protest that this is not an exclusively autistic characteristic—and indeed, researchers from Asperger to Baron-Cohen have suggested that autism may be a form of extreme maleness. Some autists may be excellent at one-way communication, speaking fluently and intelligently on a chosen subject, but when communication is considered as a two-way business, the impairment soon shows.

It's quite often said that autistic people have no imagination. This is wrong, and here I'd even take issue, just a little bit, with the admirable Lorna Wing; I'm not sure that "impaired imagination" is quite right. It's absolutely true that autistic children don't have the same imaginative play as neurotypical children. This is one of the earliest warning signs. The two-year-old who will never feed, scold, or say good night to her doll, or who will only do so when prompted, needs to be investigated. The neurotypical imagination is amazingly inventive but also, at root, extremely predictable. In the same way that there are said to be only six plots for stories, though any number of variant details, so the foundations of human imaginative play are "samey" the world over. This is because they are built on the child's own experience. The child will make toys eat, fight, hurt themselves, compete, sleep, embrace, converse, receive instruction, get lost and found again, the emphasis depending on the child's gender, life experience, and natural inclinations. Jake's teddies run races a lot; his cousin Stella's are more likely to be sent to school. Play reflects and enlarges upon what the child already knows.

Play also reinforces the child's sense of connectedness with other people. When a mother and child conspire to pretend that a teddy is alive, they are using imagination to strengthen their emotional bond through a pleasurable activity. Less obviously, the child is learning that her mother has an independent, imaginative "inner" self. Even the youngest child understands that Teddy will not really drink her juice; neither does she seriously think she's fooling her mother into believing that he does. The game is strengthening the child's understanding that other people have minds that are separate from her own, that she and her mother can collude to enjoy a "false belief." Shared imaginative play, in short, teaches the child to have a "theory of mind."

This aspect of imaginative play is almost entirely denied the autistic child. When George was little he would play with dolls; he had two baby dolls called Sam and Max, and he would accept suggestions from me—Sam needs to sleep, Max wants a biscuit, and so on. But there was no two-way play, no turn taking. Sam and Max had no characters; their activities never developed beyond a crude imitation of the kind of physical care needed by the real Sam, then a baby. "I know, Mummy, you pretend that Max is ill, and I'll be the doctor." That sort of play never happened for George. Sam's imaginative play was even less social. It was usually concerned with machines and only rarely involved humans or human substitutes.

It's very hard to write about autistic imaginings because, like their dreams, autists so rarely describe them to us. But it seems to me that they don't fully enact social situations through play because social situations have little meaning for them. A normal child uses toys to explore the ever-increasing complexities of her interconnectedness with other people. She has more control over her toys than she does over the animate world, so she is able to go over the most interesting or difficult bits to her heart's content. The toys help her to think flexibly and creatively about the social structure of which she dimly perceives herself to be a part. When she is ready, she can incorporate another child into her fantasy and accept the contributions the other child will make. It's noticeable that though two-year-olds are interested in one another, they're not good at sharing pretend play without adult help, but by five they are able to listen, take turns, and build on one another's suggestions in a mutually satisfying creative dialogue.

Toys are useful and important to the normal child, but if there aren't any, she'll provide her own. Safety pins, wood chips, bits of fluff off the carpet—once she realizes she is truly left to her own devices, she'll anthropomorphize absolutely anything. She'd rather have a doll, but a clothes-peg can become a person for her—can even become a person for whom she feels affection. I remember feeling very fond of a cupboard-full of rolled-up socks, because I chose to call them kittens. At the same time, the child is able to keep a sense of perspective. However powerful her imaginings, she knows they are different from reality. If the socks had been thrown away, I would have been upset, but not as upset as I would have been at the disposal of a litter of living kittens.

Presented with a group of mixed toys, the normal baby will handle them, mouth them, explore the sounds they make. So will most autistic babies. For the first year of life it could be extremely hard to tell the difference. There are some autistic babies who are oddly passive and don't respond to anything much, but George and Sam certainly did not fall into this category. The normal toddler will attempt to put the toys to their intended use—pretend to drink from a doll's cup, push a car across the floor, put a teddy into a stroller, maybe circle a toy airplane in the air. Gender differences will show even before the age of two, with most (though not all) boys selecting the car and plane and most (though not all) girls going for the cup and teddy. The autistic toddler *may* also use the toys "appropriately," especially if prompted by an adult. He is, however, more likely to seek out those aspects of the toys that stimulate his senses rather than his emotional intellect—he'll spin the car's wheels near his ear, or run the plane past his eyes, repeatedly, very close. The autistic toddler is also much more likely than the normal one to ignore the toys altogether.

Still, at this stage it would be quite easy to mistake autistic play for normal play. A couple of years on, the difference would be far more obvious. Presented with disparate toys, the normal child would attempt to make connections between them. She'd weave them into some kind of story—the teddy would travel by plane to a holiday destination where he would drink something unusual from a cup—the cup alone would stand in for a whole café. A little boy might make the car and the plane race, crash, or fight—with Teddy as adjudicator. If the provided toys didn't conform to the child's imaginative desire, they'd be recast; the car would become Teddy's mother; the cup could be a football for two competing vehicles.

The autistic child would not do this *at all*. Autistic children do not use toys as flexible props in the telling of their own stories. Some, like Sam, are struck by physical resemblances—a stalk of cow parsley was sufficiently similar to a vacuum cleaner to allow Sam to vacuum most of our orchard. But there was no story here. Sam was not "being a mummy cleaning the house." He enjoyed the physical behavior of the vacuum cleaner and wished to re-create this effect, but the "game" was devoid of emotional meaning.

Others, like George, become interested in the characters in stories or videos. If, in my hypothetical group of toys, the four-year-old George had found something that resembled, say, Pingu or Thomas the Tank Engine, he could have played with it. To the casual observer he would have been acting out a story in an imaginative way. But, looked at closely, the story would have been a close copy of the one he already knew. Thomas would have gotten stuck in imaginary snow, for instance—and after being dug out he would have gotten stuck again. And again. Thomas would not have been provided with any previously unscripted lines. Pingu would not have stepped, or waddled, out of role to create a new plotline. And the "story" would not have had a beginning, middle, and end. It would have been a snatch of story, a single event, isolated, out of context. And George's interpretations could be tiresomely literal. I found him, once, sitting in a pool of his own urine, quoting from *The Tale of Mrs. Tittlemouse*—the part where Mr. Jackson the toad drips water all over her nice clean floor.

George rarely "took on" a character. Sam never did. George seemed worried by the idea, as if he feared losing his own identity. Sam just didn't understand the concept. Some autistic children, however, do assume a character. When they do, it takes over. The child becomes Buzz Lightyear, 24/7. All right, says the eager mother, delighted by the emergence of some apparently "normal" play, you be Buzz, I'll be Woody. But Buzz doesn't want his mother to be Woody, unless, perhaps, she has as accurate a memory for dialogue as he has, and can reenact favorite scenes from *Toy Story* to the same obsessively high standard. Buzz doesn't need a Woody because he doesn't need to give himself a social life. Something about Buzz's appearance or tone of voice has entranced the child, and all he wants to do is relive it over and over again. Is this imaginative play, or just another stim?

When George was at mainstream primary school, aged about six, he developed an intense interest in Disney's *Snow White*. He was given photocopied sheets of characters from the film and would color these in, from memory, with complete accuracy. Dopey's hat, Doc's belt, Sneezy's boots—George knew the colors by heart and never made a mistake. And he "became" Bashful. He decided he *was* Bashful. At school, he would only answer the attendance to "Bashful Smith." This lasted for about a term. But he didn't act out the part of Bashful. He didn't alter his behavior in any way. He just announced that Bashful was who he was.

A little later, *Pinocchio* took over. This time George didn't call himself Pinocchio, but he repeatedly acted out moments from the film ("scenes" suggests a completeness that was distinctly lacking from George's performances). He put a half-lemon on top of his head, like Pinocchio's yellow cap, held a strand of raw spaghetti to his nose, and carefully threw himself down our stairs, singing a snatch of "I've got no strings to hold me down—whoops!" When Pinocchio is made to perform by Stromboli, the cruel puppet master, on his début appearance he falls down some steps, pierces a floorboard with his nose, and pulls up said floorboard, to laughter from the crowd. George would try to burrow his nose into our dining-room parquet but failed to achieve the desired result.

George thought about Pinocchio a lot, and drew pictures of him, including one of him coming down the stairs in a Duchamp-like blur of legs. It's tempting to think that he was exploring the Pinocchio story to draw imaginative parallels with his own situation; did George feel himself to be not quite human, a puppet who might one day turn into a real boy? It's possible—just as it's possible that he chose Bashful as the dwarf most emotionally linked to his autistic state (though some days, Grumpy would have fitted the bill, too). But equally, it could have been something about the smile, movements, or tone of voice that attracted him; in other words, the characters might have provided sensory rather than imaginative excitement. It's very hard to know.

Very able autists sometimes create elaborate fantasy worlds, with rules and outlandishly named countries and warring tribes. What is there to distinguish these fantasies from the sub-Tolkien imaginings of many a normal nine-year-old? One difference is likely to be accessibility. The autistic or Asperger's fantasist may decide to tell you all about the world he has created, but he's unlikely to welcome any suggestions you make. The normal nine-year-old can't wait for his friend to come around on Saturday so that they can both charge about the garden bashing orcs with sticks. The Asperger's child can't accommodate a friend, unless the friend is prepared to obey his every command. Other people are all right, says John Peters, a grandfather with Asperger's speaking on the BBC documentary *The Autism Puzzle,* as long as they do exactly what you want.

There'll be another difference, too. Normal little boys are notoriously bloodthirsty, but there will be some emotional content in their play. Goodies and baddies will be clearly distinguished, and betrayal, courage, honor, and friendship will feature in some form, however vestigial. The Asperger imagination is far more taken with rules and structures than with feelings. The imaginary world of the autist is likely to be immensely detailed, ordered, and emotionally static.

I'm only guessing. Only a handful of autistic adults have been able to tell us about what they imagine. I know almost nothing, for instance, about autistic dreams. I suspect that it is harder for an autist to know when the dream ends and reality begins. I recall only two occasions when George or Sam seemed to be telling me about a dream, and in both cases the dream seemed to have some kind of physical reality for them. Once George stood up in bed, screaming with terror, pointing to a corner of the room where, he said, he could see "Oliver the Western engine." There was no toy engine there, but George was running a fever. Perhaps this was more a hallucination than a dream. Sam once complained about "snakies and snailies in the night." I took this to be a dream, but I did discover some lumps of sucked bread in his bed—perhaps these were the snakies and snailies. Jake, by contrast, gives me regular bulletins about his dream life. He was only two when he dreamed about "a wife in my cot cutting down trees wiv a axe." Good old Freud.

To return to the diagnostic criteria—is it fair to call the autistic imagination "impaired"? It certainly operates in a very different way and is not put to the same uses. The neurotypical child uses her imagination in learning how to think and how to feel. Through symbolic play, she works out that different people have different perspectives. An idea is not a fact but something open to interpretation. By hiding Teddy and having Rabbit look for him, the child is moving away from the simple, concrete world of milk, biscuit, ball.

The autistic child cannot access the common stock of symbols. He may develop his own set of symbols, but he does not instinctively accept the transference of meanings that allow normal children to play imaginatively with one another. The autist can go some way down our symbolic path, but he will soon meet a dead end. The hardest thing for an autist to grasp is that other people have different thoughts, different feelings, from his own. Playing with toys doesn't help him to understand social complexities because, it seems, the neural pathways that should guide him to this kind of understanding are blocked.

Simon Baron-Cohen and his collaborators have devised a test

intended as an early-warning system to pick up autistic symptoms. The CHAT test (Checklist for Autism in Toddlers) is now used by some health authorities as part of the eighteen-month developmental check; it's carried out by a health visitor, who will have had some training in its use. It's a good idea, but it's by no means infallible. If I'd been asked whether, at eighteen months, George and Sam used pretend play, the answer would have been yes in both cases. A close look at the frequency and quality of their play would have revealed deficits, but it would have taken an exceptionally alert health visitor to pick them up. Did they push cars along the carpet, making "brm-brm" noises? Did they hold cups and spoons to the mouths of stuffed animals? Yes they did— occasionally and halfheartedly.

Lorna Wing's third impairment, that of social interaction, is the one most easily observable in very young children. Does a baby greet a parent with enthusiasm? Does he raise his arms to be picked up? Does he offer toys to adults as a way of initiating social contact (as opposed to needing help with the toy, for instance, to mend it, or switch it on)? Failure to do these things should be investigated.

It is unlikely that any baby, unless severely brain-damaged, will make no social contact at all. Once again, it's the quality and the frequency of the overtures that count. I've said that both George and Sam were affectionate, smiley babies, and so they were, but now I believe they lacked the automatic, instinctive social skills possessed in spades by Jake. Sometimes they greeted me effusively; sometimes they seemed to be in a kind of trance, and there was no greeting. My cousin Caroline described how, when she went away, her son Toby would "punish" her for her absence by turning his face away and rejecting a cuddle on her return. I waited for George and Sam to behave like this, but they never did. They had no awareness of the effect they could have on my state of mind.

Toby's behavior was socially sophisticated. He knew that he had a fair chance of altering his mother's behavior if he played mind games. George and Sam could express pleasure and woe, but they could not scheme, or feign, or cajole. An autistic baby is never coy.

Abnormal social interaction is likely to be the first of the three impairments to show, but it's still quite easy to overlook in babyhood. Babies spend an awful lot of time being overtired, gassy, cutting teeth, hatching colds, and so on—or at least, their mothers think they do. And interpreting preverbal behavior is difficult. I asked a friend, Elspeth, whether she'd noticed anything odd about my boys before they were diagnosed. Well, yes, she said, when Sam was about nine months old and we'd been on holiday together, she'd tried quite hard to engage him in play and had been completely ignored. Not actively rebuffed, not rejected as in go-away-you're-not-my-mother. Sam just acted as if she wasn't there. Oh, well, thought Elspeth, maybe it's just because I'm too boring. But of course, that wasn't it.

As time goes on, the impairment becomes more marked. Lack of cooperative play with other children, lack of interest in adult activity, and—in my opinion, most crucially—failure to imitate adult behavior, all indicate a fundamental problem. Poor play skills can be attributed to shyness, emotional disturbance, or lack of practice—"He'll be all right once he's at school." But social obliviousness is harder to explain. The child who sits at the bottom of the slide, deaf to the pleas of others that he move over; the child who passively allows toys to be snatched from him and exhibits no animosity toward the snatcher; the child who shows no interest in or understanding of simple social games like ring-a-roses or hide-and-seek—this child is displaying the kind of social impairment Wing meant.

Toddlers love to imitate their parents. They want to stir saucepans, sweep floors, waft imaginary razors over their cheeks. They're nosey—they want to know what's on their father's dinner plate, what's in their mother's handbag. They delight in child-sized versions of adult equipment, whether it's a tool set or a doctor's kit. The reason for this kind of imitation is obvious; it's part of the long process of learning to be an adult. George and Sam didn't imitate—or rather, they imitated a few, selected activities, but they never built up a repertoire of copied, learned skills. Sam imitated mixing a cake because the beaters excited him, but he didn't copy me when I was gardening or writing a letter. George could accurately repeat a phrase I would use, in my exact tone of voice, but he couldn't build on this to imitate my conversational pattern with friends his own age. When George or Sam imitated an action, it was in a subscribed, end-stopped way. The action was performed for its own sake, not as part of a greater, more meaningful whole. Thus George saw the Aristocats splash paint over a piano, and so he painted our own piano keyboard. Jake, though, aged three, would bash away at my word processor—"I'm writing for the newspaper to get some money for us, Mum."

Communication, imagination, social interaction—the three are, of course, closely linked. You could, however, have one impaired, with the other two pretty much fully functioning—in which case you would not be autistic. A deaf child, for instance, would by definition have impaired communication, but his imagination and his social instincts—though affected by his deafness—would remain intact. He would need help to achieve full social interaction, but his desire for that interaction would be as strong as in a hearing child, and his innate inclination to communicate would eventually enable him to find alternative ways of doing so. In an autistic child, the links between the "triad" have never been forged, perhaps cannot be forged. The autist is differently wired.

What does Simon Baron-Cohen's "theory of mind" add to the diagnostic picture? The Sally-Anne experiment, with the dolls and the marble, illustrates what Wing's impairments actually mean in terms of living a life. The autist may be highly intelligent, or mentally retarded, but what he cannot do is use his imagination to understand that other people experience things differently. He cannot communicate properly because he doesn't know what needs to be communicated. He cannot interact socially because he has no perspective on himself as a social being.

On a practical level, the lack of a "theory of mind" has many frustrations for both autists and carers. "Want it, want it," chants the child. He doesn't know that he has to tell his mother what "it" is. A child cuts his hand, badly, on the school playground. He says nothing to the teacher on duty. He can't guess that she won't know the cut has happened until he tells her. I know a little boy who developed peritonitis—he'd had appendicitis for a while, but it hadn't occurred to him to tell anyone about the pain.

I knew, for certain, that Jake wasn't autistic when he was about fifteen months old. He had just learned to walk. He had a biscuit in his hand, and he toddled off into the garden, around the corner, out of my sight. He came back, empty-handed, weeping. "Want bikkit," he wailed. He guided me, pointing around the corner, to where the biscuit was, wedged in the spout of a watering can. He knew he had to tell me where the biscuit was. He knew I didn't know.

The other two would not have done this. They might have wept; they might have used the word "bikkit," but more to imply that they should have another one than to tell me what had happened. At fifteen months, George appeared to be a gifted child, Sam seemed like Mr. Cheerful Average, but neither of them understood that, if they didn't tell me what had happened, I couldn't know.

Theory of mind is a uniquely human attribute. One animal can guess from scents or movements how another animal is likely to behave, but it can't, as far as we know, step into the shoes (or paws) of another animal. It can't make a supposition about what the other animal might have experienced, and how it might have reacted to that experience. A normal child, even one of low intelligence, can not only predict where Sally will look for her marble but also guess how Sally will feel when she finds it's missing. An autistic child, whatever the IQ level, is unlikely to be able to do this.

Does this mean that the autist is more like an animal than is the neurotypical human? Actually, the reverse seems to be the case. George and Sam are animal-like in that they use all five senses to explore their environment more actively than do most children. Their response to illness or injury is also animal-like; instead of seeking help, they lie still and wait until the pain has abated. They don't waste energy moaning and worrying, they just curl up and sweat it out. But in terms of the way they spend their time, they are further removed from animal behavior than most of us. Animals spend their time either using or practicing their survival skills. The kitten pounces on cotton spools; the cat pounces on mice. Squirrels run along walls and leap from branch to branch to exercise the muscles and balancing skills required for treetop life. Jake, in a far more sophisticated way, is unconsciously practicing his own survival skills. When he plays football, he's learning to outrun and outwit his competitors. When he plays on his Game Boy, he's honing his mental reactions. The world is too big to experience everything firsthand; when Jake reads stories he's enlarging his knowledge of the world, partly through metaphor. He's also improving his verbal skills, which are of supreme importance in twenty-first-century human society.

Very little of Jake's time is put to no kind of use. The reverse is true of his brothers. Left alone, George and Sam do little apart from "stim." They flap, twiddle, bounce, hum. George tears sweet wrappers into tiny pieces and piles them on the windowsill. Sam bangs balloons up and down between his hands to make a loud, intensely invasive sound. Apart from keeping their muscles from atrophying, it's hard to construe their repetitive self-stimulation as in any way useful or linked to any other activity. The squirrel doesn't run back and forth aimlessly along the same branch. The kitten moves on from cotton spools to mice; cotton reels are not the be-all and end-all. This leads me to the aspects of autism that I think have been overlooked by the currently accepted diagnostic criteria. Autism is a condition with physical as well as mental or behavioral symptoms. All autobiographical accounts by autists have described their heightened sensory experiences. These can be "good" or "bad"; colors may be amazingly rich and vibrant, but the noise of ordinary household appliances may cause acute discomfort.

The fact that autists sense the world differently is manifested in unusual physical behavior. Even the most able can be distinguished by peculiar gait or quirky mannerisms. Bill Gates, the putatively Aspergerish head of Microsoft, is said to rock back and forth continually, as well as having an overloud, harsh, monotonous voice. Walking on tiptoe, hand flapping, head banging, are all common. One of the first oddities I noticed about Sam was that he loved to run up and down beside a straight line—a hedge, a wall, a clothesline—with his head twisted to one side. At the extreme end of the scale, this abnormal response to sensation tips into self-mutilation. George has never gone in for this, thank goodness, but Sam began biting his hands during his big regression at age nearly six, and at one time they were always raw and bleeding.

Diagnosis of autism is always based on observation of behavior. There is no medical test that can be administered, and, at time of writing, no prenatal test. The emphasis is placed on social behavior and verbal development. I believe that more attention needs to be paid to the physical symptoms. The constraints these place on the life of an autist can be a great barrier to social integration and learning. Imagine how you would feel about going to school or to work if strip lighting caused you violent discomfort, or the smell of a certain cleaning fluid made you want to vomit. Then add the problem that you are unlikely to be able to communicate these difficulties to anyone with the power to help you. How daunting and impenetrable the neurotypical world must seem! No wonder so many autists retreat into their own.

SIX

Our Path to Diagnosis

At two and a quarter—Easter 1992—George was charming, sociable, interested in most things adults showed him, bookish, playful, humorous, and willing to perform his party tricks—singing and reciting—to any audience. Less than three months later, all this had gone.

I can be precise about the dates, because there were two trips to visit his paternal grandparents in Devon, one at Easter, one in late June. The first was a success, the second a disaster. In June, George was an unhappy child. He was clingy and fearful, he didn't want to "perform," he didn't want to be shown anything new.

There was a crucial difference between the two visits. On the second one, I wasn't there. I was working, taking a school group on an Outward Bound expedition to Snowdonia (which for me, incidentally, is atypical behavior). Min took George and Sam to Devon during my absence.

Five days is a long time for a two-year-old to be parted from his mother. I attributed George's unhappiness to that. It had been a bad idea to send him to Devon, even to the grandparents of whom he had always been so fond. He would have felt more secure, I concluded, if he had stayed at home.

I'd left him before, for work-related reasons, and he'd coped well. But he was a "terrible two" now; two-year-olds are famously moody and volatile. George's behavior didn't improve during that summer. Friends urged me to send him to nursery school; mixing with other children his own age would help, they said. He did a trial morning at nursery school and spent the whole time hiding in the Wendy House. When I came to pick him up, I heard him sobbing, "Oh, Mummy, where are you? Oh, Mummy, where are you?" (By the way, even this heartfelt cry was a quotation; he had a book of that title.) I had the distinct impression he'd kept this up all morning.

He just wasn't ready for nursery. I deferred his entry until January, when he would be three. His behavior problems continued. He was happy and lively at home, doing just what he wanted, but he couldn't cope with new places or new people. At birthday parties he would scream. On one memorable occasion he pulled the cloth with all the magician's tricks on it off the table. Hats, wands, false-bottomed boxes, all crashed to the floor.

His intellectual development, which had seemed so startlingly quick, plateaued. He still liked books and songs, but only the same ones, over and over again; he fiercely resisted anything new. His speech no longer seemed precocious; I was beginning to realize how much of it was echolalic. He was disobedient without being mischievous, as if he really didn't understand the concept of no. He had a little train, "Mike," that went round and round a track. He stared at it and put himself into a trance; it became difficult to attract his attention. Eating and sleeping were still chaotic. Potty training was a nonstarter.

He turned three; nursery school began. It was a pleasant nursery. The children's behavior was orderly, the teacher sensible and intelligent. George settled in, up to a point. He still tended to take refuge in the Wendy House and sometimes had to be coaxed out with biscuits. However, he showed enthusiasm for some activities, like trampolining, and he enjoyed learning songs with actions. "My goodness," said the teacher to me when I collected him one day, "I never knew 'Twinkle, Twinkle, Little Star' had so many verses."

But George's favorite thing at school was the attendance log. Back home, alone in his room, I could hear him reciting it to himself. His imitation of his teacher's voice was uncanny. He enjoyed the names of the other children even if he seemed shy in their presence. When our peachicks hatched, George named them after three of his classmates, Millie, Chloë, and Elliott. He would also repeat phrases he'd heard his teacher use often to dramatic effect. "Andrew, I said TAP OFF! Corinne, unlock the door!" When he was three and a half, the health visitor called for his routine development check. George was not especially cooperative, but she was satisfied with his performance. She thought he was very bright and that his speech was advanced. I pointed out to her that much of it was parroted. She produced a jigsaw puzzle, showing an elephant's trunk arching over a row of other jungle animals—monkey, hippo, snake. She asked George to name the animals. "That's an elephant," he said. "Good. And what's that?" she asked, pointing to the monkey. "That's a coffee cake," said George. The health visitor laughed. George didn't react to her laughter. "What's that?" "That's a cherry cake," said George, solemn-faced. He went along the row of animals—"That's a chocolate cake. That's a almond cake. That's a cream cake."

"Well," said the health visitor, preparing for departure, "at least he's got a sense of humor." I wasn't sure that he had. It had dawned on me that the position of the elephant's trunk relative to the row of animals was similar to an illustration in one of George's books, *The Elephant and the Bad Baby*, where the elephant reaches over a row of labeled cakes to take a bun. George had been identifying the jigsaw animals purely in terms of their spatial relationship to an elephant's trunk. He had ignored all other identifying criteria.

I explained this to the health visitor. She still thought he was fine but said that if I was worried, she would refer him to a speech therapist. I agreed. The speech therapist saw George for several sessions. I suspect she guessed the truth straightaway, but it's not her job to give a diagnosis. She referred him to our local hospital. These things take time to arrange, though they shouldn't. Our wait was much shorter than that of some parents, but it wasn't until December, several months later, that the hospital saw George and pronounced him physically fit and normal. They made an appointment to have him assessed by Dr. Gilly Baird, from Guy's Hospital, in January 1994, just before his fourth birthday.

I knew what autism was, or thought I did. In my teens I had been very struck by a book called *For the Love of Ann,* the true story of an autistic girl who had made a rather miraculous "recovery," largely, as far as I recall, through interaction with the family dog. I had seen an exhibition of the brilliant, energized, Picasso-like drawings of a girl called Nadia, and had been saddened to read that as her acquisition of life skills increased, so her remarkable ability ebbed away. I remembered a couple of autistic children at the special-needs school where I had helped in my teens—a handsome, unsmiling boy called David who didn't speak but drew pictures of electrical circuits, and a huge, frightening girl who rocked back and forth and gnawed at the scars on her hands. And of course I had seen *Rain Man*.

None of the people I had read about or met bore any resemblance to George. I can't remember what I expected from our meeting with Dr. Baird, but it certainly wasn't a diagnosis of autism. By pure chance, apropos of a conversation we were having about someone else's child, a friend lent us a copy of (I think) *The New Yorker* that carried a long article about Temple Grandin. Neither of us had heard of Asperger's syndrome before; Asperger's work was only translated into English in 1991, by Uta Frith. We discussed the article. Yes, George was quite like Temple Grandin in some ways, but in others he was quite different. As requested, we compiled a list of his main peculiarities to submit to the hospital. I reproduce it here:

Has a good ear, very good vocal imitator, but very little imitative behaviour. He is unusually good at singing.

Mixes up pronouns. Poor grammar.

He talks through quotations and by imitating adult speech, doesn't use words as discrete semantic items very much.

Has poor social interaction. Doesn't know how to play with others.

Avoids eye contact with strangers.

He is very excitable (easily aroused, not easy to calm).

Can't keep still.

He complains about strong stimuli, such as the sun, loud noises.

Sleeplessness.

He is a dreamer, living to some extent in "his own little world."

Abnormalities of attention, including the ability to shut people out and be absorbed in something trivial for a long time.

Loves nature, will stand and look at the moon for as long as he is allowed, despite freezing weather.

Good with animals. Keen on and gentle with babies.

Has a strong aversion to strangers, groups, and crowds, but manages to go to school all right.

Obsessive.

Ritualistic.

Lines up bricks in rows, or matched by color, doesn't build. Always destroys.

Poor fine-motor control, but balance and gross-motor control seem OK.

Physical contact good, embracing, etc., will offer cheek for a kiss but doesn't know how to give a kiss.

Doesn't ask for potty, seems not to know when urination is imminent. Dry at school for three-hour stretch.

Occasionally plays with feces.

"Resistant" to being taught. It is very hard to explain things to George.

Doesn't dress or undress—just beginning to put on trousers and coat.

Food—sticks to a very limited menu for a few weeks then switches to something new.

Throwing and catching poor.

Doesn't draw, doesn't hold pen properly.

Knew all colors at eighteen months, all letters at twenty months.

Could recognize simple words at twenty months.

Has a strong reaction to colors.

Can't describe an event.

Never asks questions except where is Mummy, Daddy, Sam.

Doesn't argue, simply states the contrary: "No, Mummy is NOT going to work."

Only just starting to correlate facial expression of others to emotion.

Puts everything in his mouth still.

He knows several hundred books off by heart.
Doesn't mind physical discomfort. Very brave about knocks.
  High pain threshold?
Ribena [blackberry soft drink] and (probably) most berry fruits
  seem to have a catastrophic effect on George's mood and
  behavior.
Is there a blood-sugar problem?

And at the end of this account, Min, definitely a step ahead of me,
has written "Asperger's syndrome??"

People often ask whether receiving the diagnosis was a terrible
shock. I can't honestly remember much about my state of mind,
but I don't think "shock" is the right word. There was even some
element of relief. My all-but-four-year-old was still in nappies and
still had the sleep habits of a newborn baby—now I knew this
wasn't entirely my fault. Dr. Baird said he had Asperger's syndrome (it was changed to "autism" a couple of years later) and I
took her opinion seriously, but I tended to accentuate the positive.
"He'll find easy things difficult, and difficult things easy," she said.
That didn't sound too bad. We were told that there was no cure,
that the right education was the only appropriate treatment. I don't
remember much in the way of follow-up advice as to what the
"right" education might be. When I left the room I didn't have the
impression that I had a child with a lifelong, all-pervasive disability. I just had George, and now I had an explanation for some of
his problems.

During the session, much of my attention had been taken up
with keeping George amused and under control. This is always a
difficulty when mother and child are seen together. There should
be further sessions when the parents can be seen alone, so that

the implications of the child's condition can be discussed in detail, without distractions. We were visited at home by a special-needs nurse a couple of times, but all I remember her saying was that learning to ride could be good for George, and that I shouldn't give him drinks at night. She was more concerned about Min, who had a very bad reaction to the news, and who was in fact about to have a full-scale nervous breakdown.

I do remember that we were both insistent that we had no worries about Sam. We used Sam as a point of comparison. Sam, nearly two years younger, could pedal a trike, whereas George couldn't. Sam wasn't clingy and nervous—you could take Sam anywhere. At that stage nobody suggested that we were wrong.

As the year wore on, Sam's problems did begin to emerge. But Min's and George's loomed much larger. Sam seemed a little slow, a little odd. His speech was certainly garbled. The possibility of glue ear cropped up. So, too, did the notion that George was a peculiar role model for him, that any eccentricities were a result of copying George. I don't know why I gave this much credence, as Sam's behavior wasn't like George's and nor were his speech patterns. Having had Jake, I know how strong the instincts toward normality are in a nonautistic child. Children copy, certainly—that's how they learn. But they choose their role models with care. Jake has never copied his brothers in anything other than in the most transient and superficial way.

I'm ashamed to say that I can't recall the exact chain of events leading to Sam's diagnosis. I paid so much less attention to Sam. That is partly because I was already so preoccupied, and partly because Sam has never sought attention. George does, and always has. You can't ignore George, because he doesn't want you to ignore him. Even now, when he repeatedly orders us, "Don't look at me! Don't talk about me!" it feels as if he doesn't exactly mean it.

If we truly screen him out, he redirects our attention to himself with ever-shriller commands—"Mum, I *said* don't look at me!" And I wasn't.

Sam has never been like this. Sam doesn't mind whether you look at him or not. Sam is indifferent, whereas George is thin-skinned. Sam will sometimes tell me to "Go a-WAY," and give me a push; this is either because I'm the bearer of bad tidings, for example, it's time to get dressed for school, or because he has embarked on an enjoyable course of action, such as emptying shampoo down the drain, or flushing socks down the toilet, to which he knows I'll put a stop. But most of the time Sam doesn't react strongly to the presence or absence of other people. His impassivity has always meant that he gets less attention than the other two.

So, no, I can't quite remember who first started worrying about Sam. I do remember that he was visited at home by the educational psychologist—perhaps the health visitor, or the ENT specialist, had sounded some warning notes. I do remember that he wouldn't cooperate with the activities provided by the educational psychologist—simple puzzles, handling scissors, building with blocks. "Oh, he can do all this," I assured her, "he just doesn't want to."

"The point is, he *should* want to," she said, and it was then that I realized something was up.

I raised the suggestion that some of his stranger behavior was the result of copying George. She shook her head. "You can't copy something as fundamental as eye contact." I was so used to Sam that I hadn't noticed anything unusual about his eye contact. Often, it takes an impartial observer to pick up on these things. She recommended that he go to a special-needs nursery two days a week, where he would be assessed.

The Torfield Assessment Unit, as the nursery was called, was excellent. It has since been closed, on the ridiculous grounds that because it could only serve a limited number of children, it was unfair to those without a place. Would one argue that because, say, kidney transplants could only be provided for a limited number of patients, they should be stopped altogether? I think not.

The Torfield Unit provided the kind of early-learning experience every special-needs child should have. There was one staff member to every two children, plus a speech therapist. It was housed in a sweet little child-friendly building, not unlike a dollhouse, with a different activity in each room—paint, water play, a large train set. Not all the children were on the autistic spectrum. Most, including Sam, had yet to receive any firm diagnosis. But all had language delays or developmental problems. They attended the unit for a year, and at the end, depending on their assessment, they went into either a mainstream or a special-needs primary school.

Sam did so well at the unit that his assessment tests showed him performing at nearly age-appropriate levels in most areas. The verdict was that he could cope in a mainstream school. He could not—but more of that in chapter 13.

On the days when he didn't go to the unit, Sam spent the mornings at another, mainstream nursery school. Here he did not thrive, but nor, after the first fortnight, did he show unhappiness. He was simply peripheral to most of the activities. It was a homely, unstructured place, not the right environment for someone as potentially chaotic as Sam, but it gave me a few hours to myself.

Sam still had no official diagnosis. I'd never met anyone with more than one autistic child. I'd never even heard of such a thing. I just didn't know it was possible. And the two boys were so very different from each other that my brain went on resisting the idea for far longer than it should have done. Besides, Sam was still "easy." He was odd, but his oddities didn't impinge on other people much, or make him unhappy in the way that George's did. As long as Sam was doing what he wanted, such as jumping up and down in front of washing machines, he was cheerful and equable. It was almost impossible to teach him anything new, but it took me ages to understand how deep a problem that is.

The educational psychologist, who was very sensible in every other way, said that we didn't need to "push for a label." "Let's just put down 'language delay,'" she suggested. I came to disagree. This is an issue I now feel very strongly about. Every late-diagnosed Asperger's or autistic adult I've ever come across has spoken of the relief they felt when their condition was finally identified. Luke Jackson, a teenager with Asperger's, writes eloquently in his excellent book, *Freaks, Geeks and Asperger Syndrome,* "My first reaction was relief. It was as if I had a weight lifted off my shoulders. . . . If anyone is wondering when to tell their child that they have AS, then in my humble opinion, the answer is *right now!*"

The child who goes without a label is in danger of going without the right kind of help. He may fail to qualify for a statement of special educational need. This will lead to his education being managed far worse than it could be. It's easier to convince people that the child is not just spoiled or naughty if you can say, "My son is autistic." If you've got a label, you may qualify for Disability Living Allowance. You get a disabled parking permit. What good does it do not to have these things? If there's no label to say "Please look after this bear," how is anyone to know that the bear needs help?

There are still doctors who withhold diagnosis. This is at best misjudged, at worst morally culpable. The only sound reason for not giving a diagnosis is if the doctor or equivalent authority figure is genuinely unsure. Autism, as I've stressed, can be difficult to detect in young children. There's no blood test, no absolutely defining physical characteristics. At present, autism can only be identified by observing behavior. If there is doubt, then second and third opinions should be sought before the parents are given a definite label. But those opinions should be sought as quickly as possible. The younger a child is at time of diagnosis, the better. There are several therapies and intervention programs that really help, and the earlier these are introduced, the greater the results. Why are some professionals reluctant to label a child? There are two main reasons—one, to spare the parents' feelings. This is cowardice dressed up as compassion. Autism is a lifelong condition. It is not going to go away. The parents *need* to know; how else can they do their best for their child? Of course breaking the news is hard; of course some parents will react very badly. There's not enough support for families post-diagnosis, but whoever's in charge of the child's case should take on the responsibility of ensuring that the parents have access to whatever help there is.

The best kind of help is a family support worker who visits the home, gets to know the child, puts the family in touch with local support groups, guides them through the rigmarole that establishes whether they are entitled to Disability Living Allowance, free outsized nappies, speech therapy, respite care. Parents may be too stunned to take it all in at once, but repeated visits over time can help them to accept what they may have at first rejected. We were given contact numbers for other families, but Min didn't want to use them because he thought it would be too upsetting. But eventually I did start meeting other autistic children and their parents, and found it interesting and useful.

The second main reason for withholding diagnosis is the idea that a label stigmatizes a child. This is woolly thinking, particularly in the case of autism. Autists are the group on earth least likely to care about being stigmatized, because their condition usually means that they are socially indifferent or unaware. I'd make a distinction between autism and Asperger's syndrome here. Some Asperger's children do care about what other people think of them. It might be better, in some cases, to help them keep their "label" secret if they are coping well in a mainstream environment and fear teasing if the truth is known. But this decision should be made by the person with Asperger's after a discussion of the implications. It's always wrong to withhold the diagnosis from the individuals affected if they are capable of understanding it. To quote Luke Jackson again: "I personally think that a child *should* be told, and the sooner the better. Believe me, I know!"

There may be more sinister reasons for withholding diagnosis. Some parents suspect that a vaguer label like "language delay" may turn their child into a cheaper package for the health and education authorities than "autistic spectrum disorder." I hope this is not a motivation. If a doctor or psychologist is sure that his patient has a particular condition, then it goes without saying that he should be honest about it. With Down's syndrome, the physical evidence means that no one can be in any doubt for longer than a few hours. Honesty is inevitable. With autism, in the absence of such evidence, honesty is the doctor's responsibility.

In short, I disagreed with the educational psychologist who said that we didn't need a label for Sam. I pushed for a full diagnosis, and in April 1995, when Sam was three and a half, we were seen by Dr. S, a top pediatrician at our local hospital.

Dr. S was a cold fish. I knew what he was going to say before he said it, so I was able to sit and listen to him and think, in a detached way, you're not making a very good job of this, Dr. S. "Yes, he's on the autistic spectrum all right," he said. I was sitting with my chair against the door to prevent Sam escaping. Sam was behind the doctor. He had licked a fruit pastille and was tracing patterns with it, like sticky snail trails, all over the back of the doctor's chair. The pastille was inching ever closer to Dr. S's tweed jacket. "But I wouldn't worry too much," continued Dr. S. "They can be very intelligent, you know. Some of them go to Eton." Sam began revving up to make his washing-machine noise, which was almost as loud as an airplane taking off. I smiled and nodded, but I thought perhaps I wouldn't put his name down for Eton quite yet.

So there it was. Two very different boys, same diagnosis. But knowledge is power, up to a point. Once you know what you're up against you can start planning the best ways of dealing with it.

SEVEN

Is There a Cure?

There is no cure for autism. That's a controversial statement. There are plenty of parents who believe that their child has made a full recovery from autism; there are Web sites dedicated to accounts of such recoveries. I'm not in a position to challenge these parents. I don't even disbelieve them. I think it's perfectly possible that some children with, for instance, strong food intolerances can show autistic symptoms. Correcting the diet, and providing appropriate educational intervention to make up for lost developmental time, can all but eradicate the "autistic" behaviour. It seems that the earlier the problem is addressed, the stronger are the chances of recovery. And because children with severe intolerances often manifest them early on, the likelihood that their problems will be quickly addressed is quite high.

However, I don't believe that, in the majority of cases, autism is caused by intolerances, or by inoculations. (I'm deliberately skirting the subject of the MMR vaccine, because I don't feel I've got anything useful to say about it. Both George and Sam had the usual inoculations, and appeared to be unaffected. But I wouldn't rule out the possibility that inoculations are a contributing factor in some cases. As far as I'm concerned, the jury is still out.) What I do believe is that the vast majority of autistic children are born autistic. There's a new theory that brain development may be affected by a testosterone surge in early pregnancy. That sounds plausible to me, but investigation of this idea is still in its early stages.

I believe that autism can develop in a huge variety of ways. I also believe that some of the symptoms can be made worse by food intolerances, some illnesses, or perhaps as a reaction to inoculations. In cases of extreme early neglect—the Romanian orphanages, for example—children may develop some autistic symptoms, especially self-injurious behavior, repetitive routines, gaze avoidance, and poor social interaction. I think it unlikely that such children would display autistic talents. My feeling is that these behaviors are a kind of pseudo-autism. I'm absolutely certain that full-blown autism is never created by parental abuse or neglect.

So, I don't believe there's any real cure, and I do believe that instances of recovery are extremely rare; to pin one's hopes on them would be foolish. But there are lots of therapies and interventions that may improve the quality of life for you and your child. Most things are worth trying, as long as they're safe, and as long as you feel strong enough to cope with possible disappointment.

Like dealing with sleep problems, choosing a treatment depends on the temperament of the individual parent. (It also, unfortunately, depends on the parents' budget.) No one can be sure about the efficacy of anything, because no one can know how the autistic person would have developed without the treatment. If someone has cancer, is treated, and subsequently is found to be free of cancer, it seems fair to say that the treatment has worked. If an autistic child embarks on a therapy and shows improvement, it is still only informed guesswork to say that the therapy is helping, because autism is an unpredictable, one-step-forward-two-steps-back condition. There are no certain outcomes, and no two autists are the same. The improvement might have happened in any event.

Assessing the value of any course of action therefore involves a meeting of belief and common sense. It seems likely that the parent is the best judge, because no one watches a child as closely as a parent. On the other hand, parents so desperately want things to work out that they can be tempted to over-accentuate the positive. So it's good to keep other, more disinterested adults informed of what you're doing, and ask them for their unbiased opinion. Recorded evidence is also useful. I wish I had more video footage of George and Sam, but, being a female-brained technophobe, I've never mastered a camcorder, so I've got only a few scraps here and there. Keeping a diary or notes is good, but of course they won't be free from bias.

Instinct tells some parents to leave their child alone. They feel that any therapy or intervention would put undue stress on the child, and on the life of the family too. Others—and I would guess this is the more common reaction—want to do whatever they can for their child, and can't bear to feel that they might have let something go due to lack of energy or lack of funds. I think it's a mistake to discourage such parents on the grounds that "it might not work." Powerlessness is bad for parents. If trying a diet or a behavior-modification program makes them feel that their frustrated love for their child is being put to good use, then that's a good thing.

Grandfather Clive cradles baby George. Unlike most newborns, George slept very little. This photograph captures his "overvigilant" expression.

George (in seat) is only two months old but seems highly socially interactive—not what one would expect from an autist. The bigger baby is my friend Sally's daughter Julia.

Sam is about seven months old; George is two and a half. From the start the boys were very close. Eleven years on, they still curl up in bed together.

Sam's interest in washing machines began at about fourteen months and continued at fever pitch until shortly before his sixth birthday, when all his obsessions disappeared overnight.

Sam has always enjoyed confined spaces. On one occasion he settled himself down in a badger's hole with his pacifier, Owly, and blanket and fell asleep.

Clocks were another of Sam's obsessions. Here, aged four and a half, he is turning the hands of our kitchen clock. At this stage he was extremely resistant to haircuts. . . .

George had a love affair with Nelson, a Hungarian Viszla, belonging to friends of ours. George used to gaze at a picture of Nelson and sing, "Someday my dog will come." Later, both boys became fearful of dogs.

George, pictured here with his father, has found some snails on a brick and is licking one. Sam is in the background.

George's aunt Caroline made him an exact replica of Pingu's birthday cake. George's expression is one of intense satisfaction. His hands are inside his sleeves—at this stage he wouldn't touch anything with his fingertips.

George, aged eight, on a bouncy castle. Like many autists, he is "lit up" by bouncing.

Taken after Sam's crash. Sam, aged six and a half, is now remote and withdrawn. He is camping out on the trampoline with his luggage—bottle, Owly, and blanket. He seemed to "disappear" into a world of physical sensation and became almost indifferent to human contact.

Delia, our next-door neighbor, has helped with the boys from their babyhood. This photograph shows how very much more cheerful and socially responsive Sam was before his crash.

In Dorset with our friends Caroline, Hattie, Katie, and Nelson the dog. The photograph sums up the differences among the three boys. George (nine) is aware of the camera and anxious about it. Sam (seven) is unaware of anything except the desire to escape, which is why I'm hanging on to him. He is "stimming" with his hands. Jake (eighteen months) is highly aware of the camera and is straining to be part of the action.

Both boys have spent hours on top of our Aga, which is at least as hot as a radiator. Here George, clutching a flapper, avoids the camera in a characteristically thin-skinned manner. Six-year-old Sam's heavy-lidded eyes indicate the vacant state into which he often lapsed during his crash.

Four-year-old Jake is displaying classic neurotypical behavior. He's pleased with his Christmas present, keen to show it off, and very aware of the photographer. He is composing his facial expression accordingly. Neither George nor Sam has ever been capable of this kind of response.

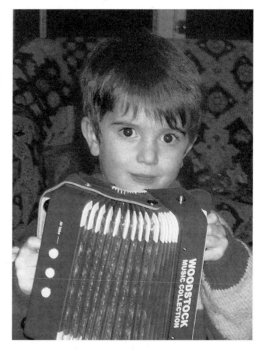

The boys at home. George is twelve, Sam is eleven, and Jake is four. As usual, George is holding his flappers.

I've tried a lot of treatments and have gained something from most of them. The usual pattern is that I'll read about something in the paper or hear about it through friends, dismiss it as too expensive or too difficult to implement, have a few conversations about it, and eventually conclude that I really ought to give it a try. At the moment, I feel I've done most of the things that sound sensible, so I'm in the happy and probably temporary position of aiming for nothing other than maintaining the status quo. The only therapy left on my wish list is swimming with dolphins, and that's only because it sounds like fun. After seven years of interventions both major and minor, the front-runner for us has been ABA therapy, which has mutated into something called Verbal Behavior. This is an effective strategy for learning, and has become a way of life. I can't foresee a time when the boys will cease to benefit from it, because it adapts to their changing needs. If—heaven forbid—I should find myself with an autistic two-year-old all over again, I would embark on an intensive ABA program in place of nursery school. I do believe it to be the best way of maximizing the autistic child's capacity for learning.

ABA stands for applied behavior analysis. It's a system devised by Ivar Lovaas in California in the 1960s, and is sometimes referred to as Lovaas therapy. Its most devoted practitioners believe that it can make even quite profoundly autistic children "mainstreamable." Useful though ABA is, I would urge that such claims be treated with caution.

It is a behavior-modification program. Learning is broken down into tiny chunks, and the child is rewarded—"reinforced"—for every success. The reinforcers are whatever motivates your child. If your child likes stickers or small toys, great. If, like Sam, your child is motivated by little except sweets, then you may have to sacrifice a few teeth in the interests of education. The point is that many autistic children don't learn because they lack motivation. Unlike mainstream children, who accept the socially imposed value of a gold star or being clapped for in Assembly, most autists are only motivated—if at all—by something in itself, not by the significance others attach to it. George chooses sticking plasters or a minute spent sitting on the heater as his rewards. Not many thirteen-year-olds would be gratified by the receipt of a Band-Aid, but then George is not most thirteen-year-olds.

Originally Lovaas used aversive techniques, including slaps, as well as rewards, but these days the approach avoids the punitive. Reinforcers may be withheld until the correct answer is given, but they will not be withdrawn for a wrong answer. "No" is used for information, not for admonishment. "Errorless learning" is the aim, so new material is embedded within what the child already knows. To give a simple example: if the task is to teach the child to identify farm animals, and he already knows horse, cow, and pig but not goat, then the goat picture will be slipped in with pictures of the known animals. As the child names the animals, the therapist will insert the word "goat" and ask him to repeat it. "Drills," as they are called, are kept short. Up to thirty drills may be covered in a two-hour session.

Several different tutors work with each child. George and Sam have three apiece. The tutors have a meeting with the consultant every few weeks; the consultant watches them in action, corrects their mistakes, and provides new material for them to work with. The consultant is specially trained, but the tutors need no previous experience—they receive their training on the job. Sam's current tutors are Delia, our neighbour; Ian, our nanny; and Andie, a friend of George's tutor, Mark. George's tutors are Mark and Jan, who are both classroom assistants at the boys' old school, and Vikki, who read an article about us in the *Mail on Sunday*, wrote to me, and discovered that the house she was about to move to was two miles away from us. Sue, our consultant, is supplied through an organization called PEACH (Parents for the Early Intervention of Autism in Children). You can use family members as tutors, which saves money, but the child might find it difficult to accept a familiar adult in an unfamiliar role. Granny Eva tutored George for a while, but George objected strenuously. Parents are often not much good at it. They are too close to the child, often not strict or consistent enough, and unable to step out of role. I use the tutor time to give good attention to Jake. For me, one of the many benefits of ABA is that it gives Jake time off from his brothers.

Verbal Behavior, which has replaced ABA for the boys, is a freer, more flexible system, but, like ABA, it aims to fill the gaps that neurotypical children fill for themselves. VB does not follow a prescribed curriculum, though it does insist that certain skills have to be mastered before certain others can be introduced. It adapts itself to what the child in question needs to learn, whether "academic" or behavioral. The first part of the training is always to establish compliance. If the child cannot sit still on request, then he cannot learn anything else until that behavior is in place. Even if it takes months, compliance has to be achieved before work can continue. The child, who all his life has successfully ducked out of adult commands, will go through "extinction bursts" at first—screaming, rolling on the floor, even biting and kicking. These have to be weathered. George and Sam, to my surprise, got through this stage in less than a day, though one may find less extreme extinction bursts recurring whenever new, unwelcome tasks are introduced.

The consultant and parents discuss what the priorities are.

Behavioral and self-care problems are tackled as well as academic deficits. So, in any one session, the child may have drills about putting on socks, eating with a spoon, and not spitting, as well as naming shapes, completing a jigsaw, modeling with clay. Verbal Behavior puts more emphasis on building up a good relationship between child and tutor, learning imaginative play, and taking the child out into the community—catching a bus, handling money, posting a letter. For a fuller account of both programs contact PEACH; details are given in the back of this book.

Both boys have therapy sessions on weekday evenings for two hours, and again on Saturday morning, which I suppose makes it the equivalent of homework. I receive no funding, except for a generous donation from a private charitable trust. It is expensive, and the more hours the boys do, the more it costs; the tutors are paid by the hour. It puts a great strain on my finances, but it is an absolute priority for me. It doesn't work miracles, but it does slowly expand the boys' range of skills. It provides them with affectionate relationships with several adults, and it chips away at the great blankness and boredom that can characterize autistic life for the child who doesn't know how to occupy himself except by stimming—that is, self-stimulatory behaviors such as flapping, hand biting, twiddling string, humming, hooting, tearing up paper . . . the list is endless. It improves the quality of Jake's life, because I can spend nonautistic time with him, and because sometimes the tutors involve him in the work they're doing with George and Sam. Jake learned to read and do sums very young, because he wanted to copy what George was doing. More important, he can see a benefit in having brothers like his, because the tutors come to the house bringing with them fun and interest and sweets.

The way we run our programs is unorthodox and would shock a Lovaas purist. But, like most aspects of child care, it makes sense to adapt the rules to what suits you and your family. For years, I put off starting ABA because I thought it had to be done for a minimum of forty hours a week, and that the child had to be taken out of school. Eventually, when George was nine and Sam was seven, I thought, no, I'm not going to take them out of school—they're too old, school's good for them in many ways, forty hours of therapy (eighty, for two) is too expensive, and I can't stand the thought of having them at home all day. So I'll just have to fit the therapy around what they already do. So that's what happens. Maybe their progress hasn't been as rapid as it would have been on forty hours a week, but there has been real progress on their limited timetable. The therapy supports and improves our family life; we'll carry on with it for as long as I can afford to do so.

When George was first diagnosed, we were told that appropriate education was the only treatment that was any use. An education program rooted in behavior management, such as ABA, is the best way of coping with the child's intellectual and social problems, but autism is also a physical condition, and some treatments can alleviate some symptoms in some cases. There are a lot of "somes" in that sentence. Caution should be urged, because it's easy to invest a lot of money and a lot of hope in a treatment that makes no appreciable difference to your child. But it does not follow that the treatment is mere quackery. George's version of autism is very different from Sam's, and so it is not surprising that they have had different responses to the same treatment.

Auditory integration therapy (AIT) is the most striking case in point. Also called light-and-sound therapy, this seeks to reduce the child's auditory hypersensitivities by "retuning" his hearing. The child is given an audiogram to assess the level of his hearing distortion, then music, altered by computer, is played to him through a headset. The child sits in a darkened booth watching a light box rotate through a color spectrum. Light and sound together seem to stimulate the brain into easing sound distortions. The child has two half-hour sessions per day for a fortnight.

George was six and a half when we set off to North London for AIT. For years he had spent a lot of time with his hands clapped over his ears. Many sounds really distressed him—crowd noises, party noises, some deep male voices, hand-dryers in public lavatories. On a long car journey it was impossible for me to use a lavatory—because of the hand-dryers, he wouldn't come in with me, and I couldn't leave him outside. He wouldn't use any kind of toilet himself, at home or anywhere else. I assume this was because of the gurgling of the cistern. A physiotherapist had given us a giant potty with built-up sides, designed to give stability to children with cerebral palsy. This was what George used, when he wasn't using the garden path or the bedroom floor.

Some kinds of music were intolerable to George. He has a strong response to music and may well have perfect pitch; he's very "controlling" of his musical environment and hates to have music put on that takes him by surprise. Before AIT, the "wrong" music would send him into a hysterical state. One year, his class had two Christmas carols to perform; one sent him into raptures, the other into a panic.

In short, George's hypersensitivities were affecting his life to a considerable degree. AIT offered to reduce them, and it succeeded. The Light and Sound Therapy Centre was an ordinary North London house, staffed by Hasidic Jews, all women. The married women wore stiff black wigs; this led George to address the lead therapist as Cruella, but either she didn't hear or she was too polite to object. George's preferred "flapper" at that time was a palm cross. I felt embarrassed when he entered the therapy room holding the cross in front of his face, as if repelling vampires, but nothing bothered the calm, good-tempered staff. Their quiet confidence must have communicated itself to George. I had doubted that he would submit to the regime of wearing headphones and sitting still, but after a few minutes of resistance he relaxed and cooperated. He seemed mesmerized by the distorted music and the glowing circle of color that moved through the spectrum. When Min joined us, after a few sessions, George, who didn't usually invite people to share his activities, grabbed his father by the tie and hauled him into the therapy room, as if to show him what he'd been doing.

After AIT, George's use of "normal" language increased hugely and never declined again. He started using the toilet for the first time, tolerating the cistern and the flush. He had usually referred to himself in the first or second person—"George is here"; "You [I] want a drink." Suddenly, he used "I" and "me" with ease. He began using words to do with feelings and preferences, which he'd always avoided in the past. In true story-of-a-miracle fashion, he said, for the first time ever, "Mummy, I love you."

The improvement was obvious to all—family, teachers, friends. And the gains held. He stopped putting his hands over his ears— when he does that now it's a sign of guilt, as if he's anticipating the telling-off he's going to get. He doesn't much like the noise of dryers, vacuum cleaners, and so on, but he'll put up with it. He never muddled his pronouns again. The sheer volume of his language continued to increase, as did his readiness to use the vocabulary of emotion—which Sam, to this day, doesn't use at all. AIT didn't remove the autism, but it broke down some of the barriers between George's world and our world. He still has supersensitive hearing—the other day he was at the end of the garden, a long way off, so I put on "The Ride of the Valkyries," which Sam loves and George detests. The doors and windows were closed, but still George heard it, and came storming in from the garden to turn it off, shrieking, "I hate this music!" But though George still has pronounced auditory likes and dislikes, his hearing seems to trouble him far less.

Sam never had this problem. He never put his hands over his ears, and he positively relished sounds like gurgling drains and helicopters. But his sensory experiences are clearly very different from ours, and he hums and vocalizes a great deal, as if to create a kind of "white noise" to keep the world at bay. When we enrolled Sam for AIT, we hoped it would reduce the humming, calm him down, and improve his concentration, which by this stage—he was also six and a half—was nonexistent. Sam was at his very worst when he did AIT. He was incapable of sitting still for a second. Eating and sleeping were terrible, he had lost all his interests, and his self-harming (mainly hand biting) was high. He couldn't pay attention to a story or even a video. Only strenuous physical activity—running, "swimming," trampolining—seemed to help him at all. So it was even more surprising than it had been with George that Sam sat and cooperated with the light-and-sound treatment.

Alas, that cooperation was the beginning and end of the treatment's success. It just didn't do anything for Sam. I thought I detected a slight improvement in concentration when he was watching TV or listening to music. He'd sit for five seconds rather than three. But it certainly wasn't twelve hundred pounds' worth of improvement. Sam's speech had all but disappeared at this time, and AIT did nothing to bring it back. For George, AIT really was a turning point in his life. If we'd "done" Sam first, we'd have dismissed it as tosh, and its practitioners as frauds.

For George the great success has been AIT; for Sam it has been the gluten-free/casein-free diet. The diet is controversial. Most parents who've implemented it swear by it; most of the medical profession frown on it. I've outlined the "opioid excess" theory on which the diet is based in chapter 12, but I do urge that, if you're interested, you use the information at the back of this book. Some of the symptoms that indicate that a child (or an adult) may benefit from the diet are a constant, restless craving for the foods containing the listed substances, a distended stomach, a pale face with dark-shadowed eyes, one or two red ears, diarrhea, constipation or flatulence, floating stools (if you're lucky enough to get a look), excessive sweating, excessive thirst, an apparent indifference or reduced response to pain, poor sleeping habits, and wild behavior, including destructiveness or self-harm.

Sam has some of these symptoms, though not all—I never noticed any sweating, for instance. By his sixth birthday, he had taken to arching his back and screaming as if in colicky pain. This happened every day, and the screams could go on for two hours. There was a lot of incoherent, tearless crying. His appetite was extremely poor. His general health seemed good in that he wasn't prone to infections, he never vomited, and his muscle tone was, as it always has been, quite splendid. But he seemed endlessly restless, physically uncomfortable. He was either hyperactive or slumped in a glazed unreachable, trancelike state. His sleeping was simply appalling, and he produced loose, pale, floating stools.

Doctors don't like the gluten-free/casein-free diet because it's hard to provide the child with the whole range of nutrients. A fair point—except that the child isn't providing himself with the full range of nutrients anyway. There are some autistic children who eat healthy, balanced meals three times a day. There must be. I'd guess it would be most unlikely that the parents of such children would consider tampering with their diet. There are many, many more children who, like Sam, live on a diet of crisps, fingernail clippings, and fresh air. When you decide to change a diet like this you've got little to lose, and possibly a great deal to gain.

I sent Sam's urine off to the controversial Paul Shattock at Sunderland University. The analysis showed a typically autistic profile, though with a much stronger reaction to gluten than to casein. This may have been simply because, through his own choice, Sam ate few dairy products—the days of swigging bottles of milk were long gone. But his diet did revolve around gluten—biscuits, bread, croissants ("squeeze-buns," he called them), grissini, and "loopy Y's" (Honey Nut Loops). On Paul Shattock's advice, I removed the gluten first. The casein, in the form of milk chocolate, ice cream, and the odd smear of butter, remained in for another year. So did the aspartame and the MSG, though I now think these are what produced the worst reaction of all.

If I had to give up gluten, I wouldn't find it so very hard, because I like the whole range of fruit, vegetables, potatoes, rice, pulses, meat, and fish. Sam never liked any of these, except for a few potatoey things and, occasionally, rice. My problems with such a diet would be mainly social. Sam has little social life and doesn't feel left out if other people are eating differently, unless what they're having is a sore temptation. We never have croissants at home, and I don't eat bread in front of him. But pasta's fine, because he's not interested in it. People often ask, "But isn't it so difficult, making separate meals for him?" The answer is no, not really, because since infancy Sam has never participated in a family meal.

Gluten is everywhere. Most prepared foods are thickened or coated with something glutinous. There are gluten-free substitutes for bread, biscuits, pasta, cake mix, and so on, but they're very expensive and, in my opinion, quite nasty. Sam nibbles the biscuits—bourbon and custard cream wannabes, pallid and brittle. Sometimes he eats rice bread dipped in egg and fried. Products come and go, irritatingly. Sainsbury's stocked some very passable gluten-free grissini for a while, but they've gone. Casein, often in the form of whey powder, is also ubiquitous. If you're going to try this diet, you have to resign yourself to reading labels carefully, and making a few more things at home.

For the first gluten-free fortnight, Sam was irritable. I started it during the school holidays so that I could monitor him closely; it was important to be absolutely strict in order to assess the effect it was having. He couldn't be taken on his usual outings to public swimming pools and play centers because he was inclined to snatch things like Kit Kats from other people. The changes happened quickly. His sleeping improved, he became less restless, his hand biting lessened. His screaming decreased; and now he never screams, though he does still cry and whinge. His stomach went flat; the shadows under his eyes faded. The craving for sugar, which had dominated his life, ebbed away. Now, he still likes sugary things, and sweets are still, regrettably, his main motivators, but that old junkie craving has gone.

His appetite improved. It's still not good. Sam, at eleven, is undersized and pale. I'm not happy with his eating; he rejects most protein, most fruit, and all vegetables except a little raw fennel and raw onion, but it really is better than it was. In any one day he'll eat a small amount of up to twelve different foods; pre-diet, it would have been two or three.

He simply can't be getting enough iron or calcium, but then he couldn't have been pre-diet, either. A dietician has been consulted—the doctor will always tell you to see a dietician before embarking—but an old adage about horses and water springs to mind. Sam's dietician provided him with a beautiful powder containing all the nutrients he wasn't getting, but inserting the powder into Sam is almost impossible. You're supposed to dissolve it into drinks, but he just tips them down the sink. The only way he gets any at all is if I freeze it into homemade ice lollies, but to give him the recommended daily dose would mean making about thirty ice pops, and even Sam would balk at that.

Since I've ditched casein, MSG, and aspartame as well as gluten, Sam's calmness and ability to concentrate have continued to improve. It would be good to take the diet still further—reduce the sugar and salt, buy nothing that isn't organic, be more stringent about the flavorings in the sweets he gets for his rewards. Perhaps, soon, I'll find the strength to tackle the next stage, but I'm not ready yet. About twice a year I think, maybe he's grown out of his intolerance, and let him have something from the proscribed list, but he still reacts badly. I always know when he's got hold of something he shouldn't have, because his eyes go red and he starts to whimper. Last Sunday he had an ice cream cone—a mini-one, in fact—and he spent the afternoon howling and throwing himself about the room.

I'm not a faddy mother. Really I'm not. I've no natural inclination toward alternative remedies of any description. I'm rarely ill, and my physical condition doesn't interest me very much. I can go for a year at a time without taking any kind of medication at all. My general attitude toward food is that you should eat what you feel like or what you're offered, depending on the circumstances. I've never consciously altered my own diet in my life, except, slightly, during pregnancy, when I followed the guidelines.

But desperation drove me to try the gluten-free/casein-free diet for Sam, and it has had a good effect. It's a bore, and expensive—or it is if, like me, you lazily buy special bread and biscuits instead of making them yourself. Some GP's let you have some of the food on prescription—not mine. But I don't begrudge the cost; the years when Sam lived on fresh air were cheap, so it balances out. The best, the noblest way to do it, would be to adopt the diet oneself, and never let the forbidden items darken one's doors, but that, frankly, would be just too disagreeable.

It would also, of course, be hard and perhaps unfair to impose the diet on George and Jake. Ironically, though Sam is more severely affected by autism than George, it's often easier to impose restrictions on Sam. I suppose it's because Sam doesn't question or challenge. If Sam's thwarted in a desire, he'll try hard to find a way around it, as when I put a new lock on the door and Sam climbed up the chimney. But he doesn't argue, even in a rudimentary fashion, and he doesn't appear to bear a grudge. Because Sam doesn't compare his lot with that of other people—because Sam has a limited awareness of the existence of other people—he doesn't have much capacity to think, it's not fair. At least, as far as I can tell.

Changing your autistic child's diet seems to me to be one of the more obviously benign interventions. If you do it responsibly, and make every effort to fill the nutritional gaps (huh!), then it can't do harm and may well do good. And if it doesn't work, well, you can just abandon it. Less easy to justify is the use of any form of drug. To date, no particular drug has been found to be of much use. Temple Grandin uses antidepressants to control anxiety, but she's an adult and can make that choice for herself. In America, I believe, Ritalin is quite widely used. Ritalin is helpful in controlling hyperactivity in some children, so when Sam was at his very worst

I approached his pediatrician about it. She warned me that it didn't have a particularly good record in managing autism but said that as it was not addictive and had no long-term side effects it might be worth a try. She added that the most common short-term side effects were insomnia and reduced appetite. Well, I thought, Sam doesn't eat or sleep anyway; it can't get much worse.

How wrong I was. In the four days that Sam was on Ritalin, the only "solid" food he ate was one ice pop, and his head barely touched the pillow. I can't remember how I got the drug down him—nowadays he won't take any medication at all—but somehow I managed. It had a noticeable effect but not a useful one. He was calmer at school, but it was a torpid calm; he wasn't able to learn anything. And in the evening, when the dose wore off, he was wilder than ever.

I threw the Ritalin away. But I was still desperate for treatment of some kind. A year later, when Sam was seven, a lot of publicity was given to secretin injections. An autistic boy in America had been treated with the enzyme secretin in connection with a bowel disorder. To his mother's astonishment, his autistic characteristics all but disappeared. Other children received the injections, often with excellent results. Parents began to clamor for this miracle cure.

The medical profession were understandably sceptical. The long-term effects of the treatment were unknown. In this country, it was never possible to treat an autistic child with secretin on the National Health Service, but a few doctors provided it privately, at considerable expense.

The way the boys are now, I wouldn't feel justified in injecting them with anything about which so little was known. But Sam's condition at that time had deteriorated so much that I'd have tried almost anything. So, off we went to London for a secretin injection. And I'm glad we did, because if we hadn't, I would always have asked myself if I had turned down the chance of a truly miraculous treatment. And though no miracle was worked, Sam did improve after secretin.

It's hard to be very clear about its effects, because I'd removed the gluten from his diet a few weeks before, so I'm not sure which improvement to attribute to which treatment. In theory they should have worked together, since they are both intended to correct a leaky gut. The doctor who administered the secretin told us to wait for a few weeks before the next injection, and to have a subsequent injection only if Sam had begun to deteriorate again. After the third shot, Sam plateaued, and never seriously regressed again, so that was the end of secretin for him.

After secretin (and gluten removal) Sam immediately started sleeping through the night. Before, he'd been going to bed at midnight and waking seven or eight times before rising at seven. This, combined with George's extreme early rising—often three or four in the morning—and Jake's normal-but-wakeful babyhood, meant that I was seriously deprived of sleep.

Since secretin, Sam has nearly always slept through. He goes to bed later than I'd like, but averages half past ten rather than midnight. I have to rouse him in the mornings, but now he wakes up smiling. Before secretin, I used to dread the thump on the stairs that meant Sam was on his way, because when he woke he was always in such a gloweringly awful mood, like an infant ogre.

Before secretin and gluten removal, Sam's hands were raw and bleeding because he bit them and banged them so much. He had deep red horseshoe-shaped weals on them, and his fingers were scabbed and swollen. Now, he still has patches of rough skin, and he'll mumble on his hands as an occasional protest against being made to do something he doesn't like, but it's nothing to what it was. He used to harm himself in other ways, too, like knocking himself under the chin and pinching and scratching himself all over. He doesn't do any of this anymore.

In March 1999, just before my fortieth birthday, Sam's physical discomfort was at its worst. He was screaming almost all the time, he would hardly keep his clothes on, and his whole body was pinched and scratched like Tom O'Bedlam. He was admitted to the hospital to be checked for appendicitis, but nothing was found. Naked and still screaming, he ran up and down the hospital corridors for half a day. He was given something to relax his stomach, which seemed to help a little, and then they discharged us with their usual sigh of relief. He had the secretin injections later that year, and he's never been anywhere near as bad again.

Secretin also seemed to clear some of the fog that had arisen between Sam and the rest of the world. His use of language had dwindled to almost nothing, and it had become increasingly difficult to get through to him. I was never sure whether he'd heard me and was choosing to ignore me, or whether it just took him a long time to process what he had heard, or whether he hadn't realized that he was being spoken to at all. After secretin (and gluten removal) his language very slowly crept back, and his responses became much prompter. Now he usually responds immediately when he's spoken to, even if the response is negative. He makes a clear distinction between remarks addressed to him and all other kinds of speech. He hardly ever reacts to what is said unless his name is used. The first time I took Sam to London for his shot of secretin, he climbed into the train's luggage rack and remained there, spitting, for the rest of the journey. He ran barefoot through Charing Cross; I had to bundle him into a taxi by main force. After visiting the doctor, we had lunch with our friends Chris and Elspeth—or rather, I had lunch, and Sam rampaged through the house and ate Elspeth's contraceptive pills. The second time, he was a whole lot calmer. He sat on the train seat, kept his shoes on, and allowed me to entertain him with toys and books for much of the journey. There's a big difference in Sam's behavior pre- and post-secretin, but what I find hard to assess is how direct a part the injections played in the improvement.

I'm out of touch with the secretin issue. I believe it's fallen from favor. It's certainly not a treatment to be undertaken lightly. Quite apart from the possible side-effects issue, it's traumatic for the child to travel to an unfamiliar place and be jabbed in the arm—though the jab itself *may* be less horrible for an autist than for a normal child, because of the high pain threshold, and because the dread of anticipation isn't there. Sam didn't seem to mind it as much as I'd expected. I was never tempted to submit the relatively calm, cheerful George to the procedure, but Sam's extreme distress called for desperate measures.

I'm even less clear about the merits or demerits of anti-candida treatment. Both boys received this—in fact it was the first medical intervention we tried. There is a theory that autistic people are more likely to suffer from candida (thrush) than others. I took George and Sam (again, privately) to a pediatrician who subscribed to this theory. He prescribed nystatin, which kills thrush, and we were told to cut yeast and sugar out of their diet, because this is what thrush feeds on.

Yeast more or less went. I didn't manage to cut sugar out, though I did reduce it. Once the treatment was under way, George's body seemed to undergo withdrawal symptoms. Thrush appeared all over his bottom, like a diaper rash. He was restless and distracted for a few days, and then his behavior and concentration started to improve. He chose a low-sugar diet for himself—for several months it was plain porridge, chicken Kiev, and very little else. He won't eat either of those things now.

Killing off the candida seemed to kick-start an intolerable sugar craving in Sam. Day and night, he thought about nothing else. He picked pockets and emptied handbags in search of sweets; he snatched lollies out of people's hands in the street. His class made peppermint creams for Christmas. They were left out to dry, and Sam ate *all* of them. He ruined pudding for the whole school; eighty portions of lemon meringue pie were laid out on trays, and Sam raked his fingers through the lot. He would break into the school kitchen and climb up into the cupboards; he would hijack the tea trolley on its way to the staff room and snaffle the custard creams. He was like a junkie in search of heroin; there wasn't enough sugar in the world to satisfy Sam's craving. And it didn't make him happy. Once he'd eaten sugar—which of course he managed to do, despite my efforts to limit it—it would make him cry.

His longing for sugar blotted out everything else. Nothing could hold his attention. The only books he'd look at were recipe books with pictures of iced cakes. All his obsessive interests, the washing machines, oasthouses, cuckoo clocks, vanished almost overnight. He no longer drew, or used toys, or danced, or even smiled.

The doctor who prescribed the nystatin also prescribed an army of supplements—evening primrose oil, magnesium, zinc, vitamin B6. At that time, both boys were still drinking out of baby's bottles. It was quite easy to spike their drinks with these supplements, so they must have received the recommended amount for at least a year. But I eventually decided to remove the bottles, for the obvious reasons that one removes baby's bottles from children of six and eight, and after that it became much, much harder to get them to take the supplements. In the end I gave up. I can't honestly say I noticed much difference.

We went through the whole business again a couple of years later, when I had their stools analyzed. Collecting the samples for analysis was not plain sailing. I'd devoted a great deal of energy to persuading the boys to defecate in the toilet rather than in nappies, trousers, beds, toy boxes, baths, on carpets, windowsills, jungle gyms, trampolines, and garden paths. Now I needed un-contaminated specimens; fishing them out of the loo was not allowed. I had to undo all the good work, and encourage them— reward them even—for pooing in accessible places.

The bath was the best bet for Sam. The samples might have been mildly contaminated by bathwater, but it was the best I could do. Samples had to be collected on three consecutive days—not too much of a problem for Sam, who produces little and often, but George only ever "goes" about twice a week. It is hard enough to get any child to change the habits of a lifetime, but autistic children are famously unpersuadable. So, I waived the "three consecutive days" rule for George. I turned him out into the garden as often as possible and at last saw what I wanted steaming on the garden path. I rushed out with my plastic scoop, then hesitated. George was nowhere in sight. What if this was nothing to do with him, but the deposit of a fox or badger? I looked forward to the laboratory report. "We recommend you no longer feed your child on slugs, earthworms and old crisp packets . . ."

Once collected, the samples had to be mixed with a special liquid until they resembled pea soup, labeled with the date and hour of production, and posted to the diagnostic laboratory. The report came back. The boys' guts were full of the bad bacteria and low on the good, though thankfully they were now free of thrush. I bought the various supplements and corrective medicines they suggested. But, alas, the boys no longer drank out of bottles. They wouldn't touch any of it. I mixed things into drinks, baked them into gingerbread, ground them up with icing sugar. No good. I stirred them into ketchup, strong enough to mask most flavors. The ketchup turned pale yellow. I gave up. So, for all I know, the boys' digestive tracts are still full of rampaging bacteria, and I certainly can't comment on the usefulness of the recommended treatment.

Some treatments may be useful in a limited, specific way. At the suggestion of various friends I took Sam to see a cranial osteopath. He was a very nice man, he struck up a good relationship with Sam, and Sam quite enjoyed our little outings. The benign involvement of another adult is always a good thing for an autistic child. Cranial osteopathy is very gentle and noninvasive. It made Sam a little more relaxed. It also made it much, much easier for him to tolerate having his head touched. From babyhood, he'd hated people to go anywhere near his head. Washing and cutting his hair, and brushing his teeth, had always been immensely difficult. After the osteopathy he submitted with a much better grace. When he was two, he screamed so much during a haircut that he gave himself a hernia. Now, it's still not easy, but it is possible. On a good day, we can even search his hair for nits.

It's hard to discuss the treatments we tried without sounding evangelical, either for or against. I can only reiterate that every autistic child is different, and that what suits one may do little for another. George and Sam, for instance, have had little need either for sign language (Makaton) or PECS—a picture-exchange system. However, both of these have made radical differences in the lives of autists who cannot achieve speech. Speaking entirely from my own experience, if I had my time with the boys again, I would put them on the diet, and start an ABA or Verbal Behavior program as early as possible. Autistic children get set in their ways; it's best if you can point them in desirable directions. The later you leave the intervention, the harder your struggle will be.

EIGHT

Sam's Crash

M um, one word from you and Sam does as he likes." George was, as usual, adapting a quotation—this time from Jill Murphy's *The Last Noo-Noo*—and, also as usual, his remark was apt. As Sam developed from toddler to child he became increasingly noncompliant. Disciplining young children relies on the removal of desired objects, or on banishment from company, or—at a more extreme level—making the child feel ashamed. Of these, only the first had any impact at all on Sam. The other two play on social sensibilities, which in Sam's case were simply lacking.

So, if (when!) Sam smashed a window, grabbed another child's sweets, cut his T-shirt to ribbons, or pulled down the curtains *and rail* in his headmaster's study, what was I to do? It was no use giving him "time-out," because he didn't particularly want "time in"—he'd just blithely wander off and do something else, something equally undesirable. Making him say "sorry" was just eliciting a parrotlike response; he couldn't *feel* sorry, because he couldn't see anything from the other person's point of view. If I removed something he liked, it would upset him, but he wouldn't learn from the punishment, because he couldn't make the right connections. "If you flush your socks down the loo, then I'll take away your Barbie Laundry Center"—Sam couldn't see any sense in that, and I'm not sure that I can, either.

When I was in Houston, staying with my friend Sally, we went to a parenting class where "behavioral issues" were discussed. We were shown video clips of various misdemeanors, such as scribbling on walls and throwing sofa cushions on the floor. (My heart began to sink as I realized that in my household, throwing cushions was regarded as good-to-normal behavior.) Then "right" and "wrong" approaches to chastisement were suggested. The "right" thing to do was to kneel down so you were at the child's level, look him in the eyes, and explain in a soft, sweet voice that you worked so hard to give him a lovely home, and when he scribbled on the wall it made you feel "kinda discouraged." This was before the boys were diagnosed, but I remember thinking that the children these people were talking about bore very little resemblance to my own darlings.

Fear and pain are, of course, the old-fashioned, politically incorrect props of infant discipline. Sam wasn't afraid of a frown or an angry voice, though George was; indeed, Sam seemed to enjoy the unusual audiovisual effects produced by an irate adult. I disapprove of smacking, but like many parents, that hasn't stopped me from resorting to it on occasion. The threat of a smack was an effective deterrent for George. But for Sam, it just didn't work at all. Autists often have a high pain threshold; to make any impact, I'd have had to hit him really hard. And besides, for most children the real pain of a smack is the humiliation—another emotion outside Sam's repertoire. I only ever smacked Sam a few times, and I always regretted it. I soon realized that smacks seemed to be something he actively enjoyed. My father is the least aggressive of men. He never laid a finger on any of us, and he would be, if that's possible, even less likely to smack a grandchild. But Sam would take him by the wrist and try to make him inflict punishment. "G'anfather Richard, smack Sam, smack Sam," he would chortle.

Autists are often disobedient without being truly naughty. They ignore your reprimand, but in ripping up a book or disemboweling a cassette they may not be showing defiance or even willful destructiveness; it just seems to be an activity that gives them some sort of satisfaction. And much of the time, Sam's wildboy behavior didn't seem to matter so very much, because he was usually cheerful with it. It's hard to feel cross with a child who's getting so much pleasure from trickling molehill earth onto his head and chanting, "It's rainin'-it's pourin'-oldmanisnorin'." "Where did Sam come from?" I asked George, to see whether he had absorbed the very basic sex information I'd given him. "Sam came out of a puddle," replied George, and yes, most of the time Sam was absolutely filthy. But he was cheery, adventurous, full of life. He loved jokes—he called our friends' oasthouse [buildings once used for drying hops] "the toast house," and laughed so much he fell over. We took him riding, and he was fearless and enthusiastic about "Orange Debbie," as he called his pony—"Get outta da way, horse, Sam's comin'!" Visiting a school, he ran into an empty classroom, sat at a table as if in a café, and said roguishly, "Right, Sam, what would you like to drink?" He had to be escorted briskly out of the flower festival in our local church, because he sat on a flower arrangement in the shape of a hassock, claiming that he was sitting on eggs in a nest.

He took an intense interest in some aspects of the world around him, though others he blanked out. We found a slow-worm in the garden: "Bye bye boa constrictor, see you next week for a cuppa tea," said Sam. A scab on his leg was a source of fascination, and he gave a running commentary on its changing colors: "Lickle bit orange . . . lickle bit green . . . bit bit purple." He stuck foam alphabet letters all over himself in the bath, pretending they were scabs. By the stream, he would pretend to be a dog, pick up sticks in his mouth, and throw them in. Colors mattered a lot. "It's a blue rainin' and a black windy," was how he described a storm, when he was aged just three. At the same age he was tearing up and down the slippery garden paths, wearing a black sweater. "O be careful, black darling," he instructed himself. If the rain was really, really heavy, he and George would strip naked and dance about in the garden. One January evening, they occupied themselves by dipping their long bangs into the icy water of the birdbath and then flicking the drops at each other, laughing uproariously.

Sam's habit of spotting visual correspondences was strong. "Look at all those lubbly worms!" he exclaimed, about catkins. He intoned "Mirror, mirror, on the wall" to a shiny circular doorknob, and pretended to blow out the hairbrush bristles as if they were candles on a cake. I offered him a plate of tagliatelle. "I like seat belts, mmm, 'licous." His word coinages were equally idiosyncratic. "Gourlagourd" and "saunters" were nouns, "ponk," "glimp," and "tuit" were verbs. I was never sure of their exact meanings, but I think Sam was.

I know he said all these things because I wrote them down. What I recorded wasn't the speech of a normal child, any more than George's utterances were normal. While Sam, aged four and five, was wittering on about gourlagourds, George, aged six and seven, was saying things like, "Oh the television is ripped and full of toothpaste," or (seeing Sam having a haircut) "All Sam's feathers are coming off." When I asked George what he'd been doing at school, he said, "Watching the shadows dance," and it transpired they'd had Music and Movement. He pointed at me and said, "She was a wonderful writer, artist, and countrywoman," which I took as a tremendous compliment until I realized it was lifted straight from a video about the life of Beatrix Potter. George used to narrate the story of his own life as it was happening, always in the third person. "He jumped into the bath with a tremendous splash." "'Where can Daddy be?' exclaimed George anxiously." "He clutched his spoon tightly. The sausage bounced off the plate, but he caught it." My all-time favorite was when he was eating a McDonald's hamburger. He pulled out the slimy, khaki slice of dill pickle and handed it to me, saying, "Mum, this is my conscience."

At this age, a great deal of George's speech was still adapted from memorized sources. As time went on, he worked in more and more phrases of his own, and his use of language has steadily become more normal. We can now have short conversational exchanges, even discussions, though he still finds it hard to cope with dissent and is very controlling of the conversation, correcting one's word order and tone of voice. Certain words and phrases irritate him, usually those that don't have a precise meaning—"Don't say 'Okay then,' say 'Yes'!" George's gnomic utterances of earlier days seem to have laid the foundations for the stronger, more "useful" verbal structures he has managed to build more recently. Sam's language, however, has made no such progress. The garbled chatter, the humor, the ability to comment on life, which were so marked at five and a half, had all vanished within six months. All that was left was a handful of syllables. These were used only to get needs met. They weren't even whole words anymore, but eroded sounds—"ju" for "juice," "'way" for "Leave me alone."

Sam was five years and five months when Jake was conceived. I was feeling quite complacent. George was increasingly settled, Sam was lawless but happy; I felt, at last, that I could take on the extra labor and responsibility of a third baby. That August, four months pregnant, I took the boys on holiday to France, on my own. I joined my mother out there, but I managed the journey with them alone, and thought little of it. Six weeks later, I could barely take Sam out of the house.

So, what happened? Regression is a common, though not inevitable, feature of autism. Usually, it happens in the second year of life. The child loses language, loses interest in play; the desire for social contact dwindles. In some cases, these skills are slowly regained; in others, the withdrawal is permanent. Sam's regression was unusually late. I wasn't expecting it, and it took a long time for me to notice what was happening, as is often the case with things that lie under our very eyes. I kept finding reasons for his restlessness, his agitation, his crying, his frantic destructiveness. It was due to illness, exhaustion, or being in an unfamiliar place, I thought. It took me a long time to realize that the old happy-go-lucky Sam had gone.

Sam's stimming was taking over his life. Proper talking was being replaced by a jumble of apparently meaningless noises. He was starting to harm himself, biting his hands and knocking himself under the chin. All his obsessive interests disappeared overnight, as I describe in chapter 7. Washing machines, vacuum cleaners, cuckoo clocks, and the like, which had made him literally jump for joy, no longer kindled a flicker of interest. He seemed to be suffering from colicky cramps, and would arch his back and scream, sometimes for a couple of hours at a stretch. Either he couldn't keep still, and just wanted to run and run, or else he would slump on the sofa, almost comatose, feeding bottle dangling from the corner of his mouth, indifferent to everything happening around him.

He wasn't like this absolutely all the time. I have photographs from this time that show the old cheeky grin (that's a cliché, but there's no better way of describing it), and there were still a few activities he enjoyed, on good days. But for far too much of the time he was aimless, disoriented, and distressed. It was terribly hard to get through to him; often he didn't even seem to hear what was said to him, let alone understand it. In October 1997, his Uncle Warwick got married. Sam's behavior at the reception was particularly difficult. The year before, Sam had caused chaos at my friend Cathy's wedding, but at least as far as Sam was concerned it had been happy chaos, borne with noble fortitude by the bride and groom. On that occasion, it had been George who was clingy and tearful, alarmed by the crowds and desperate to get back to the car. At Warwick and Heather's wedding, George was relatively relaxed and confident, surrounded as he was by familiar family members, but Sam behaved like a tiger escaped from his cage. He made constant dashes for freedom; when restrained, he would almost snarl. At one point he shook off his pursuers and careered through the massed ranks of a second wedding group, gathered to be photographed on the steps of Greenwich Town Hall. I put his behavior down to too much icing.

I may have been partly right. I don't fully understand the reasons for Sam's crash, but I'm convinced that he underwent a profound internal upheaval, and that this was linked to what he was eating, and possibly to what he was not eating. In babyhood, Sam had been placidly, indiscriminately omnivorous, but since the age of one his diet had become more and more limited and nutritionally impoverished. For a long time he had consumed mainly refined carbohydrates and quantities of milk. Had an intolerance of casein and gluten been slowly building up, to reach, suddenly, an intolerable level? This seems quite likely to me.

What, if anything, did his treatment for candida contribute?

To this day, I really can't be sure. Was I right to embark on the treatment in the first place? Was I right to continue it once such a violent reaction had apparently been provoked? Was the regression an agony that had to be gone through to reach the calmer, clearer-headed Sam we have today? I find these questions impossible to answer. Any decision making on behalf of any child involves an element of risk, however small. Have you chosen the right school, the right musical instrument to learn, the right orthodontic treatment? One can never know what might have been.

What else could have caused Sam's crash? It happened when he was unsuitably placed in the mainstream primary school, where despite everyone's best efforts he must have felt panicked and bewildered. Perhaps his language fell away because he'd gotten tired of being misunderstood; his idiosyncratic coinages and muffled pronunciations made it difficult for most people to know what he was saying, which must be disheartening, to say the least. But though these could have been contributing factors, instinct tells me that Sam was in the grip of a physical process way beyond his control.

These days, Sam is easier, more relaxed. He's more manageable than he's been since babyhood. He never runs away, and he's not seriously destructive anymore. Thanks to his ABA/Verbal Behavior therapy, he's infinitely more compliant both in public and private. His use of language is improving; he still has to be prompted to speak in full sentences, but he's light-years away from the handful of broken syllables that was all that was left to him six years ago.

Some of his humor and sense of fun have been restored. He

can be affectionate again, and just occasionally he seeks out the company of a specific person. But he is still not the bright-eyed rascal that he was before the crash. He never chats for the sake of it; most of his utterances have still to do with getting his needs met. He still has no real interests; the gap left by the white goods, oasts, and bottles of Harpic, as described in chapter 11, has never been properly filled. He spends a lot of time restlessly trying to find the thing to eat that will satisfy him—a feeling I remember from pregnancy—and he gets angry when nothing does the trick.

As a small boy, pre-crash, Sam was quite "transparent." He expressed things, reacted to things, much more immediately. I remember him aged five, on a beautiful autumn evening, running in to me from the garden—"Mummy, come and see the moon! Mummy, come and see the lawn mower!" This level of spontaneity and interaction has never returned, though he does now frequently present me with things—a crisp, a Lego brick, a balloon whisk, whatever. Sam is guarded and wary. He now keeps his inner self hidden for much of the time. People, he seems to feel, put too much pressure on him. It's interesting that the one relationship that held good throughout his crash was with George—the only person, perhaps, who exerted no pressure of any kind.

It's still hard to find things that motivate Sam, because admitting to any kind of enthusiasm would mean letting his defenses slip, and he's rarely prepared to do that. Emotionally, Sam is more "autistic" than he was pre-crash; life in the mental padded cell he has created for himself is boring, but it's more comfortable, less threatening, than the outside world.

A common belief among people not deeply familiar with autism is that there is a normal child trapped inside, struggling to get out. That's a false belief. I reiterate that Sam has no "normal" core. He is autistic through and through. But there was a time when his autism was more penetrable, when contact with the neurotypical world was more pleasurable and easy for him. That's what I want to restore. I think we're getting there. Even on a bad day, Sam is never now anything like the lost, howling child he once became. As long as I can feel that progress is being made, I can cope with most things. For me, Sam's crash had been the worst part of the whole autism business, far worse than the initial diagnosis. The powerlessness that results from finding your child in the grip of some torment you don't understand is horrible.

NINE

Off the Couch

In describing Sam's great regression I omitted one possible explanation for his changed behavior, the kind of explanation that would most readily spring to mind when discussing behavior changes in any normal child.

A psychologist would have looked at Sam's family life and suggested emotional causes for his increased aloofness, loss of language, his unexplained crying, his insomnia, his self-harm. Until October 1997 Sam, though clearly autistic and not easy to control or teach, was cheerful, busy, and, in an eccentric way, sociable. By the spring of 1998 he was all but unreachable.

What changes happened in family life during this period? Well, Jake was born, on January 26, 1998—on George's eighth birthday, as it happens. So, did Sam's behavior demonstrate his deep unease at being displaced by another baby? I might have thought that if the change had happened after Jake's birth, but it began midpregnancy. And, I would argue, my pregnancy hardly affected him. It was trouble-free. I never took to my bed, never stayed in hospital (before the birth itself) or gave up doing any of the things I normally did with Sam.

A psychologist might disagree. The child will have been affected by the news of the pregnancy. He will have overheard conversations, he will have brooded on the explanations you have given him, he will have sensed change on a subconscious level. And besides, there'll be other issues. What about tensions between me and Min, attempts to remove Sam's bottle, the changes, perhaps, of people in his life—babysitters, teachers, children at school? It would be easy to find explanations of this kind for Sam's disturbed and disturbing behavior.

Easy, but, I believe, misguided. I respect psychology. I don't dismiss it as a nonscience. Psychoanalysis and psychotherapy may be only as good as the people who practice them, but at best that can be very good indeed. No one system—no science, no religion, no philosophy—has all the answers, but I think that psychology has enhanced our understanding of human behavior to a considerable degree. I believe that aberrant behavior in children can often be attributed to emotional disturbance. And yet I don't believe that Sam's regression had anything to do with the obvious psychological upheavals. Why?

It seems to me that autism is uniquely and intriguingly resistant to psychological analysis. Autists have emotions, but they don't have the emotional instincts that are shared by the majority of the human race. As I suggested in chapter 5, they don't cotton on to the set of symbols and archetypes that form the basis for key mythologies and folktales the world over. If you read a collection of American Indian stories, another of Russian stories, and another of African, their similarities will be more striking than their differences. Of course, one can find many exceptions to every rule, but consider recurrent themes like the eventual success of the put-upon youngest son (usually the third son), the concealed beauty of the youngest (third) daughter, the cruelty of the step-mother, talking animals, forests you get lost in, the setting and accomplishment of seemingly impossible tasks. Consider child-eating ogres, magic seeds, enchanted sleeps, garments that make you invisible. Consider seven-league boots, swords that cut through anything, wishing wells, flying carpets. These devices, or their equivalents, crop up with astonishing regularity in all cultures from the Innuit to the Australian Aborigine.

Folktales are about wish fulfillment, and about the raising and assuaging of fears. They deal with all the big events and emotions of human life—love, treachery, desire, jealousy, death—and fit them into a manageable framework. They achieve this by using archetypes—the wicked stepmother, the handsome prince—and symbols—the briar rose, the red riding hood. You can take the symbols a long, long way, but while many readers will be sceptical about accepting, say, the glass slipper as a vagina, most will re-spond to the basics—Red Riding Hood straying from the path, the deceptive allure of the gingerbread house. There is a deep, wide commonwealth of imagination that links us all in our response to these stories. If you tell a tale to a group of five-year-olds, you'll get the same "oohs" and "aahs" and "no, nos!" at the same mo-ments. Normal children don't have to be taught such responses. They appear to be innate.

Normal children respond in a similar way to the pattern and shape of folktales—and most of them are highly patterned, with events falling into groups of three, or a phrase repeatedly chanted with slight variations. "Fee, fi, fo, fum! I smell the blood of an Englishman. Be he alive or be he dead, I'll grind his bones to make my bread." "Run, run, as fast as you can, you can't catch me, I'm the gingerbread man!" Presumably these repetitions were useful aide-mémoires in the days when stories were passed down orally, but there's something about them that children find deeply satisfying. Children don't like a story to be interrupted or disrupted. Even if they've heard it before, and know what happens, they want to hear it out, to savor the coziness of resolution. Indeed, when I was doing my primary-school teacher-training course, in 1981, we were told that we should never leave a fairy tale half finished, to be resumed the next day, in case the lack of resolution gave the children nightmares. This is sound advice.

As we all know, fairy tales are full of grotesquery and horror. Bluebeard's murdered wives, Hansel fattened in a cage, the wolf gobbling up Grandmother—when the real-life equivalents of these events are reported in the newspapers, we don't want our children to know about them. Shocking events such as the disappearance of the Soham schoolgirls lead to discussions about the best way to filter the information for our children, who are bound to pick up on it in this media-saturated society. Why, then, do we think it appropriate to tell stories full of horror to young children? Because if such tales are related in the right circumstances, they help the child to cope with fear. The adult teller, whether parent or teacher, should have a bond with the child, a bond of affection and respect. The telling of the story strengthens that bond. The tale addresses the child's fears, and the affection of the teller reassures the child that fears are normal, and shared. Human life does contain violence and sorrow. It also contains beauty and joy. Fairy tales shape these extremes into something the child can manage, and the telling of them lets the child know that he is not alone in the frightening, enthralling adventure of life. The adult is beside him, guiding him, consoling him, implicitly letting him know that, yes, I've felt the things you're feeling now. Fairy tales properly told are resonant and thrilling; danger and beauty are closely linked. Fairy tales should never be bland.

Fairy tales are also a receptacle for cultural memory. They pass on experience from one generation to the next. They present good advice, both practical and moral, in a palatable form: don't wander off the path; be brave and truthful. The normal child has no difficulty in generalizing the advice. She can see that "Hansel and Gretel" is not warning you against nibbling houses made of gingerbread, it's letting you know that things—and people—are not always what they seem. Similarly, the normal child has little problem in distinguishing goodies from baddies. Archetypes survive and flourish because they do have universal meaning. Even a three-year-old can detect the wiles of the smiling fox, feel anxious on behalf of the foolish goose.

And the normal child will swiftly find someone with whom to identify. She'll place herself in the story; she's not just a passive listener. A girl will usually identify with a female character, a boy with a male, though of course there'll be many exceptions. And the huge range of stories provides plenty of role-model choice. I had little time, myself, for the passive Sleeping Beauty, trapped in suspended animation until the right man came along. I identified with the brave, resourceful little girl who goes to call on Baba Yaga, the bony-legged Russian witch, and wins the support of the dog, the cat, the servant girl, the creaking gate, and the birch tree. With their aid, she outwits the witch and lives to tell the tale.

For autistic children, very little of this applies. I read the simpler folktales aloud to George and Sam from an early age, and they found favorites among them. George, far more book-oriented than Sam, had a stronger response. His favorites were—are—"The Three Bears," "The Three Little Pigs," "The Gingerbread Man,"

"The Little Red Hen," and "Jack and the Beanstalk." He quite likes "Red Riding Hood" and "Snow White," and "Beauty and the Beast" reached him via Disney. George's story choice has always tended to dominate, so, mainly due to exposure, these are also the stories Sam has shown most interest in, especially "The Three Little Pigs." The stories they like are strong on repeated phrases. "Who's been eating MY porridge?" " 'I'll do it myself,' said the Little Red Hen." "I'll huff and I'll puff, and I'll BLOW your house down." Both boys find such phrases satisfying and amusing, and for George there's also a pleasant frisson of alarm. The props are solid, and come within the boundaries of their experience—the porridge bowls, the house of bricks, the giant's egg-laying hen. The stories are linear, uncluttered, and do not rely heavily on deception and magic, both of which confuse the boys. The more complicated, fantastical tales, like "The Twelve Dancing Princesses" or even "Cinderella," fail to hold their attention, because they call on powers of imagination that George and Sam just haven't got.

So, the boys aren't indifferent to folktales. But it seems to me that the universal resonances, the powerful symbols that I've been discussing, don't do the business for them. They don't feel a shiver of fear at the thought of the great dark forest. They've no desire to right wrongs, to oust the wicked stepmother and restore the status of the displaced child. They do not instinctively see that wolves and foxes are in one camp, little pigs and hens in another. For years, George loved "The Tale of Jemima Puddle-Duck" (not a folktale, I know, but with many similarities to one). He had read it and watched it on video time and time again. One day I asked him, "George, is the fox bad or good?" "He's good," said George.

"Why do you think he's good?"

"He's smiling."

Hampered by such a profound misunderstanding of motive, and indifferent to miracles and magic (when so much of the real world is baffling to autists, how can you expect them to be impressed when a frog turns into a prince?), what's left for the autistic reader of fairy tales? A response to pattern and shape—yes, that's quite strong in both my boys. But it's a desire for pattern for its own sake. A half-told tale might (*might*) irritate George or Sam just because it's incomplete. They won't suffer from the sense of psychological disruption, the feeling that we can't leave Hansel stuck in the cage, that would trouble Jake.

A relish for quaint and repeated turns of phrase—yes, in George's case that's probably what he likes best about these stories. A means of addressing and allaying fears—no, absolutely not. Autistic people do have fears. Sometimes their lives are dominated by fears and anxieties. But these fears are rarely the ones we commonly share. In his fascinating book *Nature via Nurture* (Fourth Estate, 2003), Matt Ridley discusses common phobias—snakes, spiders, the dark, heights, deep water, small spaces, thunder. He points out that these were genuine perils to Stone Age people but are not things that most of us need to worry about nowadays. And yet we have failed to replace these phobias with more rational or relevant ones such as cars, skis, guns, electric sockets. He suggests that the human brain "is pre-wired to learn fears that were of relevance in the Stone Age. And the only way that evolution can transmit such information from the past to the design of the mind in the present is via the genes." Are the genes inherited by autists faulty in this respect? Ridley quotes experiments that indicate that fear conditioning depends heavily on the amygdala, a small almond-shaped structure near the base of the brain. The amygdala has been found to be abnormally shaped in autistic people. Perhaps heritable fears simply don't take root in autistic brains. I'm prepared to be corrected, but I haven't come across an autist who shares any of the Stone Age phobias listed above. Indeed, autists often conspicuously and inconveniently lack a fear of heights or deep water. Instead, autistic phobias tend to be one-offs, like Sam's broken chairs, or polystyrene; one boy I know was phobic about fruit, seedlings, and penises.

Of course, innate fears are reinforced by adult behavior. A mother who screams at the sight of a spider will confirm an incipient fear of spiders in her watching daughter. And as autists have a greatly reduced capacity for imitative behavior, it's unlikely that they will learn fears in this way, whether rational or irrational. It's interesting that parents can teach a rational fear to a neurotypical child, but only up to a point. They can teach the child to be wary of traffic, but they are unlikely to inculcate a deep, shuddering, giddy-making response to the sight of a car. And if their child's autistic, they'll have a hard job teaching even basic road sense.

Autists feel fear, anger, panic, joy, love. They feel most things, but their feelings are somehow displaced. Press the right buttons, with neurotypical people, and you activate certain feelings. The buttons are in predictable places, as Hollywood knows only too well. Autistic buttons are very hard to find. "How does it feel?" asks the girl, after she kisses Dustin Hoffman in *Rain Man*. "Wet," he replies.

Back to fairy tales. They are unlikely to speak to autistic fears or autistic desires. The autist is unlikely to identify with a character, because, as we've seen, he lacks a theory of mind, and he exists in the here and now. Jake might well think, I want to be like that prince, strong and handsome, slashing through the brambles and winning the prize. These are social ambitions; Jake, like many little boys, wants to be top dog. George and Sam have no social ambitions. They have no true ambitions at all. They do not place themselves in a social context. Their sense of their own identity is too frail or too rudimentary to be properly projected onto that of any other character, real or fictitious.

That business about storytelling strengthening relationship bonds—that hardly applies, either. I can see a vestige of it. George likes to choose who will read his stories to him, and he associates certain adults with certain stories. But neither he nor Sam has the sense that they are co-adventuring with the adult reader. Jake likes me to make up stories with both of us in them, he in a leading, me in a supporting, role. (He likes to have George and Sam in them too—"But you can make them not autistic, Mum.") Jake shows a very obvious, very normal, unconscious understanding of the uses of enchantment. His brothers do not.

It almost goes without saying that autists won't pick up on the practical wisdom or the moral of the story. They have a hard enough time generalizing in real life—it doesn't come naturally to them that "Don't tip Ribena down the sink" also means don't tip wine, milk, coffee, Fanta, or lemon barley water either. So it's highly unlikely that the body of folk wisdom passed down in fairy tales over the centuries will have any impact on them. To sum up, then, it seems to me that autistic people fail to respond to the symbols and archetypes that resonate for neurotypical people the world over. What has this got to do with Sam and his regression? Well, what I'm trying to suggest is that behavior that in a neurotypical person would indicate psychological disturbance does not necessarily indicate any such thing in an autistic person, because the psychology of an autistic person functions so very, very differently.

I have to be careful here, because I don't want to suggest that for autistic people behavior never reflects their experience (it does), or that they have no profound emotional life (they do). Sam has a tendency to obsessive-compulsive behavior, which increases at times of "emotional" stress. Recently, Ian, our nanny, went to hospital and was away for three weeks. Sam's obsessive behavior— opening and closing doors, taking shoes on and off, endlessly re-tracing his steps—reached fever pitch. Ian returned; the behaviors receded. Sam does care about Ian, and was made anxious by his absence. But I don't believe Sam was worried about what Ian was undergoing. He didn't think about Ian's pain, or worry that the operation would go wrong. He didn't put himself in Ian's place, thinking, I hope I don't have to have an operation. He was react-ing to the change in routine, the loss of the "games" he shares with Ian, the sense of loss of control that Sam seems to feel when unwelcome things happen.

What I'm sure about is that while many autistic behaviors may look as if they have psychological origins, the real cause is likely to be physical or sensory. A normal seven-year-old who smeared feces over his hair, clothes, and bedroom, would certainly be ex-pressing anger or upset. That wouldn't be true at eighteen months, but it would be true at seven. The seven-year-old knows what the social norms are regarding excrement. He knows that smearing will produce shock, anger, revulsion, in an adult. If he smears, then for some reason he wants to invite those responses. His behavior is a challenge to his adult caretakers. George, at seven, often smeared. He knew I would be angry, but that wasn't the effect he was after. He was interested in the physical proper-ties of excrement, and it was worth enduring the trivial matter of my outrage to explore these properties to the full. I found him watching an episode of *Pingu* when Pinga, Pingu's little sister (in-cidentally, one of *the* great characters of children's television), daubs herself all over with paint. George had done the same thing to himself, but with shit. It was the nearest thing at hand.

Where does this leave psychotherapy in relation to autism? That's an important question. Until quite recently, most health professionals believed that autism was a psychosis. It was only in the 1990s—after George's diagnosis—that the genetic component was firmly established. It's only now, in the 2000s, that the structure of the living brain can be examined, and though this study is in its infancy it looks as if autistic brains are structurally, physically different from normal ones. The child is born with autism. That's what I believe, and that's increasingly widely accepted. But in the 1960s, when Clara Park's Jessy was a child, autism, often called childhood schizophrenia, was believed to result from cold, inadequate parenting. Park cites Bruno Bettelheim, who wrote that parental rejection is an element in the genesis of every case of childhood schizophrenia [autism] that he has ever seen. Bettelheim, author of the hugely influential book *The Empty Fortress,* has been much misquoted; I believe that he never actually used the notorious phrase "refrigerator mother," which has been widely attributed to him. But he certainly saw autism as a result of nurture (or lack of nurture) rather than nature. Kanner himself considered that parents must play a large part in the onset of infantile autism. He summed up the parents of his autistic patients as "detached, humourless perfectionists, more at home in the world of abstractions than among people." And Beata Rank, an American psychiatrist, set out as her main hypothesis that "the atypical [autistic] child has suffered gross emotional deprivation . . . the younger the child, the more necessary is it for us to modify the mother's personality."

The Parks and the other parents of their generation, in addition to the hard work of looking after an autistic child, had to bear the burden of suspicion that the child got that way because of their emotional inadequacies. Never mind that they had three other happy, bright, sociable children; in the eyes of the doctors, Jessy was living proof of the emotional inadequacies that must lurk behind their façade of normality. I consider myself very fortunate that I came to autism in a more enlightened era. No one has ever suggested to me that the boys' autism is my "fault." But this pervasive assumption about the origins of autism of course led to the conclusion that psychiatric intervention, including the techniques of psychotherapy, would help.

When George was five, we had a consultation with Dr. Anne Alvarez, of the Tavistock Clinic. She is an intelligent and sensitive person, and she wrote a perceptive and thorough report on George; many of her comments still ring true. She attributes quite a lot to his difficult birth, and tactfully but clearly indicates that she regards our parenting as inconsistent and too indulgent. She underestimates—in my opinion—his echolalia, and the eccentricity of his play. She notes, for instance, that he "began mumbling . . . the Lord's Prayer to himself," without remarking on the oddness of this choice for a five-year-old child brought up in a non-church-going household. (I remember George's version of the Lord's Prayer—it included "Give us this day our staley bread," and "As we forgive those who are pressed up against us.") But she comments accurately and enthusiastically that his grasp on her hand was "affectionate, controlling, and even possessive. He's an intense, probably quite passionately attached little boy when he lets himself go, and he has a very strong will . . . he is not in a fixed state of withdrawal." She recommended psychotherapy, and we followed this up.

The ideal, in Dr. Alvarez's opinion, was three sessions a week. This was beyond our financial means; it would also have been impractical, as the nearest suitable practitioner worked thirty miles away. We compromised; George had one session a week, for several years. We gave it up when we started ABA, in the interests of redirecting time and money. The psychotherapy did George no harm, and in some ways it did some good; the therapist realized, for instance, that George overidentified with Sam, and was using Sam as a screen between himself and the real world. She worked, successfully, on decreasing his dependence on Sam. Having any bright, kind, sympathetic adult interact closely with your autistic child on a regular basis is a good thing, and so as far as that goes, psychotherapy could be of use. But I feel that, as a system, it underestimates the autisticness of autism and misinterprets symptoms that may well have an organic rather than a psychological origin. I did smile quietly to myself when George pooed in his pants in the therapy room, and his therapist told me that she was "glad that he felt able to bring something to the session." Hmm. Beware of geeks bearing gifts.

Thank goodness, no professional has ever, in Beata Rank's chilling phrase, attempted to "modify" my personality. The extremists of the 1950s and 1960s no longer operate—not in East Sussex anyway—and no one could have been more benign than George's therapist. But I do feel that, as far as autism goes, psychotherapy is based on false assumptions. There's something about autism that makes it more psychotherapy-resistant than any other condition. When it comes to the imagination, the emotions, the operation of the subconscious, there's very little common ground. The usual instincts just aren't there.

TEN

Mild Peril

Spring 1999. Sam, my Aunt Meriel, and I stood in the cathedral cloister at Hereford. Meriel, being the bishop's wife, lives in the palace; we had left George and Jake under the supervision of the palace staff while we nipped out with Sam for a change of scene. We whirled through the cathedral—Sam's wholehearted enjoyment of church acoustics keeps such visits brief—and out into the cloister. Sam was with us. We stooped for one second to examine the inscription on a memorial—and Sam was gone.

Sam had often disappeared at home, but I'd worried less about that, because he has an excellent sense of direction. When Sam is "lost" he's not truly lost, just absent without leave. But this time it was different. Sam didn't know Hereford, not beyond the palace and its grounds. We were right in the center of the city. The dangers were real—crowds, traffic, the wide, fast-flowing River Wye.

Calling to an autistic child is pointless, because even if he hears you, he doesn't usually feel any need to respond. I tend to do it anyway, because it's what mothers do when children are lost. At home, when we're walking on the farm, I can often locate Sam not because he listens out for me, but because I listen out for him. Sam may not say much, but he's rarely silent. He drones, hums, vocalizes, and bangs his hands together to the accompaniment of a nasal sound like that of a deep-toned mosquito magnified several thousand times. When he was younger, his noises bore closer relation to "real" sounds. For instance, he used to do a cheerful and accurate imitation of the torrent of bloodcurdling abuse our neighboring farmer used to hurl at her sheep. He would imitate a drill, a chain saw, or the final, climactic shudder of the washing machine. Over time, these sounds have become abstracted from their originals and now form a flow of white noise, an external tinnitus, which has the useful side effect of enabling me to find Sam even when he is some way off.

Hereford City Center, however, is crowded with sounds competing for attention. Meriel and I ran around the cathedral precinct for a while, vainly calling, and then I ran back to the palace and rang the police. It is odd, and infuriating, that when one dials 999 one is asked to supply a full address before any action is taken. I found myself having to repeat a distant postcode—"No, not *m* for mother, *n* for nutter"—while Sam, in my mind's eye, ran toward some distant horizon, ever farther from reach.

I went back out to find Meriel. She'd found a young man who had seen Sam heading for the river and had called the police. He hadn't stopped him—but why should he? Sam was seven, strong and agile; it wasn't as if he was a wandering toddler. How could a young man grab hold of such a child without fear of suspicion? And if he had gotten hold of him, what would he do with him then? No use asking Sam his name and address. It was good of the young man to do anything at all, when there was ample reason not to get involved. "I thought it was a bit unusual," he said, "because he went up to a dog, took the ball out of its mouth, and put it in his own."

We forged on. I can't remember the exact sequence of events, but before long I was touring the city in a police car, eyes peeled. At last a call came through. A woman had found Sam dancing on the treacherous bank of the Wye. She had taken him to the corner shop at the end of the nearest street. We drove there with all speed. Sam was hopping up and down in the middle of the shop, shouting, "Lollipop!" We bundled him into the police car and returned to the palace.

Sam was not hurt, neither was he frightened or even especially bewildered. The whole episode, which had seemed like an eternity to me, had taken, I think, less than an hour, but it would not have made much difference to Sam if he had been away all day. Sam doesn't get frightened because he lacks the capacity to imagine dangers. He doesn't associate me, or adults in general, with security or with protection from fears, so he doesn't mind not being with an adult. Sam does have fears, but they are not the kind that would oppress the mind of a normal seven-year-old alone in an unfamiliar city. To say that an autistic child's fears are irrational doesn't clarify the matter, because all children have irrational fears as well as rational ones. Jake won't go alone up one of our flights of stairs because he fears that Buzz and Woody (from *Toy Story*) are waiting at the top. And for a long time he made me come to the lavatory with him because, he said, Zebedee from *The Magic Roundabout* might boing up out of the pan. Honestly, Jake, I said, I *know* Zebedee isn't in there. No, said Jake, but when you were four you would have thought so. But Jake, alone and lost in Hereford, wouldn't have worried about Buzz or Zebedee. He would have prioritized his fears; his main concern would have been to get back to me, and he would have known that explaining his predicament to another adult would have been the best way to effect this. At present, Jake is worried about kidnappers, because of a note his school sent home about the strange behavior of an individual seen in the village. Jake holds my hand tightly when we're out, and if we see anyone who fits the police description ("chubby, balding, 5'5''") he urges me to ring 999. He is particularly anxious that Sam might be kidnapped, though somewhat cheered by the thought that anyone who kidnapped Sam might reconsider his chosen career path. Sam has no such worries. Sam's fears would remain approximately the same whether he was careering along through crowds and traffic or safe at home with me.

Some autists are gripped, dominated, by fears and anxieties. I remember hearing a very able autistic man, a graduate, eloquently explaining that the sight of a pencil near the edge of a table, where it might roll off, produced in him an anxiety as intense as the news of a car crash. Neither of my boys suffer to this extent. George is more fearful than Sam; his worries are more conceptual, like not wanting to grow up, and at times they do limit his activities, though they eventually recede. Sam sometimes shows distress at unfamiliar surroundings—I've noticed that he's very unlikely to eat anything away from home—but apart from that, the only true fear he seems to have at the moment is of dogs. When we walk in the woods, if a dog approaches, be it a Great Dane or a Yorkie, he will spring into my arms—so it's not quite true that he doesn't use people as protection, though I think he uses me as a physical rather than an emotional refuge. But his fear of dogs doesn't prevent him from going on the walk in the first place. The dogs always seem to take him by surprise.

The Hereford incident was the most worrying, because we were so far from home, but there have been many similar escapes. Police helicopters have been called out on several occasions.

When I was enormously pregnant with Jake, and simply couldn't move fast enough, I lost track of Sam on our farm because George was playing near water and I thought it was dangerous to leave him. My search for Sam proving fruitless, I returned to the house. I was on the point of calling the police when the doorbell rang. A neighbor, who lives a mile or so away, was holding a naked Sam. She'd taken off her coat and wrapped it around him. It was January, but Sam, naked, barefoot, and scratched by brambles, had seemed quite cheerful when she'd found him in the woods. A couple of days later, the police called. A walker had found a pile of children's clothes by a stream. A name tag had located our doctor. Police and social services made inquires of the doctor and of Sam's school, concerning, I imagine, my fitness as a parent.

Sam's youthful passion for oasthouses left him with a dominant ambition—to reach a particular oast, which stood on the top of a hill about a mile and a half away. When Sam escaped from home I think he was usually trying to reach this Nirvana. Once, he succeeded. Its owner, taking an afternoon nap, was startled to be joined in bed by a small boy still wearing his Wellington boots.

It wasn't always Sam. Devon police once retrieved George from a pig field near his grandparents' house—he'd gone out at dusk to have a wallow in the mud. George moves more slowly than Sam, who can outrun the wind, but if he gets an idea into his head, he's hard to stop. He developed a mini-obsession about Brambly Hedge, a series of books and videos about fancifully dressed mice who live in minutely detailed citadels among twisted roots. He convinced himself that Brambly Hedge could be found in a field opposite our house. This field can be reached only by crossing an extremely busy road. He also convinced himself that Danny, one of his school "friends," dwelled therein. Danny is a solid, sturdy lad; it's hard to think of a less likely resident for Brambly Hedge, unless it might be John Prescott, but George was determined to go and look for him. This caused me considerable worry as George has no more road sense than a hedgehog. Thank goodness, the dream seems to have faded.

Autists have very little common sense. In fact, "common" sense is exactly what they don't have. They may have survival instincts; Uta Frith, in *Autism: Explaining the Enigma,* has suggested that "feral" children, such as Victor, the "Wild Boy of Aveyron," were in fact autistic, and this seems highly plausible to me, not least because autism would explain (a) why the children were abandoned in the first place, and (b) why they didn't seek human help, even though in some cases they were found close to settlements. Some of these children survived for long periods using considerable ingenuity, and I don't doubt that tough, fearless Sam would do pretty well left to his own devices, though the vague, limp-wristed George wouldn't last five minutes. So autists do have sense, of a kind. But "common" sense is closely linked to social sense, and this is something they find almost impossible to acquire. They don't see the way things fall into patterns; they can't generalize from one situation to the next. If his brothers have been painting, Sam will wash up their palettes and brushes, but he'll also wash up their finished paintings. The cleaning-up process is, he knows, a way of getting rid of paint. He doesn't see that paint on paper is desirable, paint on the palette disposable. George wants to go to the shop. "Put your shoes and socks on," I say. A while later (he takes ages to do anything) George is standing by the front door, waiting. Are his shoes and socks on? Yes—on one foot.

Few autistic people are able to lead unsupervised lives as adults, almost regardless of their level of intelligence. Many lower-functioning nonautistic people with "learning difficulties" cope far

more effectively in terms of self-care and social integration, because, whatever their problems, they do have some common sense.
And they can transfer learned ideas from one situation to another.
A nonautistic person of low IQ might well grasp that "Don't touch
that broken glass" applies to all broken glass, not just that particular piece. An autist, even one of high IQ, cannot generalize in this
way. "Don't touch that broken glass" means don't touch that
piece, here, now, on the floor in front of you. The instruction will
not be retained and applied to future broken-glass encounters.
George has always loved fires. In our big, cold, old house, open
fires are not an indulgence but a necessity. George sits next to the
fire, inching ever closer; every so often I push him and his chair
back to where they started from. Once, I was upstairs bathing Jake
and forgot that George and the fire were unsupervised. I belted
downstairs to find George, both feet propped on a smoldering log,
humming contentedly and gazing at the smoke that curled up
from the soles of his shoes.

He finds it hard to resist throwing bits of paper into the fire
and watching them flare and die. The trouble is, he's undiscriminating about which bits to use. I've lost important phone messages this way; once, my address book was dangled over the blaze,
and only rescued just in time. Sam's much better about fires now,
but he, too, had a period of dangerous fascination. He used to
throw in large objects—toys, books, cushions. But though this
might seem like deliberate naughtiness, and certainly it was accompanied by roguish chuckles, I actually think it was simply
what Sam thought you were meant to do with fires. He saw me
putting logs on, so he selected approximately log-sized objects.
He didn't consider the objects for what they were, nor did he consider that burning them would cause them to disappear forever.
Sam has no sense of the future. Often, the sacrificial victims were

things he liked, and I do not feel that he was trying to destroy them. Similarly, when he pours an entire packet of salt into a pan of boiling pasta, he's not setting out to ruin our dinner. He's seen salt go into boiling water; he just thinks that's what you do.

Reading Hermione Lee's biography of Virginia Woolf, I came across Woolf's callous description of her "backward" half-sister, Laura Stephen, which persuades me that Laura was autistic. "A vacant-eyed girl," Woolf calls her, "whose idiocy was daily becoming more obvious, who could hardly read, who would throw scissors into the fire, who was tongue-tied and stammered and yet had to appear at table with the rest of us." Laura had odd vocal mannerisms ("a queer squeaking or semi-stammering or spasmodic uttering"). She was "given to uncontrolled gestures like spitting out or choking on her food," and, to the immense frustration of the whole family, had a "strange perversity," which meant she disregarded all their reprimands. Hermione Lee raises autism as a possibility; I think it a certainty. Autists ignore requests to stop not because they want to defy you but because they are socially indifferent. They don't mind about upsetting or worrying you—they are largely unaware that their actions affect you. They are driven by a compulsion to perform the forbidden action (like throwing scissors on the fire), and this compulsion is far, far stronger than any tiny amount of social or common sense they might possess.

Constant repetition of "No" will, in the very long run, have some effect. A short, simple explanation of the reason for the prohibition may also eventually chip away at the compulsive behavior. Thus George has some respect for "No, that's dirty" or "No, that's dangerous," but it has taken years to instill and is by no means watertight. George no longer smears excrement over his bedroom curtains or over radiators (the heat intensifies the smell). He no longer pulls down his trousers to urinate in public—though he does remove his underpants in public lavatories and stuff them behind the cistern. He knows it's naughty to eat out of the cat's bowl, though sometimes he can't resist the temptation. In such instances, constant nagging has succeeded in rerouting his impulses. Though he can't think things through to their consequences, he does know that certain activities will make me cross, and he doesn't like that.

Sam has only recently begun to care about whether I'm cross or not. If I really, really yell, he looks briefly cowed, perhaps only due to force of decibels. He sometimes shows defiance, which I take to be a good sign, as it indicates a dawning awareness of my reaction. Sam's ABA program (see chapter 7) has hugely increased his compliance, so it's now easier than it was to stop him from doing something undesirable, but he still has very few built-in inhibitors. Prevention is still a very important part of Sam management. There is no still, small voice within telling him not to do dangerous things with matches, scissors, and medicines. These all have to be locked away, as does toothpaste, which will be squeezed and smeared; shampoo, which will be tipped down the sink; and cosmetics, which will be crudely applied to his own face and then bitten or finger-painted onto windows. Art materials are also hidden—glue and paint for obvious reasons, felt-tips because their ends will be bitten off, erasers because they will quite simply be eaten. I have locks on my larder and food cupboard. The lock on my freezer doesn't work, so when I buy a box of ice pops I hide some in unlikely bags and boxes to make sure he doesn't eat all ten at once. At present, some are in with some frozen coffee beans, others are nestling beneath a pile of "breaded hoki loins."

The foods outlawed by his diet, such as "normal" bread and biscuits, obviously have to be locked up, but he can wreak havoc with many other ingredients. He filled the dollhouse bath with runny honey; he grabbed a kilogram bag of currants and ran around the house scattering handfuls as if he were sowing seeds. He hates to eat only a couple of biscuits out of a packet. He'd rather nibble a little of each one and trample the remains underfoot. This preference is messy and expensive. Even messier are Sam's occasional forays into cooking. Before I had locks fitted on the cupboards, Sam would pour ill-assorted ingredients into a bowl, stir or whisk them, and then put the whole lot into the oven. He once made a fairly good approximation of a chocolate pudding. I suggested that he put an egg in, so he did exactly that—put in an egg, unbroken. He wouldn't let me crack it. I surreptitiously removed it before cooking as I thought it might explode in the oven. Sam was quite keen to inspect the "pudding" once cooked, but he didn't want to eat it. He hid it, as I discovered later, under a pile of sofa cushions.

The electric beaters, the food processor, and the ice-cream maker are objects of fascination to Sam, the last vestiges of his obsession with things that spin. It is a mistake to leave the ice-cream maker unattended. Sam's additions have resulted in unconventional combinations—strawberry 'n' curry, raspberry 'n' Frosties, and banana 'n' plastic-dinosaur ice cream.

Some autists are violent. This, I would suggest, might arise more from a weak sense of cause and effect, and a very limited sense of social responsibility, than from an unusually high level of aggression. Most boys fight—most children fight—but they quickly establish rules, even without adult intervention. Biting is outlawed, faces are avoided, opponents are approximately matched for age and size. If such rules are overstepped, playing tips over into bullying, and most children understand the difference. Autistic children engage far less in straightforward fighting than normal children do, because fighting is a version of social interaction, albeit to the adult mind a rather tiresome version. George and Sam rough-and-tumble with each other, and I'm glad they do, because their other play skills are so very limited. When Jake joins in—as, to my surprise, he frequently does—they make no allowances for his size and lack of strength. Again, I welcome this interaction between Jake and his brothers, but I welcome it with gritted teeth, because while I can leave George and Sam rolling interlocked on the floor and know that little harm will be done, once Jake's involved I have to stand there, watching like a hawk.

Autistic violence can be a serious matter. A big, strong girl, intelligent and verbal, who used to be at the boys' school, has had to go to residential school, where, I have heard, she has four assistants to keep her under control. She suffered badly from premenstrual tension. Her mother asked the doctor to put her on the Pill to try to reduce the symptoms but was told that to do so would infringe the girl's human rights because she was underaged.

Pinches, kicks, and bites are common in autistic units—another reason why integration into mainstream is too much for many teachers to cope with. Granny Eva, who works in Sam's unit, wears a padded waistcoat, which she calls her body armor, to school. Though neither George nor Sam has been uncontrollably violent (yet), both have had phases of pinching or biting. The most serious wounds (not very) have been inflicted on each other, but they bear no grudges and never seem to avoid each other's company. One of the strongest motives for setting up an ABA program for the boys was the need to make them more compliant before adolescence struck. I knew that once they were bigger and stronger than me, if they posed real danger to themselves or other people, I would have no option but to find residential care for them, and I didn't want to be forced into that position. It may be that, one day, residential care is the best option for them. I can't see it at the moment—my strongest instincts tell me to keep them close to me. But if this changes, I want the decision to be made in their best interests, not as a last resort. Adolescence is only just beginning for George. As I write, he's still a lot smaller than me. I can still lift him up. His voice hasn't broken, though it can't be long now. By the time this book's in print, he'll almost certainly be towering above me. Who knows what furies the hormonal onslaught will unleash? But I'm optimistic that the system of compliance instilled by ABA will be enough to rein in the worst excesses. When George was hurting other children at school, he was given a timer. For every half hour of pinch-free time, he earned a token. Once a designated number of tokens had been achieved, he could choose his own reward—watching a video, turning on the heater, being allowed to lie on the floor in the quiet room, or whatever. Breaking the no-pinch rule resulted in the removal of a token. This worked well, and it wasn't long before the aggressive behavior had all but disappeared.

Such a system sounds obvious and commonsensical, but it's taken a couple of years of ABA to get George to a state where he can understand the workings of it. Of course, like every mother, I'd resorted to bribery and barter when the boys were little, including being driven to illogical extremes, as in, "If you sit down in the dentist's chair, I'll give you a lollipop." But I'd been surprised, and frustrated, at how difficult it was to get them, particularly Sam, to grasp the concept of a reward. For children with "weak central coherence" (see chapter 11) and severe problems with meaningful sequencing, such obvious dog-training tricks don't seem obvious at all. Sam is only beginning to respond to a "token economy"; he's way behind George in terms of timers and point systems. But, since ABA, Sam's usual response to "No" is to stop whatever he's doing, if only briefly. Before ABA, "No" was little more to Sam than a startling or amusing noise. Eighteen months ago, Sam's aggressiveness at school was quite a problem. Now, it's almost nonexistent. I think this is because ABA has increased his ability to express his desires verbally, which has lowered his level of frustration. His gluten-free/casein-free diet has decreased his physical discomfort, which obviously helps. And, though most days still include periods of unexplained crying, these periods are short. Sam's range of purposeful activity, which had contracted to almost nothing, is expanding a little. His playfulness and sense of fun, lost for several years, is returning. ABA is slowly making his life more jolly and less boring, so he has less need to liven things up with pinches and bites. And at school, Sam's got things pretty much sorted out. He knows how to avoid most unpalatable de-mands, and he's adept at risk assessment. When an adult inter-poses between Sam and his object of desire, I'm told he'll size up such factors as height, breadth, and wingspan before making a dash for what he wants.

At one time, Sam's aggression toward Jake was one of our biggest problems at home. The only thing to do was never leave them alone together, even for a second. Now this aggression has diminished. It will flare up occasionally, nearly always as Sam's re-sponse to being thwarted. If Sam's angry with me, he's quite likely to take it out on Jake, by dragging his arm or pushing him off a chair. This is no fun for Jake, but in terms of Sam's develop-ment of "theory of mind" it's quite good news; he looks at me as he does it, keen to see my outraged reaction.

We've had episodes of climbing on the roof and pulling out the tiles, unscrewing lightbulbs and smashing them, breaking windows, throwing things out of windows, flooding bathrooms, pushing the television over, tipping up heavy items of furniture.

The perpetrator is usually Sam. But the house is still standing, and we're all still alive, not even lightly scarred. I've called this chapter "Mild Peril," to quote the notes for parental guidance on video boxes, because it's my rather blithe belief that autistic behavior is not as dangerous as it looks. People do themselves most harm when they panic, and autistic people, like animals, don't panic unless they're cornered. Autists are protected from danger by their inability to think, what if? They also, in a sense, know what they're doing. Their systemizing brains seize on a detail and observe it very, very closely. Watching Sam slice vegetables with a sharp knife strains the nerves, but he manages it with (almost) a cheflike aplomb.

Of course, one cannot be blasé about danger. I have to be extremely vigilant. But I also have to trust my children's balance, surefootedness, and concentration on their chosen activity. Autists don't do things halfheartedly, if they've chosen to do something themselves. I take precautionary measures, then I let them go as far as I can without intervening. And I try to relax. I have to believe that they know what they're doing, in a physical sense at least. If I didn't, I'd be a nervous wreck.

ELEVEN

Blackberries and Tumble Dryers

When Sam was two, he would sit in the bath rotating flannels inside a toy bucket and emitting a loud, continuous drone. A little worry may have flickered through my mind; Sam's noises didn't sound very normal. But once I realized what he was doing, I was reassured. He was pretending the bucket was a washing machine. He was using his imagination—and isn't that what one wants one's child to do?

It took me a long time to recognize that Sam's imaginative play was abnormal. It was limited, repetitive, unshared. Contrast Sam, absorbed in his "washing machine," with Jake, aged three, manipulating two fronds of bracken, talking to me: "I'm a mummy wasp. I'm knitting a green jumper for my baby wasp. Mum, you be my baby wasp. No"—as the bracken becomes a steering wheel—"this is the Hungarian Grand Prix. I'll be Michael Schumacher, and you be David Coulthard's brother." On the face of it, there may not seem much to choose, in terms of the degree of eccentricity, between turning a bucket into a washing machine

and switching in a couple of seconds from being a wasp to being a
racing driver. All young children seem barmy at times, which is
one reason why autism can be overlooked. But Jake's rapid, flexible thought processes, and his desire to include me in his game,
are nonautistic. Sam, rotating flannels in the bucket, was sending
his imagination down a single track. It never broadened, it rarely
included anyone else, and it never rehearsed behavior or experiences that would be of any social use to him.

Sam played washing-machine games because he loved washing machines. Like many babies, he had enjoyed being propped in
his little chair to watch the spin cycle. Unlike most babies, he
didn't tire of watching the spin cycle for at least five years. Tumble
dryers were just as entrancing as washing machines. We never
owned one, which made it a great treat to visit the houses of people who did. Other laundry accoutrements also found favor,
though whether by association or as objects of interest in their
own right I was never sure. Clotheslines, clothespins, the basket I
kept the clothespins in, irons, ironing boards, soap powder, fabric
conditioner—Sam would show his enthusiasm by jumping up and
down in front of these things, chortling with delight. He talked
about them a lot. "G'anny Ann got red ironing board. Black
G'anma [Grandma Hilary, who often wore black] got gray ironing
board. Delia got blue ironing board." By their ironing boards shall
ye know them. I drew laundry pictures for him, putting in all the
details at his request—"Dwaw fabric 'dishner. Dwaw pegs." I usually added human figures to these endless utility-room scenes.
"Here's Mummy," I would say, brightly. "Look, here's Sam." But
Sam never requested a person.

He drew his own pictures, too. At four, he could draw a detailed washing machine, with lights, knobs, a door handle, clothes
going around inside, and soap powder and fabric conditioner on

top. These drawings weren't remarkably skillful—Sam's no Stephen Wiltshire. But they were easily up to standard for his age, and, more significant, they were by far the best drawings he's ever done. Now, aged eleven, Sam will produce a stick figure if you talk him through it. He never, ever draws unprompted. His pencil control is very poor. And yet, seven years ago, he could draw quite creditable washing machines, because the motivation was there.

Sam's favorite books all had washing machines and other white goods in them. It's surprising how many children's books do feature these things. Sarah Garland's *Doing the Washing* is particularly good because it shows an interesting arrangement of pipes draining out into the bath. We had several of those books for toddlers that encourage naming things around the house—what's in the kitchen, bedroom, bathroom, and so on. The utility-room pages became creased and grimy from much handling—or were torn out, which was the way Sam often treated his favorite things. A video episode of *Old Bear* showed, fleetingly, the edge of a washing machine in the top right-hand corner. Sam rewound the tape until it wore out.

Sam's idea of a good day out was a visit to a launderette. Faced with so many machines, he became so excited he hardly knew which way to turn. When George was doing his auditory integration therapy we spent a fortnight at my brother's house in Islington. That part of London, especially Caledonian Road, was Launderette City. We found a different launderette for Sam to visit every single day.

Once, back at home, I took the boys down a lane to gather blackberries. At that time, George's interest in blackberries was nearly as strong as Sam's laundry obsession, and he spent ages chatting to one particular bush. I failed to look around for perhaps half a minute, and in a flash, Sam had gone. Dragging

George after me, I ran up and down, checking the pond, the little wood, the place where I'd parked the car. No Sam. It was a warm afternoon. The door of the bungalow at the top of the lane was standing open. On a hunch, I looked in. There was Sam, bouncing up and down in front of a washing machine. A very old man in carpet slippers stood staring at him in utter bemusement. I tried to explain, failed, grabbed Sam, and fled.

Sam created washing machines all over the place. He would twist a sock inside a shoe, or chew an apple, spit the bits into a bowl, and shake it, making deafening muttering noises. Our rocking horse had a round hole under its saddle; Sam filled this with bits of fluff and "turned it on." Anything vaguely round would find itself filled with anything vaguely clothy. On his fourth birthday he was given a pink plastic Barbie Laundry Center, which was, as one of the party guests remarked, "almost too successful a present." Sam had eyes for nothing else—he kept it going all afternoon, hardly pausing even for the cake. His appreciative noises, combined with the laundry center's battery-powered whirrings, made conversation difficult.

Sam was famous as the Washing Machine Boy. At school, his teacher made him one out of cardboard boxes. Come the Nativity play, poor Angel Gabriel couldn't find her costume anywhere. She was about to perform, ignominiously, in something makeshift, when the costume was discovered, stuffed by Sam into his cardboard washing machine, wings, halo, and all. Washing machines were used as rewards and reinforcers. Sunday supplements and Argos store catalogues were rich sources of pictures to be cut out and stuck onto things. I remember the four-year-old Sam watching, open-mouthed, the whole of a documentary about the design of domestic appliances in postwar Italy.

And then there was Mr. Bean's visit to the launderette. It has been posited that Mr. Bean is himself autistic. He certainly uses autistic logic, as when, packing his holiday suitcase, he finds that a pair of espadrilles won't fit, so he packs only one. He shows autistic delight when one of his little plans works, and like Sam he expresses delight with his whole body. But Mr. Bean has a malevolent streak. He enjoys outwitting and discomfiting other people, and this is a very unautistic characteristic.

Sam didn't seem especially drawn to the character of Mr. Bean, but he was intrigued by some of his activities. He liked it when Mr. Bean drilled through the living-room wall, because drills excited him, and he liked it when Mr. Bean caused a baby's nappy to career through a fairground, because he had a thing about nappies, but what he liked best of all was Mr. Bean's visit to the launderette. He could see humor in the incongruous objects that Mr. Bean put into the machine—a lamp shade, a teddy, giant fluffy dice—though when Mr. Bean accidentally put on a girl's skirt Sam remained impassive. But the crowning glory of the whole episode was when Mr. Bean got stuck inside a tumble dryer. Sam's great ambition was to imitate this feat. He would open the door of the plate-warming oven of our Aga, climb inside, and beg me to shut the door behind him, which of course I wouldn't do. He imitated other actions of Mr. Bean's as well. Mr. Bean gets a raw turkey stuck on his head, and Sam tried to butt his way into our Christmas turkey. He sometimes imitated other TV characters. He used his Slinky spring as Fireman Sam uses his Bullworker, and stretched his mouth until the corners were sore, in homage to Wallace of *Wallace and Gromit*. But I don't think he ever truly identified with a character. It was more that he mimicked some actions, as George mimicked their turns of phrase.

Mr. Bean in the tumble dryer combined two of Sam's obsessions—laundry and getting into confined spaces. Daniel Shepherd,

aged ten, sent me a project he'd made about his autistic sister, Rebecca, which included a charming set of photographs of Rebecca
inserting herself into the washing machine, the laundry basket, a
large flowerpot, and so on. Sam used to lower himself into a badger
hole in our orchard and sit there in a kind of beatific trance. He
was interested in nappies, bandages, life jackets, and inflatable
armbands; he seemed to like anything that put pressure on the
body, whether his own or somebody else's. He visited his Great-
Aunt Hilary in hospital and was enchanted by the bandages she
had on her legs. That night, I found him lying in his own bed with
his swimming armbands on his legs. Aged five, he would pursue
female toddlers and lift their skirts to admire their nappies. In
one instance this led to his early discharge from hospital. Temple
Grandin has experimented extensively with the calming effects
of applying consistent pressure all over her body, and indeed has
based her career as a designer of cattle-handling equipment on
this research.

Washing machines and their ilk reigned supreme, but between
the ages of two and six Sam had many other obsessions. Grandfather clocks were sentient beings for Sam; he dreaded them as
much as he loved them. At his Great-Aunt Meriel's house, the
grandfather clock stood at the foot of the stairs. Sam couldn't get
past it to go to bed until it had been covered by a counterpane.
But on another visit, he fiddled with the pendulum and broke it.
At his Devon grandparents' house he went into the backyard and
ran all around the house to the kitchen door, rather than go
through the dining room past the grandfather clock. The clocks
didn't make him cry, but they exuded a powerful force field that
he couldn't cross.

Sam sought out grandfather clocks in books and dollhouses,
and, like washing machines, he could draw them quite well.

Cuckoo clocks were next best. "See the hen!" he would shout, longing for the little door to fly open. Alarm clocks were good, too, especially the kind with a pair of bunlike bells on top. The opening sequence of *Fireman Sam* was very satisfactory in this re- spect. Sam's favorite clock book was *The Day the Clocks Stopped*, about a clock maker called Timothy Tumblespring. Sam knew this by heart, and would "read" it at high speed, gabbling the words so they were unrecognizable to anyone not in the know. Alas, he loved Timothy Tumblespring to death. Like so many of his favorite things, including the Mr. Bean video, he destroyed it.

He liked barometers, though I don't think he knew what they were for. Come to think of it, I don't suppose he knew what clocks were for, either. He developed special words for his obsessions—to "yunk" meant to twist the knob on, for instance, a washing ma- chine. "Stonkers" were the dangly innards of a clock. "Mushroom hands" were—I think—the bells on top of an alarm clock.

Washing machines and clocks are fairly obvious autistic obses- sions. They make noises, they vibrate, they are similar but differ- ent, and therefore "collectable." Sam's passion for oasthouses was more unusual. Oasthouses are common in East Sussex, where we live. They are cylindrical buildings with cone-shaped cowls on top, once used for drying hops, now mostly converted into desirable residences. Sam would draw them, paint them, make them—he took a measuring canister, the kind with "sago," "ground rice," and "gran. sugar" marked out on it, stood it on top of a roll of kitchen towel, and announced, "Oasthouse!" He liked other odd buildings, too, like windmills and church spires, but his real love was oasts. On the morning of his fourth birthday we drove him round to visit thirty of them.

One of Sam's most idiosyncratic responses was to broken struc- tures. There was a partly demolished oast on a nearby road called

Poppinghole Lane. "Poppinghole" is the kind of word Sam incorporates into his verbal stims; the combination of the name with the glimpse of a "broken" oasthouse was irresistible, and I often found myself obliged to make this detour. Sam preferred glimpses to full-on views; he liked to look at things obliquely. A great thrill was to spy bottles of lavatory cleaner through frosted glass. "Go an' see G'anny blue bockles," he would demand, so we'd walk up the track to my mother's house and peer at her Harpic. He loved to be lifted up to look in at her kitchen window—"See G'anny ironing board peeping out."

Broken clocks didn't appeal, nor did broken washing machines, though he did enjoy seeing these things in inappropriate places. On a Dorset holiday he went into ecstasies over the sight of a washing machine dumped in the River Stour. What really did it for him was an interrupted structure, rather than nonfunctioning innards. He loved to glimpse an oast through trees, or spot the corner of a grandfather clock behind an open door. On the stairs leading up to our attic stood a chair with a broken back. Sam was drawn to this again and again. He would circle the chair, muttering what sounded like incantations. "It's as if he sees things we can't," said one of my friends. Electric beaters, food processors, ice-cream makers, vacuum cleaners, floor polishers . . . up to the age of five and three quarters it was easy to give Sam presents because he loved the plastic child-sized versions of these things. His birthday presents resembled a wedding list in miniature.

Sam was a great one for visual correspondences. The T-shaped stalk of a bunch of grapes became a folded ironing board; he filled the house with petrol via a trailing loop of jasmine. A head of honeysuckle was a helicopter. He would bend over and shake his long, straight hair until it flew about—another helicopter. I found him crooning over an apple pip—"No one seems to bother him much, please don't touch." This baffled me until I recognized it as a song sung about a hedgehog on Tots TV, and indeed an apple pip does resemble the aerial view of a hedgehog. When Sam was three, I was in hospital with meningitis. On my return he found a child's plastic brick with a straight line on it, like a subtraction sign. The straight line encased within a square structure was enough to make him say, "That's Mummy lying down in hospital." When he was two, objects were designated as helicopters, moons, washing machines, or snakes, according to their shape and action. Thus a rotary clothesline was a helicopter, a belt was a snake, a round brooch was a moon, and so on. At the time I thought this a sign of imagination; now I see it as symptomatic of the autistic need to fit everything into a system.

Sam liked animals, though not in the nurturing or anthropomorphic manner of most children. Nor did he have the junior natural historian's love of amassing information about them. As with machines, he enjoyed their sounds and vibrations—the purr of a cat, the beating of doves' wings. A trapped butterfly became yet another helicopter. The butterfly's plight was of no moment.

Poultry was a big interest. Delia, our neighbor, who has been one of my chief helps in bringing up the children, keeps lots of poultry, and both boys liked to be near, or sometimes in, her henhouses. George named the hens, eccentrically ("Stick," "You're a lovely one," "You're a no-no"), and relished calling their names, just as he relished the litany of the attendance sheet at school. Sam liked to crawl in with them, to squat down, cluck, pretend to lay eggs. His imitations were accurate. One day I lost Sam, and, like Tabitha Twitchit, I roamed the house looking for him in every room and mewing dreadfully. I found him inside a cupboard, squatting, with an expression of great concentration on his face. "Go 'way," he said. "Sam is sitting on a egg." Beneath his bottom was a golf ball.

From hens it was but a small step to worms. There seemed to be some confusion over these. Sam always liked snakes, or snake-like shapes. He enjoyed flapping ribbons or ropes or strips of seaweed. Worms came into the snake category, but they also held an association with death. I must, at some point, have mentioned that buried corpses were eaten by worms. Whenever an animal known to Sam died—usually a hen or a hamster, once a peacock, and once a cat—he would intone, "Worm ate hen" or "Worm ate Conan [cat]" with what sounded like gloomy satisfaction. He believed that worms lived in the badger holes in the orchard, and he would collect "nutkins" with which to feed them. "Nutkins," in those days, meant the discarded hazelnut shells lying on the orchard floor; these days, the word is used for any small, round edible object, for instance, Mint Imperials. Sam threw the nutkins into the badger holes as if in propitiation. Was he imagining some vast, devouring worm, lurking beneath the surface?

Unlike high-functioning autists, who are often described as "little professors" in their desire to find out everything there is to know about their chosen subject, Sam wasn't interested in facts about worms, snakes, washing machines, or anything else. Something about them gave him a buzz—something about their shape or the way they moved. The stimulus for him was sensual, physical, not intellectual. Just because he was interested in some aspects of them, it didn't follow that he had any interest at all in other aspects, any more than the fact that he liked fingering his toy Owly meant that he had any particular interest in owls in general.

This fragmentation of interest is common to all autists, but at the more able end of the spectrum the fragments tend to be larger, and arguably more useful. A high-functioning autist can develop unrivaled expertise in his or her chosen subject, but the fragmentation is still there. It's unlikely that the interest in the special subject will lead on to exploration of areas that, to a neurotypical mind, would seem related. A high-functioning autist might know, say, all the butterflies of Europe but remain indifferent to moths.

What causes this fragmentation? Probably something called "weak central coherence." Recent research suggests that differences in the structure and functioning of the autistic brain mean that the autist is incapable of seeing that details are parts of a greater whole. There is a disengagement between central and peripheral devices; the autist can pay sustained attention to one topic, or one aspect of one topic, but whereas the neurotypical brain will instinctively seek to place that detail in a wider context, to relate the part to a whole, the autistic brain confines its focus to the detail alone. In *Autism: Explaining the Enigma,* Uta Frith cites the example of a man who obsessively collected the addresses of juvenile courts. Well-wishers, hoping to expand his horizons, provided him with information about courts of other kinds. The information was rejected. When asked why he didn't want to know the addresses of non-juvenile courts, the autist replied, "They bore me to tears."

Fair enough. When George was about six, he became attached to a poster on the wall of the staff room of his primary school. It was a poster issued by the County Council, headed "East Sussex Advisory, Inspection and Training Service." It showed the photographs, names, and telephone numbers of forty-eight County Council officers—the appraisal and assessment adviser, the business education and IT adviser, the European links officer, and so on. George displayed such a passion for this poster that he was allowed to take it home with him. I still have it. I do not understand wherein its appeal lay, but I'd bet that a similar poster of, say, workers for Connex South East, or the Hastings Police Force, would have bored George to tears.

This fragmentation is both the autistic problem and the autistic strength. The intensity of the interest, the phenomenal powers of close observation, give rise to the exquisite chromatic paintings of Jessy Park, the incredible architectural drawings of Stephen Wiltshire, the virtuoso piano playing of Glenn Gould, the advanced mathematical powers of Richard Borcherds (see Simon Baron-Cohen, *The Essential Difference*). But the other side of the coin is the endless repetitiveness, the insistence on sameness, the refusal to explore and experiment. And this extends to all areas of life. If a child enjoys, say, Cadbury's Flakes, the neurotypical assumption would be that he would also like Galaxy Ripples. But no. It's quite likely that the autistic child will reject Galaxy Ripples, perhaps not even recognizing them as edible. It's also possible that if Cadbury decided to change the design of its Flakes wrappers, then these, too, will be placed beyond the pale.

Autistic interests nearly always seem bizarre. But in most cases it's not the subject itself that's bizarre (*pace* Sam's lavatory cleaner) but the narrowness of the focus. It's not odd to be interested in cars; it is odd to be interested in Peugeots to the exclusion of all other cars, or in only the hubcaps of Peugeots. It's not odd (well, not very odd) to save theater programs, or tourist brochures, or even tickets associated with expeditions of special significance or enjoyment to the collector. It is odd to save cash-register receipts. George likes till rolls. At a National Trust shop, he made a sudden plunge across a counter of fudge and tea towels and decorated gingerbread. He'd seen a piece of till roll lying on the floor beyond, and this was far more attractive to him than anything else in the shop.

George's obsessions were never as all-powerful as Sam's, and in many cases they seemed to be more closely linked to a normal child's play, or to more human concerns. This corresponds to the difference in their characters; Sam is, by and large, socially aloof, more interested in mechanical objects than in human behavior, whereas George has strong social instincts, which fit Lorna Wing's category of "active but odd." Many of George's obsessions have involved characters from children's books or films. I've described his attachment to Pinocchio and Bashful in chapter 5; he also had a big Mickey Mouse phase. This was when he started primary school, aged four and a half. He was the Mickey Mouse Boy; the other children, who were attracted to George and wanted to be friends with him, bought him many Mickey-related gifts. He would smile shyly at the children when they handed these over. He liked to have a few Mickeys on the table where he worked, or beside him at lunchtime. Mickey became something he could hide behind—he often seemed to use characters in this way, including going through a phase of claiming to be Sam—but I think he was initially attracted to the large eyes and the wide, unequivocal smile. George, atypically, has always been interested in facial expressions, though sometimes he finds them overwhelming. He both likes and fears strongly delineated features; if he sees a picture of Cherie Blair in the newspaper, he'll pile lots of things on top of it. Her dark, wide-apart eyes and pillar-box mouth are just too much for him. His fear of men with beards arises, I think, because he finds their faces confusing. They look as if it wouldn't make much difference which way up you turned them.

George also had his Thomas the Tank Engine phase. An admiration for the works of the Reverend W. Awdry is almost a diagnostic requirement of autism; Thomas was chosen as the icon for Autism Awareness Year in 2002. It's easy to see why the engines appeal to a systemizing brain. They each have a name, a number, a color (though sometimes, alarmingly, they go for a respray), a similar-but-different shape, a designated function. They are predictable; the pattern of their behavior is interrupted by small mishaps, but these can result in interesting visual variations—Percy's face reflected in a pool of water, James's red paint smeared with coal dust. Their faces are broad and clear, their range of expressions limited and well defined. It's easier for the autistic child to see that Gordon is cross or Percy is mischievous than it is for him to judge the moods of his own mother. George liked all these features of the engines, but because use of language particularly excited him he also latched on to the Reverend Awdry's characteristic turns of phrase. " 'Stow it, you two,' protested Bert. 'I don't know whether I'm standing on my dome or my wheels.' " George used to chant these and other phrases constantly, and they still occasionally surface to this day. He developed a particular liking for one of the engines, but, being George, it couldn't be one of the main players, like Henry, Edward, or Thomas himself. No, it had to be Douglas.

Douglas is Scottish, and his speech is heavily accented ("Then awa' wi'ye, Donal', an' tak' yon guids"), which meant reading his dialogue aloud was jaw-achingly tedious for me. He is also relatively obscure, and appears in only a handful of stories and video episodes. In the early 1990s, images of Thomas and friends abounded, but could you purchase a T-shirt, mug, or pasta shape in the image of Douglas? You could not. Douglas is also a twin. Donald is No. 9 and Douglas is No. 10. They are both black, always an important color for George. Apart from their numbers they are identical, at least as far as I can see. But George only liked Douglas. He wasn't interested in Donald. Donald bored him to tears.

Despite his singling out of Douglas, George usually liked twins, or pairs. He was intrigued early on by the twinness of his cousins Will and Kate. My friend Elspeth gave birth to identical twin boys, and George found them enchanting, as indeed they were. He liked to carry around pairs of things—two toy engines, James and Mike, a bottle of shampoo and a matching bottle of conditioner, a pair of wooden cutouts of boys playing soccer, which he named Adam and William. He also developed mild obsessions about color and at one stage would only wear black or red. At the moment he favors pink, which isn't that easy when you're dressing a thirteen-year-old boy. He decided that Sam's color was green, and luckily Sam seemed to concur. If asked to choose something for Sam, George will still usually select something like a green lollipop for Sam, and a pink or red one for himself.

He designated a balloon of a different color for each of the people in his life. These balloons were imaginary; he would sometimes draw them. He would chant, "A red balloon for George, a green balloon for Sam, a blue balloon for Mum, a yellow balloon for Delia." Sam enjoyed this recitation, and joined in. When he ran out of colors, George would introduce a "stripey" balloon, or a "spotty" one. By and large he would eat only red food, and to this day he uses ketchup to mask unwelcome colors.

I call his color obsession "mild" because I've heard of far more extreme cases. George always retained some measure of flexibility. Even at the height of his red/black craze, he would consent to wear his school uniform, which was royal blue and gray. For a while, he liked to carry a small red object—a brick or a car—but it was never hard to separate him from these. I've come across children whose color obsessions rule their lives, and those of their families.

Some of George's obsessions seemed to develop from fears. It was as if he could master the fear by dwelling on it, never letting it out of his sight. He had a great interest in sea life, particularly whales. He had several factual books with titles like *Creatures of the Deep*, and he would require me to read every word of these aloud, over and over again. "The ocean is the most varied habitat on earth. . . . The different kinds of plants and animals living at various depths have adapted themselves to their surroundings in astonishing ways." I don't believe he understood much of this sort of thing, but he liked hearing it. Whales were tops, followed by dolphins, which fulfilled the criteria of being similar to whales, only satisfyingly different. George invented a third member of this group, the "wophin." He talked about wophins with such conviction that his teacher checked on their existence in an encyclopedia.

He was very frightened of sharks and stingrays. When I reached passages in the books that dealt with these, he'd clap his hands over his ears and make loud "la-la" noises to drown out the dreaded words. But he didn't want me to stop reading. His love of whales and dolphins arose partly from his dread of sharks and rays. By poring over the one, he could reduce his terror of the other.

The sea-life obsession was also linked to his fascination with water, which had been present from the beginning of his life. I dreamed, once, that George was rocking astride the branch of a pine tree just outside our house. The branch transformed into a dolphin, which bounded off into the twilight, George safely on its back. The dream felt peaceful, and appropriate. I've just watched a friend's old home movie, which shows us in the gardens at Sissinghurst. George, aged six, lies down without warning on the path and stares into a pond, keeping his eyes as close to the water's surface as he can. He remains in that position for some time. People walk by him, even step over him, but he remains oblivious. We took him to garden centers so that he could stare into tanks of tropical fish. I considered buying fish for him, but decided that his love of dropping small objects into water would make life too scale-raising for them.

A strong reaction to water—either for or against—is common in autists. With their highly developed sensory responses, sparkles, ripples, bubbles, or crashing waves are experienced more intensely by them than by the rest of us. Only yesterday, Sam was transfixed by raindrops splashing onto the surface of a horse trough; he stood watching the circles spread and fade, unmindful of the fact that he was soaked to the skin. George used to spend hours muttering by the edge of the pond on our farm. One evening he wanted to walk there, but I explained that it was too late, we'd have to go in the morning. The next day he said, on waking, "The water lilies have opened their eyes now." This was his way of saying, "It's morning, remember what you promised." He was four.

It did seem as if water lilies had characters for him, or at least sensate life. He never seemed clear about the difference between things that could feel and things that could not. I remember him rebuking me for ironing: "Too hot! Poor shirt." Blackberries became important to him, almost to the point of obsession. He endowed them with semihuman characteristics. He would stand in front of blackberry bushes, repeating phrases over and over again until he'd shaped them into a kind of poem. I noted down one of these "poems," composed when George was four years and eight months:

> Just look at all those blackberries.
> They want them to pick
> And they want them to grow.
> They want them to pick
> And they want them to grow
> The blackberries smiled.
> Pick them down to the ground.

This seems to express his rather Keatsian ambivalence about black-berries. He liked eating them (the only fruit he did eat), but didn't like them to be picked—he used to urge me to "stick them back on the white sides," that is, the white patch left when one is picked. There was also a lot of chat about the berries as though they were people. "The blackberries have woken up. They come downstairs. They put food in their mouths."

Nature—weather, seasonal changes, atmospheric effects—held George in thrall. He loved dawn and dusk—we saw rather more of dawn than I might have wished. He made up several twilight "poems"—"The sky is washed. The sky is clear. The prickly leaves are turning black," was one. Another was:

> *The light is fading fast.*
> *All the beasts can talk in the night,*
> *"Brm brm," called out the silver car,*
> *"All is ready for the morning."*

Once, waking to find a late fall of snow covering the daffodils, he said, "We're lost because the spring has gone." Such remarks were not addressed to anybody, and he had no interest in recording the "poems." He would repeat them over and over to himself, not to me, and he always knew when he'd finished with them.

The "poems" contained phrases from his usual sources—books, songs, videos. The one about the silver car, for instance, owes much to *The Tailor of Gloucester*. But he would customize these sources, rework them until the sound and shape gave him satisfaction. He tried to do this to most things that caught his attention; he seemed to be constantly trying to reshape the world the way he wanted it. He had a mini-obsession with lions and other big cats, which arose, like the sea-life obsession, out of fear. For a long time the

Sainsbury's Book of Big Cats was a favorite, but unacceptable passages had to be altered. Thus "lions often kill zebras" became "lions often play with zebras," and "Pumas leap on to the backs of animals they want to kill" became "Pumas leap on to the backs of animals they want to see." In other stories, the changes were not so obviously made for the purposes of consolation. In Arnold Lobel's Frog and Toad stories, George simply reversed Frog and Toad. (These stories were great favorites, because Frog and Toad were a pair, one green, one brown, the-same-but-different.) Often, a minor character would be promoted to a major role. I did my best to follow George's instructions, but I drew the line when his championship of Moppet and Mittens led him to demand that "The Tale of Tom Kitten" be read without reference to the eponymous hero.

It's hard to know when an interest becomes an obsession, and when an obsession becomes a stim. Everybody has interests, and the existence of a great and dominating interest does not in itself indicate autism. But what the autist does with his interest, what function it fulfills for him, is, I believe, qualitatively different from, let us say, my Uncle Norman's interest in dragonflies. Norman enjoys dragonflies for many reasons, but he does not enjoy the isolated fact of them. Quite the reverse. To Norman, dragonflies demonstrate the importance of biodiversity, and for Norman, as for many people, understanding the need for biodiversity is crucial to understanding human existence. Our survival depends on biodiversity; our moral sense, the sense of responsibility that is a by-product of civilization, obliges us to respect it. Norman has concentrated on dragonflies, but they are the gateway to profound, far-reaching ideas. His interest in them connects different parts of his mind and character, sensual, intellectual, aesthetic, moral, and emotional.

As far as I can tell, autistic interests never provide this kind of connection. The obsession seems to assuage the rage for order, or to satisfy some almost physical craving for stimulus. It never unlocks a morality, a philosophy, a worldview. This may explain why autistic interests disappear as quickly as they arrive. Norman's interest in dragonflies is only the most specialized part of the love of natural history that has been observable in him since early childhood, and that has directed his career, his choice of dwelling place, his holiday destinations, even, to some extent, his choice of clothes, food, and furniture. Barring some catastrophic brain injury or disease, it's inconceivable that he will ever lose interest in dragonflies. Not so with autistic interests. Clara Claiborne Park describes how Jessy reached degree level and beyond in mathematics but has now lost all interest in the subject except in totting up the checks she receives for her paintings. Other autists seem to experience the same cutoff. Tree frogs one day, manhole covers the next.

George, who is less deeply obsessive than most autists, now has a few mild interests—dogs, their gender and breed; poultry, ditto; vehicles—when is a truck a lorry, when is a coach a bus? These are the subjects he most often mentions, but they don't dominate either his life or mine. Sam has no interests. The washing machines, cuckoo clocks, oasthouses, fabric conditioners, fell from grace in the autumn of 1997 and have never been replaced. Their disappearance marked the beginning of Sam's huge regression. He seemed to move into a world of physical sensation. So distracted was he by the humming and buzzing inside his body that he seemed incapable of thinking about anything at all. I never thought I'd say this, but I miss washing machines. At least they were something you could talk about.

TWELVE

Ketchup with Everything

I like food. I consider my relationship with food to be uncompli-
cated. Unusually among my female acquaintances, I've never
been on a diet. I'll try new dishes with alacrity, and I'm a reasonably adventurous cook. By choice, I eat quite healthily. I particularly like vegetables, and I'm not tempted by junk.

It seems to me indicative of the power of autism, therefore,
that the diets of both George and Sam are eccentric, unbalanced,
nutritionally impoverished, and strongly oriented toward junk. I
started out with the usual middle-class intentions about feeding
my children. Breast was best; solids should be introduced slowly;
fruit and vegetables were important; additives, salt, and sugar
should be kept to a minimum. I was far from fanatical. I had no
objection to the odd biscuit, and happily used jars of baby food to
save time, particularly when I was working. But during their
babyhoods I was careful to introduce a range of tastes and textures, and though I wasn't prepared to eat my evening meal at half
past five I did try to be with them and talk to them while they ate.

I would have been astonished, and horrified, if I could have seen into their nutritional future. This morning George breakfasted on six After Eights and some lemon barley water. I was pleased—*pleased*—because lately he hasn't been eating anything at all. Sam had no breakfast. This is common. I set out some Frosties (dry) and a beaker of orange juice, but he tipped the juice down the sink and ignored the Frosties. The only thing he ate before the school taxi arrived was a sugar mouse, which was the bribe I used to get him out of bed.

Sam takes a packed "lunch"—a bag of plain crisps, some gluten-free biscuits, some raisins, an apple, a bag of Whizzers (dairy-free Smartie wannabes), and a small marzipan cat made by my mother. He will eat about half of this. Guess which things he'll leave. George doesn't have a lunch box, because at the moment he chooses to deny that he eats anything at all. So I smuggle supplies into his taxi on Monday mornings. On arrival, Pat, the taxi escort, conveys the supplies to George's teacher by similar sleight of hand. They are kept in the classroom in a drawer to which George has unrestricted access. Most days he won't eat unless nobody's looking— or until everybody's pretending not to look. The drawer contains Twiglets, crisps, Aeros, and Bourbon biscuits—George is not on the gluten-free/casein-free diet. Some days he gets through quite a lot of these, but today was not one of those days. The note in the home-school book says, "G. has eaten nothing except a small tube of Parma Violets."

I don't think Parma Violets count toward the recommended five daily portions of fruit and veg. For years I've been mentally straining to accredit goodness to the horrid things my children eat. Crisps are only potatoes, really, I tell myself; ketchup is a vegetable. It had better be, because it's the only one George eats.

When George is in eating mode—and after five or six days of

starvation he'll usually have a kill, like a python—he eats meat smothered in ketchup. Burgers, sausages, bacon, ham, mince, casseroled lamb, sometimes roast meat, chicken curry; he covers all these, including the curry, with ketchup so thick that you can't see what's underneath. Occasionally, chips or potato waffles or even roast potatoes will get the same treatment. I slip a few slivers of vegetable matter in with the mince or the casserole, but as often as not these will be removed, even from deep within the ketchup, wiped clean, and left in a neat row on the kitchen table. George eats no fruit except, in season, blackberries. He does like lemon sorbet, and if he's in top form, he'll eat *fromage frais* in those little pots, raspberry flavor only. Jake gets tired of having to finish up their strawberry-flavor conjoined twins.

There are a few other foods that enjoy bursts of favor—Coco Pops (dry), toast and Marmite—but meat is George's staple and always has been. It isn't the limitations of this diet that concern me most. I've heard of worse—indeed, I've experienced worse, like the period of several weeks when the only solid food to pass Sam's lips was the top part of Jaffa Cakes. (I threw the pallid sponge bases out for the birds. They bounced, and the birds weren't keen.) More worrying, to me, than the restricted, protein-heavy, over-salted range is the pattern of semi-starvation that has been going on for the past eighteen months.

George's attitude to eating has something in common with anorexia. He has linked eating with growing; well-meaning adults, myself included, have made the usual remarks along the lines of "Eat that up, it'll turn you into a big strong boy." But George doesn't want to be a big strong boy, and he certainly doesn't want to be a man—"I won't be a horrid man with a big black beard." Eighteen months ago, George changed schools. Like most autists, he finds it hard to cope with change. He wanted to put things back how they were, and as he knew that the new school was for "big" children, he decided to stop growing.

He has now accepted the change of schools as irreversible and no longer wants to return to the old one. But the obsession with staying small has remained. Daily, he begs me to tell him that he will not grow up. It's tempting to lie to him in the hope that this will make him more relaxed about food, but though lying may be a successful short-term strategy, it stores up trouble for the future (as well as being, well, wrong . . .). His teachers and I attempt to reassure him that though his body will change, the "George-ness" of him will not. He doesn't find this wholly satisfactory, but it's the best we can do.

When George is in starvation mode, he fights for control over his hunger. "No tummy, stop rumbling," he says. "Be quiet, my tummy. You're not hungry." He woke me this morning at five-thirty, weeping, demanding, "Don't cook for me! Never cook for me again! Take that bacon back to Sainsbury's!" He tries to control what others eat, too, putting food in the place where Sam sits at table, or saying, "Those are for Jake, not for me." When the food phobia first emerged I did the thing that child-care experts tell you not to do but that suggests itself naturally to mothers: "Eat that, and then you can have this." In George's case the "this" was Refreshers or Softmints. The strategy not only didn't work, it backfired. George began to refuse Refreshers and Softmints and came to regard them with fear and loathing. I then decided to re-move all pressure and offer George no food at all, ever. I made sure that food was left out in places where he could reach it, but I never set it near his place at the table. I stopped asking him to sit down. I tried to make no reference whatsoever to food.

This was more successful. Like a shy animal, George would inch toward the food and take a nibble before darting away again.

I made no comment and pretended I hadn't noticed. But one can't instruct other people in all the niceties of one's apparently barmy autism strategies. "Hello, George," say cheery visitors. "What are you eating? That looks delicious. Do you like it?" Piercing shrieks from George. "It's not mine! I don't like it! I'm not eating!" Food pushed aside; down the snake he slides, back to square one. It's not clear to me just how damaging the boys' eating habits are to their physical health. Not very, the evidence suggests, at least in the short term. Both boys have less than their share of minor illnesses; they almost never have a day off school. Sam has had only one course of antibiotics in his whole life, George only three. Admittedly, this is partly due to the difficulty of getting them to take medicine, but I've never felt that they've missed treatment they desperately needed.

Their hair is thick and glossy, their eyes clear and bright. Sam is small, but he still has his splendidly delineated musculature, and he has enormous stamina. George is exceedingly thin. He was last weighed in April 2002, when he'd been denying himself food for about four months; he weighed fifty-nine pounds, which for a twelve-year-old boy about five feet tall is very, very little. It was around this time that I asked the doctor to look at him. "He's thin," he said, "but he's not in danger. Give him another month, and if he hasn't started eating, we'll take action."

He did start eating, and the only legacy of this, his most prolonged fast, was constipation, which took a few days to sort itself out. On non-eating days, George is floppy; bursts of activity are followed by slumps. He becomes irritable and sleeps badly—but that's been true all his life; the not eating isn't wholly to blame. At nearly thirteen, he's poised on the brink of his big growth spurt, and I'm hoping his appetite will win the battle with his neuroses. But I can't be sure.

Sam's eating habits and problems are very different from George's, but they're just as hard to correct. Sam was my heaviest toddler by far, and up to the age of two he ate pretty consistently, in his placid, undiscriminating way. The first peculiarity I noticed was when he refused to be spoon-fed, well before his first birthday. He managed his own spoon quite well, ate lots of finger food, and glugged away at bottles of milk, so I didn't see it as a problem. Much later, I realized that this spoon business was not so much a manifestation of independence as his deep dislike of having his head touched. He just couldn't bear the sensation of having someone poke a spoon into his mouth.

At two, Sam rejected all meat, fish, eggs, cheese, and vegetables. Increasingly he would tolerate only dry, crispy food—toast, biscuits, crisps. He didn't want milk on his cereal, though he drank it in huge quantities via his bottle. Milk and fruit juice; I told myself that he must be getting the nutrients he needed, even though he no longer ate "proper" food.

The number of acceptable foodstuffs steadily dwindled, until we reached the tops-of-Jaffa-Cakes-only phase, which must have been when he was about four. He had an appointment with a dietician around this time. She asked me to keep a food diary for four days, to record absolutely everything he consumed, and what it weighed. The diary got off to a flying start: "Monday. Breakfast—one chocolate-flavour shape out of Advent Calendar. Weight—?" Whatever the dietician's advice was, it didn't come to anything. You can take an autistic child to broccoli, but you can't make him eat.

Like George, Sam has been through phases of eating virtually nothing, but whereas George has powerful psychological motives for starving himself, in Sam's case I think it's mainly a physical problem. Sam seems to find chewing and swallowing difficult.

He'll gag and spit things out, even desirable things like sweets. Sam enjoys quite a wide range of flavors. He'll bite into most kinds of fruit, and even into raw vegetables if I leave them on a chopping board rather than offering them to him directly, but the textures seem to defeat him, and he won't swallow them. Fruit can be ingested only in the form of juice or ice pops.

It's common among autists to favor certain textures. Sam's preference for crisps, Frosties, and Japanese rice cakes is typical— thin, dry, crispy, yellowy brown is often preferred. As one might expect, autists want sameness in their food; one of Leo Kanner's two defining characteristics of autism was "desire for the preservation of sameness." Sam likes food that's the same all the way through, like Pringles or popcorn. He also likes food that comes in a packet, and he hates to leave the packet half finished. But he can't manage a whole packet of, say, biscuits, so he'll take one bite out of each. He likes food with a clear beginning, middle, and end. The textural surprises of something like a casserole are anathema to him.

When Sam was tiny, he would drop food from his high chair, as most small children do. As soon as he was released he would scramble under the high chair and eat the bits he'd dropped. Crumbling and scattering food has been one of Sam's abiding features. He'll nibble around the edge of a cracker, then break it into little pieces and sweep them onto the floor. He takes little snatching bites, very fast; for him, food is an enemy that needs to be subdued.

On the rare occasions when Sam will eat a sausage or a burger, it has to be smoking hot. Like many autists, he has a high pain threshold; he snatches burgers out of the frying pan with his bare hands. Then he will lick the fat out of the hot pan. He eats ice cream with his fingers and likes to dab blobs of it all over his

sweater. For years he wouldn't use cutlery; we're currently working on reintroducing spoons. Again, a dislike of cutlery is quite
common. Thérèse Jolliffe, a very able autistic woman who became
a university researcher, says that she has never been able to see the
point of cutlery. She made the conscious decision to conform to
the inexplicable habits of the neurotypical world where possible,
so she has trained herself to use cutlery. Sam has made no such
decision.

Once he outgrew his high chair and its constraining straps, it
became more and more difficult to persuade Sam to sit down to
eat. Again, this problem is widespread. The dilemma for the
mother is, do you prioritize social training and "manners," or do
you just try to get food into the child by hook or by crook? I went
for the latter, which I now regret. At one stage Sam ate so very,
very little that if he opted to eat anything, anywhere—on the
floor, in the garden, in the bath—I tended to concur. He liked to
sit on top of a large court cupboard in the kitchen. He was often
naked; he would take his Rice Krispies up there and rain them
down like some kind of hobgoblin. For years he most commonly
ate while sitting on top of the Aga.

Just as I lost control over *where* Sam ate, so I felt powerless
about *what* he ate. I am very far from being alone in this. At gath-
erings of families with autistic children there will always be several parents holding Tupperware boxes containing cold toast and
Marmite, or beakers full of a certain obscure brand of herbal tea,
which is the only fluid their child will accept. George once had a
craze for a kind of cereal called Bran Buds—like All-Bran cut up
into tiny bits. Bran Buds were not readily available, so family and
friends were under instructions to buy up stocks whenever possible. Em, George's godmother, came across them in Nine Elms
Sainsbury's. She filled her trolley. At the checkout, the assistant

gave her a pitying, inquiring look. "Oh, they're not for me," she hastily explained. "They're for my godson." Autistic children are very powerful and controlling. Most of the mothers clutching strange specimens in Tupperware boxes have other children who eat an unexceptional balanced diet and have no special provision made for them.

I've never met an autistic person who ate completely normally, although some come close. Most are extremely picky, but a few go to the opposite extreme and eat indiscriminately, without stopping. Obesity can become a problem in such cases, but many of the "faddy" autists are noticeably thin. Typical fads involve number—it has to be five sausages and ten chips; color—only red foods will do, and by red we're not, alas, talking about tomatoes, peppers, and red mullet, but red Smarties, red jelly, Hula Hoops in a red packet; utensils—food can be eaten only off a Thomas the Tank Engine plate; shape—pointed chips must have their ends squared off, toast must be cut into squares of equal size; brand— "He'll only eat Birds Eye fish fingers, and, yes, he can tell the difference"; packaging—the whims of food manufacturers, who endlessly alter their packaging, are the despair of many mothers who've relied on frozen lasagne that looks like *this,* and find it won't be touched now that it looks like *that.*

Many seem to like extreme flavors—in George's case, curry and ketchup; in Sam's, lemons (biting into the peel), marzipan, and ferociously salty foods. Some will eat most things as long as they're coated with the preferred flavor. Saskia Baron's brother, Timothy, ate little apart from lettuce, until it was discovered that the vinaigrette dressing was what really attracted him. Now he has a good mixed diet because he'll eat most things if they've got vinaigrette on them. Many eat, or at least taste, substances that aren't food at all—soil, coal, soap, paint. George used to raid the cat's bowl. I had a brain wave and offered him mashed sardines, which to me smell similar to cat food. It worked, for a while.

The best outcome is when an autist can be persuaded to eat certain foods because of their healthy properties. This cuts no ice whatsoever with George and Sam, but I have come across intelligent, hyperlogical people with Asperger's syndrome who will diligently consume the recommended balance of protein, carbohydrate, unsaturated fat, fruit, vegetables, and so on. The Asperger's brain likes to systematize things; if applied to diet, this can be good news. Asperger's eaters like this are likely to be odder in their eating habits than in their choice of meals. Thérèse Jolliffe, for instance, dislikes "mixed-up" food, or disguising sauces. She eats one thing at a time; carrots, then meat, then potatoes. The neurotypical habit of loading a fork with several different items seems to her unnecessary and unpleasant.

Drinking is nearly as fraught as eating. It's only recently that the boys have begun to drink plain water, unless you count bathwater. As a toddler, George was addicted to the blackberry soft drink Ribena, which had a bad effect on his mood and behavior. When I bravely removed the Ribena and substituted red grape juice he improved to the extent that I thought his difficulties were at an end—this was when he was about two and three quarters, pre-diagnosis. Sam can't drink anything without spitting some out and tipping some more down the sink. If given straws, Sam blows bubbles. If allowed to pour his own drinks, he fills the cup until it overflows. Sam likes wine. If I set my glass down for a moment, he'll take a swig, swill it around his mouth, and spit it back into the glass. A flyer arrived advertising a local wine-tasting event. Jake drew my attention to it, earnestly suggesting that it would be something Sam might enjoy.

Many normal children are, of course, faddy eaters. My cousin

Henry went through a stage when he would eat only sieved raspberry yogurt and Kraft cheese cut into the shapes of First World War biplanes. Such peculiarities should not be taken as symptomatic of autism unless there are similar eccentricities in other areas. Four-year-old George would ask for a boiled egg, weep when the shell was broken, demand that I "put the bits and pieces back on," eat the egg, then turn the empty shell upside down so that it looked whole. Jake, at the same age, cried when I threw crusts to the hens, "because we'll never see that poor toast anymore."

In chapter 7, I described Sam's gluten- and casein-free diet. Life with and for Sam has changed immeasurably for the better since I implemented this. His stimming has reduced; he is far more sociable and playful; his ability to process what is said to him is much better. I intend to keep him on the diet for the foreseeable future.

More information about this diet can be found via the addresses and reading list at the back of this book. The opoid-excess theory on which it is based is, at time of writing, only a theory; no scientific studies have, as far as I know, proved or disproved it. I have no scientific ability, and I don't want to make the diet into a soapbox issue. All I can say, in common with many parents, is that Sam's pre-diet behavior fitted the description of a child suffering from opioid excess, and the improvements following the diet have been obvious to everyone who knows him. The theory, in brief, argues that the guts of some autistic people cannot properly break down gluten and casein. The fragments of these proteins—peptides—pass through the wall of the gut; autistic gut walls are more likely to be damaged than most. The peptides travel around the body, damaging the central nervous system and the brain. The gluten peptide is gluteomorphine, and the casein peptide is caseomorphine—as the names suggest, the action of these peptides is similar to morphine, which is why the pre-diet behavior of children like Sam can resemble that of a junkie.

My assumption is that the unsuitable foods slowly harmed Sam throughout his early life until at nearly six he overloaded. It took me a while to get the diet going—I had to cross all the usual mental boundaries, thinking it was too difficult, too expensive, too time-consuming, not nutritionally balanced, and so on, but once I'd actually started, improvements were evident within a few weeks.

So, what can Sam eat? In theory, any meat, fish, fruit, or vegetable. Eggs, rice, maize, potatoes, nuts, pulses, beans, tofu, soy . . . the permutations are endless. The snag is, of course, that Sam doesn't recognize most of these things as foodstuffs. At the moment he relies heavily on rice crackers, gluten-free breakfast cereals, extremely expensive gluten-free biscuits, and "potato products." The "best" things he eats are eggs, in the form of a biweekly omelette, and gluten-free sausages and burgers—maximum once a week. He eats a daily vitamin tablet but won't touch the special nutritional supplement provided by the dietician. But I don't feel guilty about the low nutritional value of Sam's diet. In nearly every respect, it's nutritionally superior to the junk he ate when he was free to choose. Sam now sleeps soundly. His stomach is flat, he never screams (though he does still cry, usually once a day), he can sit down and concentrate, and his bitten hands have nearly healed. He still likes sweets, but this terrible restless craving has gone. Why, if this diet works so well for Sam, have I not implemented it for George? Partly cowardice. George, being so much more vocal than Sam, would put extreme pressure on me were I to interfere with his eating arrangements. Partly because George has a little bit more of a social life than Sam, and it's much harder to say "No, you can't have that" when you're eating outside the home with other people.

Partly because George has such a complicated psychological relationship with food that I don't want to risk rocking an already unseaworthy boat. But most important of all, I don't believe that George has the same digestive problems as Sam. He has never had a swollen stomach, loose stools, or screaming fits. He has never exhibited any junkie-type behavior. He has never mutilated himself; his pain threshold seems to be much lower than Sam's. In the case of diet, as in most other things, they're worlds apart. Two very different boys; same diagnosis.

THIRTEEN

Education, Education, Education

When George was diagnosed by Dr. Gilly Baird, she told us that the right education was the only effective "treatment." Chapter 7, on interventions, makes it clear that I consider several other treatments worthwhile, but in essence I agree with Dr. Baird. No diet or vitamin supplement is going to magic away true autism. You use diet, or supplements, or AIT, or whatever, to get your child as well as you can, and that will help him to learn as well as he can—but that may still be not very much.

What is the "right" education, though? That's a subject of much debate. At the time of writing, national and local government favor a policy of inclusion; special-needs children should be included in mainstream schools if at all possible. I believe this policy to be wrong—wrong as in misguided, and in some cases wrong as in immoral. I also believe that current practice is storing up enormous problems for the future.

All case histories are different. But I feel able to speak with some authority, because I've tried both mainstream and special education for my boys. George, as outlined in chapter 6, started in a mainstream nursery school, aged three. At that time, pre-diagnosis, we were hoping that the routine of school and the contact with other children would iron out some of his peculiarities and antisocial behaviors. Of course it did nothing of the kind. It was a lively, well-run nursery, one I'd have warmly recommended for any normal child. And George was not so "lost" that he couldn't get something out of it. He enjoyed some of the activities, shied away from others. He learned to write his name, very large, on two sheets of A4 paper taped together. After the trauma of the first few weeks he seemed quite happy; he learned new songs and rhymes and reproduced these at home with pleasure. He memorized the attendance log, and seemed to relish the fact of the children's names. He even seemed to single out a couple of children as "friends," though these friendships didn't extend as far as inviting anyone home for tea. On sports day, when George's autistic lack of competitiveness and team spirit were clearly apparent, he cheerfully allowed himself to be towed up and down by one of those kind-but-bossy little girls who in later life will run the PTA with aplomb.

I don't think that George's mainstream nursery experience harmed him, except that by keeping him there we deprived him of special help, of the kind of intensely structured, individually tailored learning that would have targeted his deficits and smoothed out some of the bumps in his intellectual and social development. But such specialized nursery teaching is not easy to come by, and besides, by the time George was diagnosed he had less than two terms left before he reached the age for "proper" school. If we'd been very, very clued up, we'd have either found him a special-needs nursery or started a home program for him ourselves, but for a long time we'd believed that our son, far from being handicapped, was in fact exceptionally bright. It would have taken a great leap of imagination to look at George aged three and declare, "This child is wholly unsuited to mainstream education."

The educational psychologist assessed him and judged him ready for mainstream primary school, starting in the kindergarten class at the age of four and a half. He received a Statement of Special Educational Need—which is, I gather, increasingly hard to obtain—this meant that he was entitled to a certain number of hours per week of extra help. His helper was Ruby Cruse, who worked at the school as a dinner lady and classroom assistant. Ruby continued as his helper throughout his time at the school, and once our ABA program was running she became one of his tutors. She was a great friend to George and a huge support to us all. She died of cancer a couple of years ago, and her loss was deeply felt.

We chose our village school, where my brothers and I had been pupils in the baby-boom 1960s. In those days the classes were huge—up to forty children, with just one teacher and no assistant. We sat in rows and trilled "London's Burning" on our recorders as our free milk stood in a crate by the radiator, the cream rising unappetizingly to the top of the third-of-a-pint bottles, each lid pierced by a paper straw. We learned our joined-up handwriting in great loopy swirls, rows and rows of *f*'s and *g*'s of almost Elizabethan elaboration. Girls and boys separated for needlework ("binca") and woodwork ("balsa"). The playgrounds were segregated, of course, and the lavatories were all outside; the boys peed against a wall into an open drain. In Assembly we sang our way through *Hymns Ancient and Modern* and recited the Apostles' Creed. I was put in a corner for whispering during a tracing lesson. Even aged five, you could be rapped on the knuckles by a ruler, and for grave misdemeanors the older children were hit by the headmaster, who kept a slipper for the girls, a cane for the boys.

It was a happy school; we took the cane and the slipper (which were sparingly used) absolutely for granted, in the way children do. I daresay much of the teaching was fairly humdrum. Math was still mainly about a farmer taking his wheat to market to sell at sixpence ha'penny a bushel; if he sold nine bushels, then . . . We wrote it all out in laborious columns. I remember being forced to insert adverbs into a story I'd written, and being aware, even then, that they were injurious to my prose style. But the work didn't concern me much; I lived for the life of the playground. I spent six years there, and they were rich and vivid.

So I was pleased, for sentimental reasons, to be sending George to the same school. It had changed a great deal. By the 1990s, primary schools had become much more child-oriented. The classes were much smaller—I think there were only twelve in George's year. The old hierarchies had gone. The staff were more affectionate and involved with the children, and the older children had a lot more to do with the younger ones. The three R's were still taught effectively, but in interesting and creative ways. There were computers, a library, a cooking area. There was more to art teaching than the three pots of primary colors and the single sheet of paper clipped to an easel that had characterized the Friday afternoons of my childhood.

Of course, the school wasn't perfect. But it was pleasant and busy and it had a positive atmosphere. The headmaster hadn't come across autism before, but he was keen to learn, as were the other staff. When I described George's condition, the head asked whether he was likely to wander off, perhaps try to walk home? I said it was a possibility. "Then come and look at our locks," he said. "If there aren't enough to keep George safe, we'll have more put on."

George started at the school surrounded by goodwill. This continued to be the case. I can't fault the teachers in terms of their attitude toward him, nor of the effort they made. George has always been an attractive child, and the other children were disposed to like him. Many made particular efforts to be kind to him. There were some disagreeable moments; there always are, with children. There was some teasing, and I'm sure George was called "mental," not that he would have noticed or minded. But there was no sustained bullying, and George was carefully watched and protected by adults.

Bullying is usually a problem when autistic children are included in mainstream schools. Autists, with their naïveté, their odd mannerisms, their failure to understand social rules, are obvious victims. And when they are bullied, they have no idea of how to deal with their aggressors. At best, they won't notice or care; it'll be water off a duck's back. But, more often, they *will* notice; they will be hurt and frightened. They won't understand the nature of the attacks, whether verbal or physical. They won't know how to alter their behavior to make themselves more acceptable. And above all—and this has to be borne in mind in every instance of mainstream inclusion—it won't occur to them to tell an adult what is going on. Remember, they don't know that the adult doesn't already know.

Luke Jackson, in *Freaks, Geeks and Asperger Syndrome*, is unequivocal. "All my life I have been bullied," he states. "I never knew why. Everything at school was so loud and so complicated." What was bearable at primary school—just—became unbearable at secondary. Luke ran away, never to return to that school. Clare Sainsbury, in *Martian in the Playground*, quotes many high-functioning autists on the subject. The conclusion is inescapable; for a pupil with an autistic spectrum disorder in a mainstream school, being bullied will become a fact of life.

Luke Jackson says that the ASD child is an easy target, as well as an obvious one, because he is often alone. He reminds his readers of the literal-mindedness of the ASD child—"Bullies don't actually say, 'Now I am going to bully you.' Therefore your child may not realize that the torment they are suffering is bullying." He also points out that "there is another side to the bullying problem . . . some bullying may not actually be bullying! AS kids don't always realize when friendly messing about is actually friendly stuff." Most of us know that fighting and the exchange of insults are part of the bonding mechanism of male teenage friendships. Controlled, playful aggression is an acceptable disguise for affection and intimacy. But this kind of behavior has specific and subtle rules, and the autistic child, who finds it so hard to pick up social rules of any kind, has no hope of learning these, which flourish in a subculture largely untouched by adults. I started this digression by stating that George was not bullied at school. Nor was Sam. But they left mainstream school when they were eight and six respectively. I have no doubt that if they had stayed, they would have become victims, as their contemporaries grew more powerful, more concerned about what is or is not socially acceptable, and moved further away from adult control.

However, during the boys' period at the village school, bullying wasn't something I had to worry about. On paper, if any mainstream setting was appropriate, then it was this one. Small classes, dedicated support workers, intelligent, well-intentioned teachers, a supportive head, a short journey from home to school—the setup was benign and cozy, and communication between home and school was good. The teachers paid home visits and discussed strategies with me. And yet the school could not serve the boys' needs beyond a certain point. Why was this?

I need to backtrack here, to include Sam. As mentioned in chapter 6, Sam was lucky enough to go to a special nursery-assessment unit from three and a half to four and a half. Here he prospered, to the extent that at four and a half the gap between his accomplishments and those of a normal child of his age seemed really quite narrow. Socially, too, it was a good time for Sam. He joined in group activities. He particularly liked songs with actions, and a kind of mini-aerobics exercise; he would come home and practice his movements. To say he made friends would be putting it too strongly, but he noticed the other children, and sometimes mentioned them at home. (Only the other day, seven years on, he started talking about "Treesa." Teresa was a girl who shared his taxi to the nursery. I asked Sam a couple of questions, and his answers indicated that he was, indeed, remembering that child.) He got on well with the staff, and had a particular favorite, Maureen. He named his hamster after her.

Sam was cheerful and equable and he enjoyed school. This, coupled with the fact that he cooperated with the assessment tests—cutting, sorting, drawing, and so on—led to the conclusion that he was suitable for inclusion in mainstream. This turned out to be a mistake, but it would have been hard to see that at the time. And besides, there was no special provision for autistic children at that time. If the boys hadn't gone to mainstream, they would have gone into a school that catered to a variety of special needs, many of them not remotely similar to autism.

So in September 1996, the term Sam turned five, he joined George at the village school. He, too, received a Statement of Special Educational Need, entitling him to a certain number of hours with a helper. Kim, like George's Ruby, was a classroom assistant and dinner lady. Like Ruby, she stayed in touch after Sam left the school, and became one of his ABA tutors.

From the start, Sam's integration was trickier than George's. Despite Sam's apparently sunny nature, he was much less aware of other people than George was. George showed some desire to do what the other children did—he'd sit at his desk, get his work out (though he'd only complete it under strict surveillance), sing in Assembly (sometimes), sit on the mat at story time. Sam didn't. Sam has never compared himself to anyone. He never got into the rhythm of classroom life. He just did his own thing. His teacher would set aside time in which to pay special attention to Sam, and then find him intractable. Without the careful, unvarying structure of the assessment nursery, Sam's progress slowed and then went into reverse.

In common with many parents, one of my complaints about the system of "statementing" is that the hours of help the child receives don't cover playtimes and lunch breaks. That arrangement would be appropriate for a condition where the problems are primarily academic. But it cannot be emphasized strongly enough that autism is a social handicap more than it is an academic one. The most social parts of the school day, such as the dinner hour, are the times when the autistic child is likely to be most at sea. Sam's dinnertime behavior became so wild that, for his last term, I had to collect him every day, take him home, and return him an hour later.

Yes, it would improve matters if the statemented child had a dedicated helper for every minute of the school day, though few authorities would fund it. But that wouldn't address the underlying problem about mainstream inclusion, which is that very little of normal school life is appropriate for or applicable to an autistic child.

When I came to choose a primary school for Jake I looked for a caring, supportive atmosphere above everything else. But I also looked for liveliness, variety, bright wall displays, music and drama, outings, links with the local community, sporting opportunities, playground games. I wanted—and got—an environment that would be visually and mentally stimulating, teaching that would be enterprising and imaginative. Nearly all of this runs contrary to the needs of an autistic child.

When George and Sam started school, I had underestimated their sensory abnormalities. Having now read many accounts by adult autists, I know how difficult and distracting the physical features of a school environment can be. Strip lights flicker, radiators hum, the chatter of other children is bewildering and incomprehensible. The walls are covered in a confusing jumble of color and sparkle. Classrooms are rearranged—you've just gotten used to one layout when you have to start all over again. Smells of cooking or cleaning fluid, or even the teacher's perfume, are overpowering. You can't take in the teacher's instructions—she talks too fast, and her earrings jangle.

The ideal autistic environment looks dull to neurotypical eyes. Plain, pale walls; floors evenly covered without changes in carpet or tile design, to help those who, like Sam, have problems with depth perception. Displays, whether of art or of information, kept to a minimum—the autist often inadvertently notices every tiny detail, which can lead to "overload." Soft, non-flourescent lighting. No harsh bells marking the end of a lesson. Ideally, no abrupt end to the lesson at all, which should finish when the task is completed. As few transitions as possible from one room to another. A simple, coherent timetable, presented in pictogram form; deviations from the timetable to be kept to a minimum. Plenty of space between the work area of one child and the next. No disruption of routine for sports days or Christmas shows, events that are important to neurotypical children but meaningless to the autist. All this would be on my wish list.

At George's present school, each child has his own workstation, a V-shaped structure where the child works facing the wall, with his back turned on the others. The aim is to cut down distraction, to aid concentration, rather like the blinkers on a horse's harness. But isn't this just strengthening the child's isolation? No. It's creating a feeling of calm and security, which puts the child in a better frame of mind to cope with the social demands that will, inevitably, be put upon him.

The environmental needs of an autistic child, then, are not compatible with neurotypical needs. Academically there will be a little more overlap, but even so, the differences will be profound. As we've seen, the intellectual profile of the autist is characterized by peaks and troughs. All teachers have to cope with a wide range of ability within the same class, but in the case of an ASD child she could be faced with, say, mathematical skills approaching A-level standard in a child who can neither read, write, nor wipe his own bottom.

Good mainstream teaching makes links between subjects. In primary schools, project work dominates; you choose a subject like "the Romans" and from it develop exercises in all the disciplines. Creative writing—imagine you are a galley slave. Math—calculations using Roman numerals. Geography—a map of the Roman Empire. Technology—make a scale model of an aqueduct. Art and craft—DIY mosaics with squares of colored paper. Even cookery—there may be no larks' tongues or honeyed dormice to hand, but let's find out how the Romans made their bread. A good teacher can turn a single subject to endless use. The children learn that the past affects the present, that one culture gives birth to another, that you can combine using your imagination with your practical skills and your powers of logic, that the world is wide.

To the autist, this fluid, creative approach may well be baffling. Autists like to compartmentalize. They are likely to prefer the certainty of traditional, rigid, academic boundaries. Just as the ideal autistic environment looks plain and boring to us, so the repetitive sheets of sums or lists of memorized facts in which some autists delight may seem dry or sterile. These comments don't particularly apply to my sons, who have never achieved much academically, but the nearest equivalent would be George endlessly coloring in the same photocopy of the Seven Dwarfs. Isn't that getting boring? Wouldn't he like to color something else? No, and no.

I'm not suggesting that the autistic student should be endlessly indulged in his taste for repetitive exercises. New subjects, new skills, have to be introduced. But what I am saying is that the swift changes of subject, the creativity, the diversity, of good mainstream teaching is likely to be so bewildering to the autist that he may withdraw altogether.

One argument often put forward to support the inclusion policy is that ASD children will benefit from the example of mainstream behavior. Well, if these children could learn by example, they wouldn't be autistic. When autistic children imitate others, they do so only in the most superficial and transient ways. They don't relate behavior to the underlying social structure. George's time in mainstream was far more successful than Sam's, but he still never learned in any meaningful way from the play of the other children. This isn't surprising—if you think about it, most autistic children have had a "mainstream" home life, and they haven't learned from that.

Thérèse Jolliffe, an autistic woman who has become a university academic, has written a brief account of her life. She states,

> I hated school. Parents of autistic children should never think about sending their children to ordinary schools, because the suffering will far outweigh any of the benefits achieved. . . . Although ordinary schooling enabled me to leave with a dozen or so O-levels and a few A-levels and then to obtain a degree, it was not worth all the misery I suffered. . . . I was frightened of the girls and boys, the teachers and everything there. I was frightened of the toilets and you had to ask to use them, which I was not able to do, also I was never sure when I wanted to go to the toilet anyway. . . . When I attended a place for autistic people, life was a little more bearable and there was certainly less despair.

This was a girl with spectacular academic gifts who didn't have the social skills or the word-finding ability to ask to use the toilet. That's autism in a nutshell.

Am I suggesting that inclusion in mainstream is always wrong? Not quite. But I do believe that the cases where it works well are hugely outnumbered by the cases where it fails. At the heart of the government's inclusion policy are two fundamental misunderstandings. One is that normality rubs off on abnormal people, to their benefit. It doesn't. The other is that intellectual ability is a more important educational criterion than social ability. It isn't.

Many parents will disagree with me. I would have disagreed with myself, when the boys were first diagnosed. Like the majority of parents of autists, I believed, for a long time, that I had normal children. Autism isn't like Down's syndrome, which is identified from physical characteristics in the first few hours of life, if it hasn't already been picked up by prenatal screening. The parents of a Down's baby can't fully imagine what life's going to be like for them or their child, but at least they will never harbor the mistaken belief that their child will have the same needs as everyone else's. They can make decisions about the child's education from a position of some knowledge.

When "autistic" parents come to choose the first school for their child, it's likely that they will not long before have received the diagnosis. It can take years for the full import to sink in. It's hard to shift that bedrock expectation, that illusion that nothing is wrong with their beautiful, healthy, loveable child. When George and Sam were first diagnosed, I think I saw their autism as a kind of cloak, a covering of their true selves that might one day fall away. I didn't recognize that they are autistic through and through.

So, when the educational psychologist or the person from County tells you that your child is suitable for mainstream, you're happy to believe it. I've often heard such authority figures say, "We always try to put the parents wishes first." Fine—but how does the parent know what their child's needs are? Giving birth to an autistic child doesn't make you an instant expert on the subject. Parents at this stage are vulnerable to suggestion. They jump at the chance of mainstream, thinking that it means their child's difficulties are superficial, curable. When the boys were four, it was impossible for me to foresee that they were as deeply handicapped as has proved to be the case.

This is a sensitive area. It would be wrong to come down heavily on the parents, to tell them that their child will inevitably be severely handicapped, that he has no hope of functioning in the "real" world. Autism is a highly unpredictable condition, as we've seen. My boys, to date, have done far less well than would have been predicted, but there are plenty of cases where the reverse is true. What does need to be explained carefully to parents is that autism is an all-pervasive condition. Whether a child is high- or low-functioning, there isn't one aspect of his life that won't be touched by it. And most mainstream schools are not adapted to take account of autism *in any way*.

It was really the deterioration in Sam's behavior that led me to take both boys out of mainstream. George could have carried on. True, he wasn't learning very fast, but he didn't learn much faster after the move, either. George, in contrast to his infant precocity, was on an intellectual go-slow from which he is only just beginning to emerge. But at the age of eight, when he left mainstream, he was quite manageable in the class. He needed Ruby, his helper, but with her support he didn't cause undue problems for the teacher or the other children, except on the odd occasion, as when he pulled up a hedge, newly planted to commemorate an important date in the school's history. But increasingly he was a satellite to the activities of the others. As their work and play became more sophisticated, there was less and less with which he could join in. The move would have come sooner or later, but George was quite happy; it wasn't a matter of urgency.

Sam, though—Sam's position at the school had become untenable. During his first year there he had been blithely impervious to instruction, restless and unfocused, but jolly enough, motivated by washing machines, and with the odd flash of responsiveness. In his second year, the great regression happened. As I suggested in chapter 8, his inappropriate educational placement may have played a part, though I suspect that the causes were mainly physical. But Sam's huge shutdown, his loss of all motivation, his seesawing between torpor and wildly destructive behavior, was too much for the school to cope with. As for peer-group interaction, Sam no longer had anything in common with the rest of the class other than that they were all housed under the same roof.

My instinct has always told me to keep Sam and George together. They've always been close, perhaps because they are the only people in the world who put no pressure on each other. The bond between them will be important to them throughout their lives; a decision about one involves a consideration of the other. I hope I'd be flexible enough to respond if their needs diverged sharply. But when it became obvious that Sam had to leave mainstream, I decided to take George out as well. George's move, I realized, was going to happen one day; why hang on and watch him fail?

Luckily for us, autistic provision in our area had improved. Torfield School, a special-needs school seven miles away from us, in Hastings, had opened an ASD facility, where no more than eight children were taught by experienced staff. There was a part-time in-house speech and language therapist, and a high staff:pupil ratio. The boys would be able to stay in the same place until they went to secondary school, aged eleven. And they would be together.

So in September 1998, aged eight and nearly seven, that's where they went, and that's where they remained. George has moved on to a similar arrangement, a facility attached to Saxon Mount, a special-needs secondary school. Sam will join him there very soon. They'll stay there until they're sixteen, and then—well, who knows?

The experience of the last few years has convinced me that an autistic environment is the right environment for them. There have been plenty of problems. George took ages to adjust to the change to secondary school, and became aggressive and semi-anorexic, but now he loves school and is settled and manageable.

Sam is still resolutely unteachable—as Mark, the classroom assistant, says, "No one is better than Sam at being autistic." He has a knack of deflecting all attempts to coerce him into constructive and meaningful activity. But he feels secure at the unit; he runs out to his taxi every morning with alacrity. Removed from the bewildering pressures and mental and sensory overload of mainstream life, he is calmer, happier, and less destructive.

And the boys need that high staff:pupil ratio. All autists do. Most of them can't learn anything in a group. Everything has to be presented to them individually. Indeed, learning to tolerate sitting in a group at all, even for the attendance, is difficult. They can't be expected to follow any kind of generalized curriculum. Only an individual education plan makes sense. Ideas about what an average ten-year-old (or whatever) should or should not be learning just don't apply. And the comments I made about autists failing to pick up the "good" habits of mainstream children applies in reverse as well. Parents fear that their child will learn to be "more autistic" from being in a class with other autistic children, but this doesn't seem to happen. Autists take so little notice of one another. Neither George nor Sam has ever imitated a new "autistic" habit in anything other than a fleeting, superficial way.

It's lucky for me that both boys are sufficiently handicapped to qualify easily for special-needs provision. It's much harder to find an appropriate placement for a more able autistic or Asperger's child. Sadly, the common pattern is that the more able child more or less makes it through mainstream primary school, where smaller numbers and a more protective attitude among the staff give the "different" child some degree of shelter, only to find everything falling apart once they move on to middle school. That big change at eleven, from a smallish, cozyish school where you are taught by the same teacher for nearly everything, to a large, split-site middle school

with a complicated timetable and a different teacher for every subject, is daunting for most children. How much worse it must be for
the ASD child, with his impairments of communication and social
interaction, let alone his anxieties and hypersensitivities. It's like
parking a child in a wheelchair at the bottom of a steep flight of
stairs and expecting him to climb them.

Arguably, the whole concept of school is wrong for children
on the spectrum. Any school, even the most specialized, involves
some degree of social cooperation and space sharing. One of the
motivations behind home education programs, such as ABA, is
the impossibility of finding any school environment in which an
autistic child can thrive. Luke Jackson, now at a gentler, more tolerant school, still has many difficulties, and takes comfort from
the knowledge that, if things get really bad, homeschooling is a le-
gal option.

I think schools can be adapted or created to suit ASD children.
Opting out altogether has its own pitfalls. The current provision is
woefully inadequate, and I could go on for pages about necessary
improvements, but I'll confine myself to main targets. First, all
special-needs children diagnosed before the age of five should have
access to special-needs nurseries with trained staff. Nursery education is hugely important. With autistic children, it'll be much
easier to work with them later on if they have been expertly di-
verted away from their rigid routines and antisocial behaviors at
an early age, before these get "stuck." It's not realistic to expect
the parents to do all this. Sticking an autistic child in an ordinary
nursery is often pointless and can terrify the child and confirm his
isolation.

Second, local authorities should be prepared to fund home-
therapy programs such as ABA for families who feel that their
children are not suited to any kind of school setting. If, as its most

devoted practitioners claim, ABA given young enough can turn an unreachable child into one ready for gradual integration into school, then it's money very well spent.

Third, the provision for high-functioning autistics and Asperger's children is worst of all. Such children need academic teaching, in some cases to a very high level. They also need careful and sensitive teaching in social skills and self-care. It's vital that the authorities recognize that a high IQ has very little to do with common sense or the ability to communicate. A unit attached to a mainstream school might be a good option, where the able pupils can access the academic expertise of the main school but where they are also protected from the hurly-burly of school life, and where they can be given help in their specific areas of weakness. The current "sink or swim" attitude to inclusion is extremely harmful.

Fourth, the government needs to invest in training teachers to work with autistic children. The odd half-day course here and there isn't enough. Teaching autists is very different from teaching mainstream and requires almost opposing skills. Teaching autists can also be a rewarding, interesting, and important job. If the current estimates are correct, and nearly one in a hundred children are on the spectrum, then we need a huge expansion in expertise.

Autistic children don't need much in the way of special equipment. They need computers, but then who doesn't, these days? Most of them are physically healthy. A sizeable minority suffer from epilepsy, but apart from those, few cost the state in terms of drug treatments. What they do need is man- and womanpower. It's ironic that this most unsocial of conditions is best tackled by constant input from a large number of people. No man is an island, though most autists would probably think otherwise, were they capable of conceptualizing in that way. These little would-be islands need to be surrounded by bridge builders who know what they're doing. People cost money; there's no getting away from that. But effective input early on may lead to savings in the future. The better, the more purposeful, the child's early education, the more likely he is to achieve some degree of independence in adulthood. The current inclusion policy dooms many children to failure, and in the long run, failure is expensive.

FOURTEEN

Did You Sleep Well, Dear?

The last time I could rely on an unbroken night's sleep, the Berlin Wall was tottering, Nelson Mandela was still (just) on Robben Island, and Dirty Den (from *Eastenders*) held sway at the Queen Vic the first time around. If anyone had told me then, at the end of 1989, in those last restless nights of late pregnancy, that I would not be allowed to sleep through the night until well into the twenty-first century, I'd have—well, what would I have done? Simply not believed them, I expect.

I'm writing this in February 2003, and the sleeping's a whole lot better than it's ever been. Sam now goes to sleep before eleven and never wakes before seven. George retires at about ten-thirty; most mornings he joins me in bed at about three, but he usually falls quickly back to sleep. Sometimes he even stays in his own bed all night. Jake, asleep by eight-thirty, crawls in with me at about two, tells me his dreams, and then sleeps again until seven. It's rare for me to wake alone in my bed in the mornings, but it does sometimes happen.

It would be tedious to recount all the variations of nocturnal disturbance I've encountered over the last thirteen years, but I'm by no means the only sufferer. Sleep is a problem for many autistic children—or rather, it's a problem for their parents, since the children don't seem to care. It's certainly the aspect of life with the boys that wins me the most sympathy, though it's not the one that bothers me the most. "Oh, I just couldn't do without my eight hours," people say, considering my plight with pity and horror. I might well have said something similar myself, pre-children. But of course you can do without your eight hours, or even your six hours, if you have to.

I can't say exactly why autists should sleep badly, but as they do nearly everything differently, it seems unlikely that their sleep habits would conform to ours. They are often highly tense, anxious, overstimulated people; relaxing isn't usually part of their repertoire. Their heightened senses may mean that they find it difficult to block out intrusions of light or sound. They are often dependent on rituals, and the disruption of a ritual may prolong wakefulness. Jacqui Jackson, four of whose seven children are on the spectrum, says that Ben, her youngest, is very hidebound by routine. If he's missed his pudding, he'll scream for it in the middle of the night, not because he especially wants the pudding in itself, but because he can't bear to have his routine altered. And of course, having defective social wiring, autists fail to conform to the sleep pattern society expects of them, just as they may fail to conform to the pattern of greeting people on arrival, wearing warm clothes in winter, or wiping their bottoms after they've been to the lavatory.

Very new babies don't seem to distinguish between day and night. They feed, sleep, feed, sleep, feed, have a little look around, feed, and then sleep again. However, it doesn't take long for the normal baby to be nudged into the habit of sleeping more during the hours of darkness and having wakeful, playful times during the day. Even poor sleepers—and Jake was (is!) one—soon follow this pattern. It's common to find a six-month-old who wakes several times a night, much less common to find one who is fully alert, playful, and ready for action at all times of the night. By this age most babies have settled for a longish night and two naps a day, even if the night is not as long as the parents would like, and of a somewhat ragged texture.

I have already described the newborn George's superwakefulness, and the lack of pattern or coherence to his sleeping, even after many months. George really didn't seem to know night from day. His sleeping and waking remained entirely unpredictable, and unpredictability is very exhausting.

Like all new mothers, I had listened with a kind of smug horror to tales of other people's sleepless nights and had privately decided that my baby would be different. My baby would sleep through from early on, because I would do all the right things. I had, of course, reckoned without the baby's force of character, and my own lack of resolution; if giving it yet another feed and taking it back into one's own bed is the only way to grab a few more minutes' sleep, then that tends to be the path one takes.

As George grew older, the problems changed. He did, at last, accept the difference between day and night, but he would become very uptight at bedtime. He had to fall asleep in our arms; we could never just lay him down and leave him. And when he woke during the night, he could never put himself back to sleep without our help. I remember doing feeble things like buying sheets with little pictures on them in the hope that he would occupy himself with looking at them, but George was not to be fobbed off with anything like that. As soon as he could pull himself up to stand, at six months, he devoted his energies to working out how to escape from his crib. At ten months, he succeeded. I remember with a shudder the rattle, the thud, and the pad of tiny footsteps hurrying toward our room.

Sam seemed to be a sleepier baby than George. Certainly, you could put him in his crib and leave him; it wasn't until I went on holiday and had him in the room with me in a travel crib with transparent sides that I realized what a lot of time he spent awake, fingering Owly, staring at the ceiling. Unlike the social George, he didn't call for me, but he didn't sleep, either. Once Sam had graduated from a crib to a bed, things became a lot worse. It dawned on him that he had no need just to lie there anymore, so he didn't. He ran up and down the corridor, chuckling. Putting him to bed in the evening was the worst part. We tried to do what the baby books suggest—return him to bed, cover him, reassure him, make a decisive exit. We did this over and over again—forty, fifty, sixty times. Often, the evening would end with one of us taking him out and driving him around in the car—another failure.

The sleep issue probably caused more friction between me and Min than any other. Since I've been on my own, I've changed my attitude, and nights have improved. I never try to stop them from coming into my bed anymore. Nighttime is full of fears for any child; how much worse for one who can't express his terror? If George finds comfort in the pressure of my inert back, then why should I deprive him of it? In *Nobody Nowhere* Donna Williams writes about her night terrors: "I had become literally terrified of falling asleep and then, frightening as my mother had become, I would go into her room and stand there watching her sleep, feeling secure in the knowledge that if anything was to get me it would have to get her, too, and she knew how to fight. . . . Unknown to my mother, I lay stiff and silent under her bed, almost too afraid even to breathe." Donna Williams's mother was a violent drunk, and yet Donna still sought her as a refuge. How can I possibly deny my children access to my bed?

Having children in bed with you isn't great for a marriage, but the loss of evenings is worse. Sleepless autistic children can be with you for eighteen hours a day; the lack of adult, child-free time is more of a deprivation than the lack of sleep. Now, I'll often choose a late night, reading or going out with friends, over extra sleep. I read stories to George and Sam, sit with them until they finally subside, fall asleep on the sofa in their bedroom, then wake an hour later, read for an hour, then sleep again. When I go out, I stay up later than is strictly sensible. I need the mental space, the change of scene, more than sleep itself. Since I've been single I've been able to suit myself in this respect, and it works much better. Experts are divided about how much sleep we actually need. I suspect most adults need less than they think. You get used to it. I don't think I'm any more haggard or less energetic than my sleep-fulfilled friends.

Acceptance is the key—for me, anyway. Once I'd let myself stop fighting the boys' sleep habits, everything improved. One should set oneself realistic targets. I put Jake to bed at eight-thirty because I know I can. Plenty of children his age go to bed at seven. I know he and I can't manage that, so I don't try. Ten-thirty to eleven has become feasible for the other two, so that's what happens. It's not too bad.

The worst time of all was when Jake was a baby, and waking for breast-feeds at all-too-frequent intervals, and Sam was at the height, or depth, of his regression, the strange physical and mental disintegration from which he is still not fully recovered. At midnight Sam would still be racing up and down, whirring, humming, hooting, and flapping. His hands were bloody from being bitten, his fingers were swollen like sausages from being banged repeatedly against hard objects. Once asleep—often with the aid of a car ride—he would jump up as if woken by an electric shock seven or eight times before morning. Each time he would drink a bottle of milk or juice before going back to sleep. When I had to get him ready for school in the morning, he would be a lowering zombie, groaning, barely conscious. Astonishingly, he never wet the bed.

Desperate times, desperate measures. I'd already, years before, begged the doctor to give me a sleeping drug for him. At last she handed over some Phenergan, with the warning that, in a small percentage of cases, it had the opposite effect. Well, guess which category Sam fell into? I laced his bedtime bottle with Phenergan, and his head hardly touched the pillow. Autists seem to have an ability to override conventional medication. When Sam had a general anesthetic, he was up and running minutes afterward. It's an interesting area, and one into which there's been little research.

My experiment with Ritalin, the hyperactivity drug, is described in chapter 7. Once the Ritalin was in the bin, I knew I could no longer delay what I had been dreading—the removal of gluten and casein from Sam's diet. This is also dealt with in more detail in chapter 7; here, suffice it to say that nights improved pretty quickly once the diet was under way. Sam is now the soundest sleeper of the three.

I'm not the person to ask for advice about sleepless children, but I suppose I do have some views about what not to do. I do think that past early babyhood it's a bad idea to give them drinks at night. For years I was tyrannized by horrible, scummy feeding bottles lined up in the corridor outside the boys' room. I'm pleased with myself for never putting a bottle (or a pacifier) into Jake's mouth. He went from breast to beaker, and once he was off the breast he never, ever had another nocturnal drink. It's easy to be smug about doing without a pacifier, but I have to admit that Jake's thumb was in his mouth from the word "go." But the great thing about thumbs is that they don't get lost.

Giving children bottles at night does send them back to sleep, but it's habit-forming, and I suspect that it messes up their appetites and makes it harder to stick to a three-healthy-meals-a-day routine. It's also bad for their teeth, of course—though Jake has managed more cavities than the other two, despite no bottles and a relatively healthy diet. Bottles are depressing and squalid and oppressive, but in dealing with sleepless children, it's hard to reject instant assuagements and take the long view.

Personally, I wouldn't bother with books about how to make children sleep. I had a horrid book called *Healthy Sleep Habits, Happy Child*, which just made me feel worried and inadequate. I would also ignore, or heavily edit, advice from friends and family, especially from the older generation, who often recall the infancy of their progeny through a rosy and inaccurate glow. The main thing is to get in tune with yourself, with what you can and can't tolerate.

Having a reason for a problem helps a lot. Once I knew the boys were autistic, I found it much easier to accept their unsleepiness. It was a symptom of their condition, not a failure on my part. Once I'd given up any expectation of a good night's rest, I found it didn't affect me as badly as I would have expected. Luckily, I'm a good sleeper; I don't lie awake worrying, and I can usually get back to sleep quickly after a disturbance. If I've had a truly terrible night, I try to snatch a nap of five or ten minutes during the day. One of the very few things for which I'm grateful to Margaret Thatcher is the concept of the "power nap."

When I was an undergraduate, my preferred modus operandi was to go out in the evening, come back late, write an essay in the early hours, and then sleep until noon. I was outraged at being expected to attend a tutorial at nine in the morning; it felt like an abuse of human rights. These days, I couldn't sleep all morning even if I got the chance. I like early mornings now—this morning, yellow leaves and crimson berries glowing through furry frost, and the sun, shorn of its rays, a giant red eye bouncing up through the orchard. Intimately acquainted as I now am with every stitch in the weave of the twenty-four hours, I've grown fond of the declining moon, of foxes barking at midnight, of the predawn crowing of the cocks. Would I swap all this for a solid, predictable eight hours a night? Well, perhaps I would—but I'm not quite sure.

FIFTEEN

What Do They *Do* All Day?

F ive in the morning. George is up, and has been for some time. He's longing to jump on Sam, but I'm not going to let him. So I put a video on. After eleven years, it's still the most reliable way of keeping George out of trouble at times when I'm prepared to give him rather less than full attention.

He chooses *Kipper the Dog: Looking after Arnold*. Kipper is designed for four-year-olds, but George doesn't know that, and if he did, he wouldn't mind. No normal thirteen-year-old boy would be able to watch Kipper (or Teletubbies, or Tweenies, or Bob the Builder) other than in a spirit of irony or nostalgia, but irony and nostalgia are strangers to George. Irony depends on playing off one point of view against another, but George can only ever hold one point of view in his head, which is, of course, his own. Nostalgia requires that you look at the past and make a misty-eyed comparison between yourself as you once were and yourself as you are now. For George, time past and time present are the same thing. He's troubled by suggestions that he was once different, or that change is in store in the future. He can remember the past—he remembers everything. For most of us, the operation of a shared culture externalizes memory, edits and shapes it. George undergoes no such sorting process. His memories seem almost as present, as real to him, as what's happening here and now. When he started school, there was a little boy in his class called Adam Perry. Not long after, Adam left the school. George asked about him frequently, bothered by this disruption in the attendance. Two years later, Adam returned to the school. "Here's Adam Perry!" said George, as if Adam had never been away.

This idiosyncratic sense of time may be one reason why George returns to the same videos over and over again. *Looking after Arnold,* this morning's choice, might have been selected during any of the intermittent Kipper phases that have recurred throughout the last six or seven years. George has "customized" his video watching in the same way that as a three-year-old he customized his books; he selects certain key moments (not complete enough to be called scenes) or snatches of dialogue, and rewinds them. At other moments he'll enact the video—if a character falls, he might cast himself off the chair (or push Sam off), or if Kipper switches off the light, George will do the same. And then at other times he'll run out of the room. You'll think he's lost interest; he's sitting on top of the Aga, or on the garden wall, twiddling a flapper. But if you turn off the video, there'll be a shriek of protest. Running out during certain scenes is not a sign of lack of interest, it's all part of the elaborate choreography that video "watching" has become for George.

His treatment of his videos goes beyond any normal interest in narrative and characters. It's hard to explain what he gets out of them, because I don't exactly know. Of course, repetition of any kind is soothing and reassuring. George likes to know that you only have to press a button to see, for the umpteenth time, Kipper blowing out his candles, Arnold sucking his lollipop. But there's more to the endless rewinding than a simple desire for repetition. An American author, Robert Hughes, has written a memoir of life with his autistic son, Walker (*Running with Walker*), another champion rewinder. Hughes presents Walker's favorite videos as if Walker himself had written a guide to them for other autists, including "great rewind ops.": "Highlight: The scene where Cinderella's cute little creature friends sing 'We Can Do It' . . . All those friends! All that happiness! It's a terrific rewinding moment!" Hughes believes that, for the largely nonverbal Walker, the most rewound moments are passages of special emotional significance. He may well be right. It's possible, as I suggested in chapter 5, that George identified with Pinocchio, for instance; that he, like Pinocchio, yearned to be a "real boy," and that he rewound bits of the film in order to learn how to do it. It's also possible that he made no such connection.

George was less than two when he received his first video. It was *Pingu: Barrel of Fun*, and it was given to him by his godmother, Em, whose daughter Sophie was just ten months older. "You'll love me for giving him this," she said, and I did. *Pingu* hollowed out a forty-minute oasis of calm in George's highly colored, energized, chaotic world. I bought it for several friends expecting second children. I didn't really see how, without *Pingu*, one had any chance of breast-feeding a new baby.

Pingu seems to have fallen from favor with the general public, but he was very big in the early 1990s. He is an animated clay penguin who lives with his parents and little sister, Pinga, at the South Pole. He's a brilliant creation—a funny, mischievous, sometimes insecure little boy penguin whose adventures are rooted in domesticity without ever being dull. Each five-minute episode deals with one of the minidramas of a young child's life. Pingu tips his chair over backward, pretends he's brushed his teeth when he hasn't, spits unwanted vegetable matter into the toilet, fights with his sister, eats too much popcorn, wets himself. His parents are sentimental, quarrelsome, inconsistent, and slow-witted, just like real parents. An astonishing amount of personality is conveyed by each twitch of a flipper, each prod of a beak. Pingu and his companions converse in a kind of quacking gabble, with all the rhythms and intonations of real speech but with hardly any recognizable words. Despite this, each narrative is entirely comprehensible. Anyone interested in linguistics would do well to study *Pingu*.

Barrel of Fun was followed by many other Pingu tapes. Sam joined George in adoration. "'Gu! 'Gu!" Sam, aged two, would demand, and both would solemnly imitate the penguins' actions as they watched. As usual, different aspects appealed to each of them. Sam enjoyed spotting his objects of desire re-created in clay—a cooker, an ironing board, a washing machine. George was fascinated by the quacky language. With his good ear for mimicry, he became completely fluent in Pinguese, and would quote large chunks of "dialogue." It's hard to tell whether he attached meaning to the sounds he was hearing, but my guess is that he did.

Pingu certainly had emotional significance for George. Sam was indifferent to scenes of naughtiness, jealousy, punishment, or affection—though he did find some things funny—but for George, all that was important. There's a character called Mui in Timothy Mo's novel *Sour Sweet,* a Chinese woman newly arrived in 1960s London, who watches *Crossroads* intently in order to learn the social habits and moral values of westerners. For George, *Pingu* fulfilled a similar function. George, with his socially active but odd variety of autism, was intrigued by social behavior, even though he didn't understand it. Here, the rewinding comes into its own. Rewinding helped George to learn at his own pace. In real life, people won't rehearse their emotions for your benefit. Videos gave George time to sort out the action in his own mind. Pingu's mummy's cross. Yes. Why is she cross? Better check. Rewind. Because Pingu broke a plate! Hmm. Thought so.

Rewinding can also be used to create stimulating visual effects—stimulating to autists, that is; numbing to neurotypical viewers. Both boys went through a stage, early on, of preferring the credits to any other part of a film. Sam, aged three, would imitate this effect by holding a sheet of paper with writing on it close to his face and moving it quickly upward, rolling his eyes at the same time. He found a tiny, tiny label with the Disney logo on it, and this, too, he ran upward in front of his eyes, "singing" as he did so. Some of the boys' videos were made by a company called Pickwick. At the end of the tape, the viewer's eye would be directed as if into a keyhole, then the solid white letters of PICKWICK would disperse and whirl through space. This was one of Sam's "great rewind ops." He would also reenact the whirling of the letters using his own hands and body and his long, flying hair—"I a white Pickwick," he used to say. Yes, he sometimes used the first-person singular in those days.

There is a remarkable consensus of opinion among the autistic "community" about their viewing matter—remarkable because, unlike neurotypical children, they rarely converse with one another and are highly unlikely to give one another recommendations. Casey Junior, the steam train struggling up the hill in *Dumbo*, is a favorite autistic rewind. So is the "pink elephants on parade" sequence—a surreal dance hallucinated by a drunken Dumbo. Will and Kate, the boys' twin cousins, got frustrated when George kept rewinding the pink elephants—for them it was the dullest part of the film, because they, with their neurotypical plot-and-character motivations, wanted to get on with the story. Finding out what happened was rarely of interest to George and Sam. I remember observing the twins and George as they watched *Dumbo* together, and thinking how different they were. They were three at the time; this was before George's diagnosis. The twins cuddled together and wept when Dumbo was parted from his mother; George, oblivious to suffering, danced with delight in front of the psychedelic pink elephants. At that stage I didn't realize quite how profound the difference was. I recalled this years later when Jake, also aged three, watched *Dumbo* for the first time. "They've taken his mummy away," he sobbed in outrage and disbelief. "This can't be for children." It was another year or more before he felt brave enough to watch to the end.

Pingu was quickly joined by various Beatrix Potters, *Rosie and Jim*, the unavoidable *Thomas the Tank Engine*, *Spider in the Bath*, which particularly excited Sam, and *The Magic Roundabout*, which provided George with some of his best lines: "This will make *Ben-Hur* look like a vicarage tea party!" he would exclaim, at the sight of me and my friends drinking tea. "This will make Ken Russell spit with jealousy!" he declared, spitting on the floor. Some of these lines are still in use. "I've been let down by the government," George recently told his trampoline teacher, who was startled by the apparent profundity of the remark, not knowing that it was borrowed from Dougal.

There was *Fireman Sam*—during that emotional half-light through which mothers of toddlers grope their way, I remember idly wondering which was the more fanciable, Fireman Sam or his sidekick, Elvis Cridlington. *Noddy* had a burst of favor, and for George, the dire *Tots TV* was enormously influential. The three rag-doll tots live in a cottage, a sort of care-in-the-community arrangement, where they witter and fuss all day about spillages and breakages and whose turn it is to use the bathroom. Sometimes they totter out on their woollen legs to have educational encounters with harmless animals. This was absolutely on George's level. Their banal, repetitive exchanges resemble much ordinary human discourse; they provided useful conversational models for George. Later, *Bananas in Pyjamas* reared their ugly skins; "Big blana! Big blana!" Sam would shout. George became addicted to a strangely mesmeric set of glowing balloon bears called Jellikins, each of a color linked to a personality type. Pepper was red and assertive, Denny was blue and dreamy, Coral was pink and vain.

You'd be hard put to find an "autistic" family that wasn't in thrall to the Disney empire. I have reservations about Disney, myself, and I've tried to minimize Jake's intake. I dislike the way faces and emotions are stretched out of shape, the way the dialogue has one knowing eye on the adult audience, the way ancient myths and folktales are remodeled to express middle-American values. I find the colors unsubtle, the wisecracking unfunny, the romance unstirring, the pathos misplaced. And I've never been able to find cartoon characters cute. But I'm also grateful to the Disney Corporation for the hours of entertainment it has provided for my hard-to-occupy children. I know most children like Disney—most adults, too—but there does seem to be something about it that is particularly attractive to autists. Perhaps the exaggerated emotional responses are easier to understand. Perhaps the swooping, swirling movements provide special visual stimulation. The music is certainly important; no one knows better than Disney how to make a tune stick in your head, and autists tend to be even more responsive to this than the rest of us.

Whatever the reasons, you'll rarely come across an autistic

child who hasn't had some kind of Disney fixation. In our household, the front-runners have been *Dumbo, Snow White, Pinocchio,
The Aristocats, Fantasia, Beauty and the Beast, The Jungle Book,* and,
for Sam, some of the early Silly Symphonies, especially "Pig-Net
Machine" (*The Three Little Pigs*) and a marvelous sequence about
Easter Bunnies painting chocolate eggs. In all of them, the most-
rewound moments involve an intriguing visual effect, like Mowgli's
eyes mesmerized by Kaa, the *Fantasia* fairies coloring the autumn
leaves, or Snow White peering at her reflection in the wishing well.

The more recent, more sophisticated Disney / Pixar productions,
like *Toy Story* and *A Bug's Life,* are more acceptable to adults—well,
to this adult, at any rate. They're too complicated for Sam, but
George was very taken with them, even going so far as to experiment with some limited pretend play with toys modeled on the
characters. But the play never went beyond reenacted fragments.
I've never known George to improvise on character and motivation.
I think he is, at last, able to recognize Flik the inventor ant as a
goodie and Hopper the cruel grasshopper as a baddie in *A Bug's Life*
(or *Three Bugs Full* as the toddler Jake used to call it), but it would not
occur to him to invent his own acts of aggression for Hopper or
heroism for Flik. Nor does he display any fear of the one, or admiration of the other. George's response to favorite videos is enthusiastic but essentially dispassionate.

Toy Story and *A Bug's Life* are the nearest to age-appropriate that
George gets. Attempts to interest him in feature films about "real"
children—even Harry Potter movies or *Chitty Chitty Bang Bang*—
have largely failed. He is interested in real children—he loves the
activities of children on *Teletubbies* or his various nursery-rhyme
tapes, and likes to know their names. When he was younger he
wanted these children to step out of the television and join him.

My attempts to convince him that this was impossible were thwarted when we went to a friend's house and met another visiting family. The sons, Oscar and Felix, were the very boys who George had watched over and over again as they read "The Gingerbread Man" in an episode of *Teletubbies*. George recognized them at once. "Here are Oscar and Felix!" he trilled, delighted. The encounter gave him food for thought. If Oscar and Felix could turn up in a Sussex garden, then clearly I was wrong about the non-transferability of TV or fictional characters. "Mum, the Cat in the Hat *can* come to our house," he stated on the journey home.

So, George is far from indifferent to seeing "real" children onscreen—indeed, they exert considerable fascination. But it's difficult to interest him in a full-length feature film with child stars because he has no curiosity about what happens to them. They talk too much and too quickly, and one's understanding of the film is too dependent on listening properly to what they say. And again, there's this failure to identify. Normal children cast about constantly for role models. When Jake was three, he was gripped by Shirley Hughes's books about a little boy called Alfie, because Alfie was very like himself. Alfie had a security blanket, Jake had his hankies. Like Jake, Alfie wanted to go to parties but found it difficult to let go of his mother's hand. Alfie admired a more boisterous child—"rough, tough Bernard"—but his admiration was tempered by shock. Alfie reflected and enlarged upon Jake's own experience. His mild adventures led Jake's imagination just a little further than it had been before—a few steps beyond the garden gate—and gently expanded Jake's sense of his own potential. Aged five, Jake now happily identifies with a range of characters from books, videos, and real life. Whether it's Harry Potter, soccer star Michael Owen, or Danny, the John Travolta character in

Grease (yes, I'm afraid so), he can annex aspects of other characters to explore facets of his own personality.

George has very little of this capacity. Sam has none. Nor do either of them use television, as Jake does, to find out about the adult world. Jake is a big fan of quiz shows. "Mum, I support the clergy," he called out the other day, which baffled me until I realized he was watching a special edition of *University Challenge,* the clergy versus the lawyers. When he was three, he would arrange his toy engines in a semicircle and announce that he was playing "The Leakest Wink." He fired questions at the engines (Q: "What does get brown when you do wee on it?" A: "Grass.") and dismissed them with scorn when they gave the wrong replies. Just the other day, he memorized the telephone number to apply for *Who Wants to Be a Millionaire* and rang it. ("Mum, I'll just ring Chris.") I heard him talking to the recorded message: "My mum could be on your show. Then we could afford a new kitchen bin."

It doesn't matter to Jake that he can answer few, if any, of the questions. He likes quizzes because he likes scoring, he likes winners and losers. And he is fascinated by adults, their concerns and preoccupations, the way they interact. He watches quiz shows, and *Top of the Pops,* and *Neighbours,* partly because, he thinks, they allow him an enticing sneak preview of his own future. To George, thinking about the adult world is difficult and disturbing. For Sam, it's simply irrelevant.

Other parents of autists report similar viewing habits to those of George and Sam. Videos are always preferred to television. Short, simple episodes, prefaced by a catchy theme tune and peopled by a small predictable cast, form their foundation of video watching; *Postman Pat* and *Bob the Builder,* it seems, can be enjoyed anytime, anyplace by most autists, regardless of age or IQ level. Regardless of gender, too; the teenaged Walker Hughes's favorite Disneys include *The Little Mermaid, Cinderella,* and *Alice in Wonderland,* whereas a neurotypical male Disney enthusiast would surely be shy of confessing to such preferences after the age of, say, seven. Indifference to gender is a common autistic trait, and yet another example of how autists don't perceive the same patterns that give life its coherence for the rest of us. George can always tell the difference between men and women and is interested in categorizing male and female animals ("Is that a daddy cow?"), but he chooses a pink Barbie cupcake at the baker's and has little idea that some toys, sports, or activities are associated with one gender or the other. Sam doesn't seem able to tell the difference between the sexes. ("What is Grandfather Clive, Sam?" "A mummy.") He uses "he" and "she" indiscriminately.

The boys' taste in books is even more infantile than their taste in videos. At three, George's appetite for stories and poetry was prodigious and precocious. It hasn't progressed much since. There's a cycle of old favorites that never seems to weary him. At the moment we're back on the tank engines (the black twins to the fore again, but this time with a more prominent role for Donald). Other hardy perennials are the Dr. Seuss books, some Beatrix Potters, Eric Carle (highly colored, highly patterned books, usually about insects), Arnold Lobel's Frog and Toad stories, and Allan Ahlberg's Funnybones skeleton family. Then there are a few oddballs, like *Rumples and Tumbles Go to the Country,* which is so dreary that the author has declined to put his or her name on the cover. Rumples is a pink toy rabbit, Tumbles a blue one. They spend a day in the country learning facts about wildlife. This little volume has exerted a powerful hold over both boys since early childhood and is now so patched with tape that it has swollen to twice its original size.

The fact that the rabbits are a not-quite-identical pair appeals strongly to George. He is almost equally devoted to an Enid Blyton book called *Bimbo and Blackie,* about a pair of kitten cousins, one white, one black. The best bit is when they change colors— Blackie gets covered with flour, Bimbo with soot. George's love of pairs has been a consistent theme throughout his life and is in some way linked to the way he sees himself and Sam.

Sam is much less likely to request a book than George, though if I put a selection in front of him, he'll leaf through them with some slight interest. If he were able to select a favorite author, it would be Dr. Seuss. *Green Eggs and Ham* would be found under the palm tree on his desert island, along with the Bible and Shakespeare. Sam appreciates bouncing rhythms and rhymes, and Dr. Seuss is good at both. Sam also finds these books comical. When I first started reading about autism, the received wisdom was that autists had no sense of humor, but this isn't true. Humor was one of Sam's strongest characteristics from the earliest age. Of course, autistic humor isn't the same as ours, but that doesn't mean it doesn't exist.

Nursery rhymes have been important to both boys, perhaps most markedly to Sam. When Sam was at his very worst, veering between hyperactive and destructive one minute and catatonic the next, nursery rhymes and their accompanying tickling games ("This Little Piggy," "Round and Round the Garden") were one of the few remaining ways of making contact with him. He still likes to climb on my knee and play "This is the way the ladies ride"; he's small for his age, but all the same, it's getting tricky to manage. He knows a great many rhymes by heart. He'll rarely repeat a whole one, but if I pause in my recitation, he'll supply the missing word, or an approximation. This may not sound like an impressive skill for a boy of eleven, but it's way ahead of many of Sam's other attainment levels.

I love nursery rhymes, too. I'm fascinated by their mysterious power to restore the equilibrium of a fractious toddler. When a two-year-old wakes, cross, after a nap, there's no better way of bringing him or her around than to sit together for half an hour reading nursery rhymes. Something about them operates on a level below consciousness—it's akin to the soothing experience of sitting near a fountain, or listening to the wind. For normal children, nursery rhymes operate on many levels. The vocabulary, imagery, and characters stock the store cupboard of our imaginations and continue to nourish us throughout our lives. They are a kind of quintessential poetry—the best possible words in the best possible order. They provide us with an immense wealth of shared experience. It's extraordinary, given how short the rhymes are, how strong a sense we all have of the personalities of Little Jack Horner, Miss Muffett, Bo Peep, and so on. "Hey Diddle Diddle" is the essence of a good party, "Humpty Dumpty" expresses the randomness of disaster, and what could be more melancholy than the second verse of "Polly Put the Kettle On"?

I'm not at all sure that Sam and George tap into this. I don't know whether they see anything in their mind's eye when they hear nursery rhymes recited. George, with his greater interest in people, may have some degree of response to Bobby Shafto or Mary Mary as characters, and his love of phrases may mean that the words resonate for him in an almost visual way, but for Sam, I have a feeling that they don't operate at this level at all. I don't know that Sam sees Humpty Dumpty as an egg, or can imagine what skipping over water and dancing over sea would be like. The impact of nursery rhymes, for Sam, lies in their rhymes and rhythms and pleasing word sounds, which is not to say that they are any the less intense for him than they are for normal children.

As with books and videos, neither boy has any inkling that nursery rhymes are inappropriate for their age. Sam doesn't know what his age is. I have no evidence that he's aware of being younger than George or older than Jake. He just doesn't fit himself into any frame of reference. Much of the boys' taste in music would seem to be age-appropriate, but if so, this would be purely by chance. Both of them like a range of rock and pop, but neither has any idea of what's hip or cool (which is just as well, because it means that I can impose my very uncool tastes upon them), and neither makes any connection between music and clothes, hairstyles, or modes of behavior. Most autists seem to be strongly affected by music; perfect pitch, which George may have, is not uncommon. Neither boy plays an instrument, but listening to CDs is an important part of their day. As a way of keeping them entertained, music is on a par with videos, and far more important than books. At school, music therapy has been, for them, one of the most successful parts of the curriculum.

George segues effortlessly from his nursery rhymes to Bowie, the Police, the Rolling Stones, Elvis, the Beach Boys, and others. He loves *Peter and the Wolf,* and a few classical pieces—for a while he was gripped by Stravinsky's *Rite of Spring.* He likes the blues, especially Robert Cray, and he loves Christmas carols performed by cathedral choirs. He goes through periods when he wants to hear the same CD over and over again—it's the Bee Gees at the moment—and finds it difficult to tolerate anybody else's choice. He throws unwelcome CDs down behind the bookcase. His aversions are strong. He abhors Queen ("Bohemian Rhapsadaisy," as Jake calls it), which is a pity, as Sam is quite a fan. Sam has cruder tastes than George and enjoys anything with a thumping great beat. Status Quo would be exactly Sam's thing, if I could bear it. Both boys like reggae and ska—Desmond Dekker's "Israelites" would be one of Sam's desert-island choices.

Both boys "dance" as they listen; their dances are quite like running on the spot and have no reference to anyone else, either as a partner or as an audience. George shrieks at me if I try to dance with him. He can recognize all the tracks on any of his CDs from any part of them, and is just as likely to be heard singing the bass line as the melody. He also likes lyrics, and sometimes quotes them, as when I told him to hurry up and get into bed, and he replied, "I can't, I'm a rock 'n' roll suicide." Sam has less musical subtlety than George, but he does distinguish between tracks. He can't ask for them by name, but he reserves his most energetic dancing and his loudest participatory squeals for a few particular songs—Cockney Rebel's "Make Me Smile," Jimmy Cliff's "The Harder They Come," and Elvis's "Long Tall Sally" among them.

One might assume that George's musical ability meant that he could join a choir or a dance class, or at least learn to play an instrument properly. But that assumption fails to account for the disconnectedness of the autistic experience. Being able to sing well doesn't mean that you want to sing with other people. It doesn't mean that you want other people to hear you singing, or even that you want to sing at all. George has a good voice, but he can go for months without using it. Besides, joining any class or group requires a basic acceptance of the rules of herd behavior. It would be possible to train a child like George to conform to these rules, but it would take a long, long time, and the training process would be disruptive to the rest of the group. George can learn a new song after a couple of hearings; to learn to follow a choir leader's instructions would take him a couple of years.

What about an instrument? Many autists become proficient

players; why not George? Given the right teacher, that should be possible, and it's something we'll try one of these days. It would be hard for George to read music—it's been hard enough to teach him to read words—but his musical memory is so good that he could probably learn by ear. So, why didn't I start him on an instrument years ago? There are two, linked, reasons. One is motivation. George, as a rule, resists learning *any* new skill. As Clara Claiborne Park describes in *The Siege,* the autistic child finds her contentment, her Nirvana, in nothingness. Jessy Park spent hours circling a spot on the carpet. Any attempt at redirection was a disruption of her inner peace. I'm reminded of Malvolio in *Twelfth Night*: "Let me enjoy my private." Jessy's parents' difficult task, at which they ultimately succeeded, was to lay siege to the walls Jessy had erected to protect that core of nothingness. George was never as sealed off as this. He was, as I've described, a highly proactive baby. But, past babyhood, George's behavior did often display large "Do Not Disturb" signs. I was wary of introducing new skills and ideas because I didn't want to prod the oversensitive George back into his shell. Autistic children overload quickly. Once they crash, the restoration of harmony can take a very long time.

Alongside this lack of motivation, there's a problem best described by Jessy Park herself as the feeling of "too good." Some things are experienced too intensely, enjoyed too acutely. Pleasure tips over into pain. Music, for George and for Jessy Park, can become "too good," and then it can no longer be borne. (This doesn't seem to be an issue with the more phlegmatic Sam.) There is some kind of self-protecting mechanism at work. Music, painting, even some people—once they begin to overwhelm, they need to be put away. Attempting to participate in George's activities is the surest way to precipitate shutdown. If you praise George for his singing, or admire his painting, he'll swiftly retreat from both.

There are signs, though, that George's skin is growing thicker, and it may soon be possible to introduce "proper" music lessons. He enjoys music classes at school—in fact he takes charge of them, telling the other boys what to do and what their favorite song should be. He seems happy to sing alongside familiar people. He goes to a mainstream trampoline club; he still has to be supervised, but he is now able to follow the teacher's instructions almost as well as the other children. In the past, painting was a private activity for George, but now he'll allow his tutors to sit by him and make suggestions as he paints. It's encouraging to hear from older parents that learning doesn't seem to have a cutoff age for their autistic offspring. Some of the skills and experiences missed in childhood can, it seems, be recovered or introduced in later life.

George started painting "properly" when he was five. Not drawing; it puzzled me, early on, pre-diagnosis, that my amazingly intelligent child showed little interest in or aptitude for drawing. George's early drawings of people were all in bits. He'd draw eyes, legs, hands, and so on, separately, scattered across the page. Neurotypical children's drawings develop in a remarkably consistent way. Drawings of people by Chinese four-year-olds, I gather, look very similar to drawings by American four-year-olds. First there'll be a circle with eyes and legs; later there'll be an ellipse for the body, and the addition of hands, fingers, hair, ears, and so on, will all happen in the fullness of time. I've never come across another child who failed to link up the features as George did. When Sam was three and a half, I asked him to draw a picture of Grandma. He'd never attempted to draw a person before *at all*, but he immediately drew a fully fledged figure, with features like hair, fingers, and toes. "Draw Grandfather Clive," I said. He complied. On request, he added Lulu the dog and Vinnie the cat, and the tumble dryer. The dog and cat were different from the human figures, and different from each other. Sam had missed out all the developmental stages in infant drawing; from nothing, he produced a drawing that was easily age-appropriate. I tried to get him to reproduce this feat on other occasions, but he never would.

Now, at thirteen, George will draw on request or command, but never spontaneously. His figures have a certain energy and charm, but his skill level barely exceeds Jake's, and he rarely places his figures in any sort of context. His paintings, however, absorb considerable amounts of thought and care. I don't think they are ever intentionally representational, or at least, they're not planned as such. If asked, George may say that he's painted a storm or the sea, but I have a feeling he's being wise after the event. All his paintings are explorations of color, and always have been.

Both boys have always been strongly responsive to color, George especially. Both of them could name every color well before their second birthdays. I remember George, aged two and a quarter, in his stroller, looking at a donkey. "What color is the donkey?" I asked him. "Gray," he replied. "No, browny gray. No, pinky browny gray." This acute color sense is shared by other autists. Jessy Park, now in her forties, uses color ranges in her minutely detailed paintings where the gradations in shade are so subtle as to be almost invisible to the neurotypical eye.

At five, George painted round discs of color, some free-floating, some overlapping. He limited his own color range. In one painting, he would work his way through every combination of red, white, and yellow; in another, he'd stick to blue and green. The discs would be joined by a few vertical stripes. He painted on a little easel; he'd walk around it, peering at his work from every angle. Then he'd lie on the floor looking up, apparently admiring the way the light glinted on the fresh paint. He always knew exactly when he'd finished. This wasn't when the paint ran out, or when some alternative activity suggested itself; it was when he'd done whatever he felt he had to do to the painting. After that, he lost interest. I stuck his best ones on the wall, but he didn't look at them again.

He then abandoned paint for a couple of years, perhaps in reaction to too much praise. I can't remember why or how painting crept back in, but the pattern in recent years has been a burst of intense interest followed by a fallow period. Since the discs, he has been through several "styles": stormy Turneresque vortexes, thick Van Gogh coils of ridged, textured color, late Kandinsky battlefields of converging stripes and dashes. He goes through phases of preferring different media—poster paints, powder paints, acrylics, heavy finger paint (always applied with a brush), thin paint box watercolors. One summer, he switched to felt-tips, which he mixed with pencils and wax crayons to create dense "scribble" pictures, the colors converging on, or radiating out from, a dark center. Occasionally he'll use something other than a brush, like a potato to make a print, and he'll sometimes turn his brush around and make scratchy patterns with the end of the handle. Today marked a new departure—graded color, from pale green to deep crimson, crossed by regularly spaced black horizontal bars. This, George declared with more certainty than I'd heard him use before, was "a sunset."

Poor deluded woman, my readers must be thinking. Only mother-love could turn these splotches and dribbles into Turner and Kandinsky. Yes, of course I'm biased, and George is not a phenomenal autistic artist like Stephen Wiltshire, Jessy Park, or David Braunsberg. But he does have a real affinity for color and, to a lesser extent, texture. He works with great purpose and concentration; he always seems to know what he's doing; and, like a true expressionist, he incorporates drips and other minor accidents into the overall scheme. And despite the fact that he's usually working with basic children's materials, the results have a depth and brilliance of color that I, for one, couldn't possibly achieve.

Sam still eats paint. He loves mixing colors, and he splats his brush onto the paper with relish, but he has little awareness of any visual effect. Leave Sam alone with paints for thirty seconds and the kitchen will have been redecorated. He has a similar attitude to Play-Doh and cooking ingredients; it's almost impossible to get him to concentrate on the end product. Handling materials, squidging, slicing, smearing, is what interests Sam. Since the demise of his obsessive interests, Sam has been much, much harder to occupy than George. I'm writing this in the middle of August; the summer holidays can seem very long indeed.

For Sam, strenuous physical exercise is important to fill the time as well as keep him fit. He has the physique and stamina of a sportsman without any of the team spirit or ability to practice techniques. It will never be possible for either boy to participate properly in a game like soccer or cricket; they will never develop the capacity for social cooperation that such activities require. Luckily, neither of them shows the least interest in team games. Solo activities, like trampolining, swimming, or riding, are usually a better bet for autists. I'd certainly advise any family with a big-enough garden to invest in a proper trampoline if they can possibly afford it. It's been the single most important piece of play equipment for my boys, though a swing runs it close.

During the holidays Sam gets taken for a long walk every day, like a dog. We go to woods, beaches, parks, or public gardens. Sam can outwalk anyone; I've never known him to run out of steam. When he was fifteen months old, he walked unaided to our bluebell wood, a distance of about three quarters of a mile. George, though not quite so sturdy, was also an uncomplaining walker.

Before Jake was born I would spend hours out with the pair of them, enjoying their enthusiasm for the wind in the long grass or the ripples on the water's surface as they threw acorns into the pond. George and Sam were the most undemanding companions on these walks, completely absorbed as they were in the physical experience of grass, trees, water, and mud. I was free to watch them and to think my own thoughts. Jake, alas, has all the normal childish reluctance to walk unless there's a specific end in view. More than two fields' worth of walking is usually accompanied by demands to be carried and a litany of complaints about physical discomforts.

Sam runs as much as he walks—doglike, he covers about five times as much ground as I do. I like walking too, so when I'm out with Sam I'm happy to be looking at beautiful places, albeit at high speed. It's hard to judge whether or not Sam has a sense of natural beauty, but he certainly seems internally calmer and happier when he's charging along a woodland path or leaping back from crashing waves. And he always knows exactly where he is. He won't necessarily be able to name the place, but his behavior shows that his sense of direction and ability to recognize landmarks is extremely strong. We take the boys on lots of trips to castles, children's zoos, rare-breeds farms, steam trains, and the like. We need to fill their days; they are very much more aimless than normal children, and left to their own devices will quickly revert to stimming—hand bashing, stick twiddling, or tearing up valued garden plants. Their social life is limited and almost entirely engineered by me. There are no sleepovers, no camping expeditions, no chats on the telephone. But neither are there the grumbles and clashing schemes that accompany normal childhood occupations. A couple of weeks ago, George announced, "I'm so bored"—it was the first time any of my children had ever said such a thing.

George himself looked startled, even as he said it. I don't mean to suggest that autism and boredom are strangers to each other. Far from it—I think autists often suffer from ennui without knowing what the feeling is or what to do about it. But they don't have the neurotypical preconceived ideas about what's boring or uncool. Almost no conversation means almost no arguments, and speaking as a parent, that's not entirely bad.

SIXTEEN

God and the Tooth Fairy

When George was four, we asked him what he wanted for Christmas. "Aphids," he replied. His kind godfather provided a box of stick insects as an approximation. The stick insects did attract George's attention—he liked to watch their moon-walking progress from one side of their box to another—and they lived for several years in a corner of the bathroom in seeming contentment. But I now realize that George hadn't actually been asking for aphids at all. When asked what he wanted, he had replied "aphids" simply because he associated the word "aphids" with the word "want." This was because in Eric Carle's story *The Bad-Tempered Ladybird* the protagonist repeats the phrase "I want those aphids." George's "request" showed that despite his apparently precocious vocabulary and speech patterns, he profoundly misunderstood the intention behind much of what was said to him.

It also showed that he had little, if any, concept of what Christmas was all about. This wouldn't have been because he couldn't remember the previous Christmas. George's memory is extraordinary; I sometimes think that he's never forgotten anything at all, and that his lack of an ability to edit or organize his memory is one of his main problems. No, George certainly remembered Christmas. He didn't understand the standard "What do you want for Christmas?" question because he hadn't cottoned on to the giving-and-receiving idea. He didn't know what presents were for, either practically or symbolically. He didn't have the slightest notion of what he was supposed to want.

Never is the difference between the autistic and the neurotypical child more pronounced than at Christmas. Neurotypical children pick up the Christmas behavior patterns—the rituals and traditions—really, really fast. By four, all neurotypical children understand presents. They enjoy the expectation, the novelty, the surprise; the act of unwrapping is in itself a pleasure. They know that a particular present comes from a particular person; they are capable of rudimentary gratitude, and some appreciation that a gift is a token of affection or goodwill, though they may not be able to mask their dismay if the present doesn't satisfy their expectations. They are just about old enough to enjoy giving something in return, and they are gratified by the expressions of delight on the part of the recipients. They are also old enough—just—to feel envy if another child has received something more desirable. And they will have no difficulty in distinguishing their own new possessions from those of their siblings. Jake's capacity to distinguish one trifling item from another—say, the bottle of bubble mixture found in his stocking from the one found in Sam's—never ceases to amaze me.

Autistic four-year-olds have very different reactions to presents. Some—usually lower-functioning, like Sam—will sniff each package and, if it smells of chocolate, will rip it open regardless of who it's intended for, social rules blithely ignored. The more able may be worried by presents. This was certainly true of George. They may come to like the toy inside, though with their restricted play skills it's harder to find toys that will appeal. But they won't like the element of surprise. They won't see the point of wrapping paper, unless they enjoy the physical sensation of tearing it off. Most of them would much rather be handed their Thomas the Tank Engine video in an unceremonial, straightforward manner. And if they understand the connection between present and donor at all, they'll be bothered by the pressure of expectation. Some sort of social response is expected of them. They don't understand which response, or why. The whole business makes them agitated and confused.

It's hard for an adult to accept this reaction. It's deeply ingrained in us that children want *things,* that acquisition is central to every child's enjoyment of life. Many adults aren't confident of giving pleasure to a child, or being liked by a child, unless they have brought them something. This is a pity, but it's common. The autistic child's indifference to, or active dislike of, being given things is yet another barrier to forming relationships. My Uncle Norman, on a recent visit, wanted to give each boy a five-pound note. Their reactions were entirely characteristic. Jake wanted to put his into his piggy bank straightaway. George squealed, "No, Norman, I don't like money." Sam simply threw his back across the table. Norman, who is used to the boys, was more than able to cope with rejection, but for less well-prepared adults such a reaction could be surprising and upsetting.

I couldn't quite believe, myself, the depth of George's antipathy to Christmas presents. (Sam, as usual, was more indifferent than hostile, and besides, in the days of his obsessions it was relatively easy to find things that would give immediate satisfaction, like toy helicopters and rubber snakes.) When George shrieked with horror at the sight of a parcel, or clapped his hands over his ears—which is what he still does if he wants to evade social demands—I would often conclude that he must be ill, or overtired. No child, surely, could be *frightened* of presents? And there were plenty of things he liked—some books, some toys, some videos. Could he really be so bitterly opposed to getting more? Yes, he could. Or rather, I failed to recognize that what George was objecting to was the ritual, the social palaver, that surrounds present giving, rather than the toy inside. If I unwrapped his presents myself, and left them lying about, getting a little battered and becoming part of the landscape, they eventually became acceptable. Then, perhaps, in an offhand manner, I would introduce the concept of giving. "Grandfather gave you that," I might remark, weeks after Christmas; "Caroline chose that for you." Depending on mood, such comments might be met by a quick shriek of disapproval or by quiet acceptance, even interest.

What should you do about a child who expressly rejects presents? You could, I suppose, ask family and friends not to waste their time and money on buying them anything at all. But this doesn't take into account the fact that most adults want to give things. People want to be kind, and the more handicapped the child is, the kinder they want to be. You could ask them just to give the cash equivalent, so that you can choose something acceptable, but this seems too functional and joyless. The best way, I think, is to explain the child's likely reaction, and ask people not to take it personally when a proffered gift is dropped straight into the wastepaper basket. (This has happened!) It's hard for feelings not to be just a teeny bit hurt, but, well, they're adults.

I think that people should go on giving presents, and the parent should stage-manage their distribution in whichever way is appropriate. Despite their negative reactions, nearly all the toys, clothes, books, videos, CDs, tapes, and so on, that give the boys real pleasure have been given by one generous person or another. I rarely have to buy them anything. Over the years, grandparents, godparents, aunts, uncles, cousins, and friends have shown great ingenuity in the presents they've found for the boys. I'm very grateful. I can't pretend that gratitude is a concept that George and Sam have grasped as yet, but I like to think we're inching toward it. It's unusual that I, as a parent, have to train my children to learn to tolerate presents, but if they can master it, it'll bring them a few steps closer to inclusion in the "normal" world. For the same reason, we celebrate their birthdays in a fairly conventional way, with guests, presents, cake, and candles. By making the celebration predictable, the boys have learned to do more than just cope with their birthdays—they actually enjoy them in a mild way.

Donors who have been discouraged in the past by the boys' less-than-gracious reaction to their offerings should take heart. Because, in autism, play skills are delayed, many toys are still in use that would ordinarily have been consigned to formless ruin or oblivion. When Aunt Caroline gave the infant Sam twelve wooden men in a boat, who could have foreseen that he'd be doing math with them at age eleven? Who could predict that thirteen-year-old George's preferred reading would be inscribed, "To George, with love from Granny Eva, Christmas 1993"? The boys' condition dispenses with ideas of what age—or gender—is appropriate. If they can use it, then it's very welcome, whatever it is. Jake, going through a toy box recently, said, "I've grown out of this rattle. I think I'll give it to Sam."

It's not only present giving that makes Christmas different or difficult for autistic children. Most people's Christmases involve increased sociability, more visitors, noise, and chatter that will be incomprehensible or even alarming. Few autists understand the point of conversational exchange in its own right. Then there's the special food and drink, which may appeal to some, but for most, Kanner's "desire for the preservation of sameness" will not be waived for Christmas fare. As a family, we go in for Christmas dinner in quite a big way. Stuffings, sauces, homemade pudding and mince pies, a different wine for each course—our Christmas meal takes no prisoners. But there's nothing on the groaning table that Sam actually wants to eat, except the outsides of the sugared almonds, and the icing on the cake. For most autists, their idea of a satisfactory Christmas meal is whatever they usually have; three fish fingers cut into quarters, dry cornflakes in a green bowl, orange squash with two bendy straws, or unrestricted access to a tube of Pringles.

Is that sad? Not necessarily. I see no need to deprive the neurotypical members of the family of their feast. Sam's enjoyment of his Alphabites won't be enhanced if we all eat them with him. I try to make him something that looks a little festive—say, a jelly decorated with a few sweets—but by and large, his social aloofness is quite handy. He doesn't begrudge us our gourmandizing, doesn't feel excluded because none of it appeals to him. He's got his eye on that cake icing; nothing else matters much.

Some aspects of Christmas do appeal strongly to the boys. They like decorations—glittery, sparkly ones, but also the branches of holly and yew, the trails of ivy and swags of bay, which we use to transform the house into an indoor forest. The boys, by autistic standards, aren't particularly resistant to change of this kind—perhaps they can see it's only temporary. George loves the Christmas tree. One year, in October, he sat himself down in the room where we normally put it, and announced that he was going to stay there until the tree arrived.

For George and Sam, Christmas is a pagan festival of light, heat, and color. They both love fires and candles and bits of ribbon and tinsel to flap. If the weather is icy or stormy, so much the better; both of them respond to elemental extremes. As a parent, I have to say that there are some advantages in the autistic attitude to Christmas. Alone among my friends, I'm not beleaguered by requests for expensive rubbish advertised on television or discussed on the school playground. I don't have to cope with the covetousness, disappointment, and hysterical overexcitement that so often tempers the normal child's genuine enjoyment.

George is capable of accepting some changes in routine as exciting. Sam is more troubled by the disruption, but even for him, there are aspects of Christmas that he welcomes. Not Father Christmas, though. Like most mothers, I introduced the idea of Father Christmas early on. George was appalled. A man with a deep voice and a beard? Like that terrifying individual who came to service the boiler? In *his* bedroom? At night? "No, Father Christmas is NOT coming to George's house," he stated. The terror has lessened over the years, and now, at thirteen, he shows some mild enthusiasm for Santa. He even wrote him a letter. "Dear Father Christmas. I would like a stick of rock and some firewood. Love from George." Sam remains impassive. When F.C. visits his school, he hardly reacts. Why should he? It's just another incomprehensible adult.

If I'd known the boys were autistic, I don't think I'd have let Father Christmas into their lives in the first place. The point of him is to give delight, a delight that comes not just from the bulging stocking but from the magic and mystery, the sense of a benign presence who is ungraspable, but who has the child's best interests at heart. Autistic children don't want to be singled out by a bearded stranger, and they don't collude in magic because it involves the use of mentalizing skills they simply don't possess. A normal one-year-old doesn't understand magic either, because she hasn't yet grasped the concept of shared belief. In this respect many autists never progress far beyond that one-year-old level. To appreciate magic, you need a firm grasp of what's normal, what's expected. Autists, who see the world in disconnected detail rather than as a coherent whole, lack that overview of normality.

Now, we continue with Father Christmas mainly for the benefit of Jake, who at five is still a staunch believer. He'd be outraged if his brothers didn't get stockings. It's taken me years to train the boys to put their hands into their stockings. For a long time, they never thought of hunting for anything that wasn't on view. Out of sight was out of mind. If a favorite book was in a different place on the bookshelf, they couldn't find it. They never rummaged through a toy box (though they did, and do, rummage through handbags in the reasonable expectation that they will find Life Savers and chewing gum). So it was with their stockings. Father Christmas would leave a lollipop sticking out of the top. They would pull these out, grin, and eat them. But it wouldn't occur to them to look further. I must be one of the few mothers in the land who is still urging her children to pull things out of their stockings well into the New Year.

The Father Christmas business also raises the problems of instilling beliefs into autistic children. In a normal child, the gradual waning of belief in Santa is a rite of passage. I've never come across a child who felt cheated or deceived by finding out the truth. The child seems to understand instinctively that the whole thing is a friendly deception well suited to infancy. Children are not deeply rational; they want to believe in magic, but, at a certain stage, guessing the truth gives them a pleasing sense of importance. They recognize that the nature of their collusion with adults has changed.

They recognize that to expose the deception to a younger child is unkind and unfair. But none of this applies to an autistic child. A more able autist, with typical literal-mindedness and regard for accuracy, may object to having been told a lie. The less able will simply accept whatever they're told without question. George's early fear of Father Christmas didn't prevent him from believing in him. George believes everything he's told. His intellectual passivity, his very limited ability to question things, may mean that he never will stop believing that Father Christmas rides on a sleigh and comes down the chimney.

What of the other big issue of belief—the Christmas story itself? Whatever your own beliefs or nonbeliefs, if, as I have done, you send your children to Church of England primary schools, there's no avoiding the "true meaning of Christmas." Nativity plays bring a mist to the eyes of the stoutest atheist, and it's a stern parent indeed who throws cold water on his five-year-old's enthusiasm for Baby Jesus. "He who mocks the infant's faith / Shall be mocked in age and death," wrote Blake. I'm an agnostic, but Jake is devout, and I'm happy for him to be so. Never are the consolations of religion more obvious than when one attempts to explain the mysteries of life and death to an anxious child. Jake has curiosity about the numinous, the intangible; he wants to know what happens beyond the here and now. Besides, his understanding of culture, history, and politics would be terribly diminished if I withheld religion from him. I tell him Bible stories, and though I do punctuate discussions about the afterlife with riders along the lines of "Some people think . . ." I try to leave his core beliefs intact.

For George and Sam, it's a different matter. When Sam was at the mainstream primary school, he received a report that simply said, "Religious knowledge: Not Applicable." How do you approach the idea of an afterlife to a child who seems unable to think outside the present? How do you explain the central moral tenets of Christianity—or of any faith—to someone who does not relate his behavior to that of anyone else, someone who cannot commit an altruistic act because he cannot think himself into the position of another person? Even the most rudimentary religious understanding involves contextualizing. It involves curiosity about the origins of life, the nature of death. It involves using one's imagination.

I'm not saying that all autists are incapable of religious experience or religious instinct. Some, I expect, would appreciate the way a religion provides a clear code of conduct, a set of rules to organize behavior. Others might enjoy the ritual of religious ceremony, a pleasingly reliable pattern with room for those slight variations that seem to fascinate some autists so much. And there may well be an element of aesthetic response. Both George and Sam like going into churches and cathedrals. George looks up at the ceiling and says, "Wow!" and Sam tests the acoustics with his verbal stims, which means our visits tend to be brief. George likes "church music" (including "You Can't Always Get What You Want" by the Rolling Stones, because it features choirlike chanting), and, to a limited extent, he likes the reliable cast of characters who turn up in paintings or stained-glass windows—he's certainly able to identify Mary, Joseph, shepherds, kings, and so on. But the normal range of childish questions about who made the world and where we go when we die remain unasked.

Jake and I have just been on holiday in Italy. A great thrill was putting a coin in a box and lighting an offertory candle. It took Jake no time at all to grasp the concept of asking God for something special, and he knew that "something special" didn't mean a new Game Boy, either. I remember Sam, at a similar age, spotting the bank of candles at the end of a church in France. With a roar of "Cake!" he ran the length of the church and blew the whole lot out.

God, Father Christmas, and the Tooth Fairy worry and baffle George and make almost no impact on Sam. The Tooth Fairy we can dispense with; the boys don't want money, and besides, I've hardly ever seen any of their milk teeth once they're out. I think they must have all been swallowed. With Father Christmas it's a case of "I've started so I'll finish," though I do feel it might have been better never to have started. As for God, I feel wary of attempting to introduce an idea that, if it were grasped at all, would be swallowed whole. Belief in God has many uses for Jake, and I'm happy to concur with him. When he's older, he'll have a sufficiently broad experience and understanding to make his own mind up, and I hope I'll respect the faith, or lack of faith, he chooses. Belief has no uses for George and Sam—though this could change with time—so I leave it more or less untouched.

If I were a firm believer, would their imperviousness to religion worry me? I don't think so. Autists present a fascinating challenge to the theologically inclined. Their absence of altruism, their underdeveloped moral sense, is balanced by an absence of malice, an almost prelapsarian innocence. George once said to baby Jake, who was crying, "Jake, Tinky-Winky created you for good, but you've turned out evil." This sounds profound, but it is in fact an adaptation of a line from *Wallace and Gromit*. George does not truly understand the meaning of good and evil, nor is he (as yet) capable of implementing either. Most of the Ten Commandments are easy for the boys to keep. The Seven Deadly Sins are largely an irrelevance. The boys might covet their neighbor's ox—or their neighbor's ice pop—but the desire would be purely for the ox or ice lolly itself, unaccompanied by any desire to get one over on the neighbor. Any temptations they feel arise from their overriding private preoccupations, not from the kinds of torments that neurotypical flesh is heir to. I met a very intelligent Asperger's boy in his late teens, who was a fanatical Lib Dem (if that's not a contradiction in terms) and followed the workings of Parliament with close attention. At the time, a number of sexual scandals among politicians of the Chelsea-strip variety were coming to light. This boy, who wanted to become a politician himself, had the answer. "I know how to avoid a sexual scandal!" he announced. "If somebody said they wanted to suck my toes, I'd just say, 'No, thank you.'"

Wise words. This boy would not have been remotely tempted by any of the usual pitfalls, though when it came to resisting the temptation to recount everything there is to know about the Russian Revolution, he was as weak as water. What would a Christian theologian make of George and Sam's absence of sin? Though the Ten Commandments would pose few problems for them, Jesus's most important commandment—that one should love one's neighbor as oneself—would be impossible for them to attain, having so little sense, as they do, of what Uta Frith calls the "last visible self," the tiny homunculus who oversees all the executive operations of the brain.

In the instance of religion, as in so many other ways, autism challenges our assumptions about what it means to be human.

Christopher Smart in his poem "My Cat Jeoffry" describes his cat as "an instrument for the children to learn benevolence upon." Perhaps this is the most comfortable way to consider the boys, from a Christian point of view. Good and evil may be closed to them, but they can be instruments for us to learn benevolence upon; unwittingly, they provide a yardstick for neurotypical moral behavior.

SEVENTEEN

Wear and Tear

I'm making a visitor a cup of coffee. "Sugar?" I ask, silently willing the answer to be "No." "Yes, please," comes the reply. I fish my tangle of keys out of my pocket, move quickly to the cupboard and unlock it, trying not to attract the attention of George and Sam. I fail. They leap down from their vantage point on top of the Aga and bound across the kitchen. I reach for the sugar, keep the boys at bay with swift jabbing movements of my elbows, spoon the sugar into the coffee, and return the bowl to the cupboard as if I were a wild dog protecting a zebra haunch from a swarm of hungry rivals. In an autistic household, the physical and emotional effort involved in performing the simple acts of everyday life can be considerable.

What would happen if I do what normal people do—leave the sugar bowl on the table, or on a shelf, or in an unlocked cupboard? Well, the boys would help themselves to it, sometimes with spoons, sometimes with their hands, sometimes sticking their tongues straight in. What they didn't eat would be scattered far and wide, so there'd be a patina of stickiness to clear up, as well as no sugar left for anyone else, and a pair of buzzing, hyperactive boys. My hypothetical visitor may be startled by my defensive elbow action, but he'd be even more startled, and disgusted, by the sight of the boys licking spilled sugar direct from table or floor. And he wouldn't know about the advances I've already made with coffeemaking. Time was when the coffee and milk would also have been locked up, not because the boys wanted to eat them, but because they loved tipping them over the floor or down the sink. I now have a shelf next to the Aga on which jars of spice and bottles of oil are placed in full view. That's progress. I still shudder at the memory of the gallon can of olive oil that Sam upended; I came into the kitchen to find oil creeping across the floor, an advancing golden tide.

Both boys have a habit of putting things into an approximation of the right place. One of them—I don't know which—filled the kettle with orange juice. Liquid does go into a kettle, doesn't it? I didn't realize and switched it on. The air filled with the aroma of cooking marmalade. I sometimes dry out wet boots and shoes in the very coolest oven of the Aga. George popped his trainers into the roasting oven. The stench was indescribable.

I'm so used to the need for constant vigilance in small matters that I no longer feel the strain of it. It's the same kind of vigilance that any parent of toddlers needs to exercise, but in our case the "toddlers" are strong and agile, and the need to supervise them will continue indefinitely. Though it has to be said that they're much easier than they were. They'll still appear as if from nowhere when they hear the click of the food cupboard being opened, but they're far more responsive, post-ABA therapy, to the word "no." They have no conscience, no inner voice to tell them that they mustn't touch this or that, but if an adult's there to give commands, they'll usually desist. The hundreds of tiny rules and tricks that have to be observed in order to keep home life from degenerating into chaos have become second nature to me and to the other adults who spend a lot of time with the boys. Visitors, however, constantly underestimate their speed and cunning. "I'll just put my tablets out of reach," they say, putting their little vial of poison on a shelf a couple of feet up, not realizing that Sam has the climbing skills of Spider-man. "I didn't think he saw me put it there," they confess, referring to George, whose eyesight would put the average eagle to shame.

I can't think of any aspect of daily living that hasn't been encroached upon by autism in some way, at some time. Take the car. George used to jump up and down on the roof, making huge dents. Both boys like sitting inside the car. Sometimes, to give myself a few minutes' peace, I'd leave them in there for a bit, but if I didn't remember to remove any cassettes, I'd come back to find them all eviscerated. Once, Sam ripped up the car tax sticker disc. I painstakingly pieced it back together, but was told that mosaic-effect tax discs weren't recognized by law. Then there were the more obvious hazards of letting children play in cars, like lights left on and twisted mirrors. And once or twice I've come back to find the seat smeared with excrement, though this hasn't happened for ages.

What a useless mother, you're thinking. Why did she let them play in the car at all? Well, because they wanted to. And because at the stage when they were wreaking most havoc in the car, they'd have been wreaking equal amounts of havoc in the house, and I prefer my house to my car, by miles. Smearing excrement, for instance, could happen anywhere. It's a popular hobby within the autistic community, especially at the lower-functioning end of the spectrum. I met the mother of a severely autistic sixteen-year-old, and asked her, nervously, about the problems of adolescence.

"Oh, masturbation's a godsend," she replied breezily. "It's so much better than smearing." Oddly, it was the more superficially socialized George, rather than Sam, who had the more passionate engagement with feces. Touch wood, he's left that stage behind, but I still have to check the lavatories regularly. There are messy seats to be wiped, blockages caused by overenthusiastic bottom-wiping to be shifted. Sometimes George uses a whole, unraveled roll of paper to wipe his bottom, and then replaces it. Hand towels can also be used for this purpose. Donna Williams explains that it's easy for the autist to confuse the functions of slightly similar items. If it's whitish and squarish and lives near the lavatory, then it'll get used as lavatory paper. Alien objects are sometimes inserted into the pan. George put the video of *A Bug's Life* down the toilet the other day. *"Why?"* I bellowed. "Because I didn't want to watch it," replied George, only mildly abashed. Well, ask a silly question.

Sam went through a phase of flushing underwear away. It was hard to prevent this. My usual answer with Sam is to keep things locked away out of temptation, but it's not realistic to lock up every item of clothing, and you can't lock lavatories from the outside, because if the boys can't gain immediate access to them, they'll use something else instead. Sam has had periods of weeing in alternative receptacles just for fun—tooth mugs, toy boats, that kind of thing. Unfortunately, his choices are often insufficiently capacious. This habit is clearly not one to encourage, so the lavatories needed to stay unlocked. Like most of Sam's "challenging" behaviors, the interest in underwear disposal ran its course. When he was down to his last pair of pants and socks, he stopped doing it. Months later, when we had work done on the drains, the builders were surprised to find a couple of garbage bags' worth of stagnant undies.

I do now lock the bathroom from the outside. There are just so many enjoyable activities, from flooding to squirting toothpaste and shaving foam to running a bath and getting in with all your clothes on. George likes to wash his trainers, which involves immersing them in water and rubbing them with a bar of soap. He doesn't always take his feet out first. If he can't get into the bathroom, he'll perform this operation in the washing-up bowl or the garden water tank. Then there are medical supplies. George once dressed a small finger wound with forty Band-Aids. They made a rather neat globe, like a harvest mouse's nest. Sam once ate one hundred vitamin pills. I rang the hospital; apparently it doesn't matter as long as they haven't got iron in them.

Small irritations are more characteristic of life with the boys than major panics. Luke Jackson says he can quite understand why his younger brother Joe takes the laces out of everybody's shoes, and the batteries out of their toys—Joe enjoys chain reactions, and holding a battery is like holding "a little piece of power." I suspect there are reasons behind all the strange things the boys do, although George can rarely explain, Sam never. As I write, I'm looking through the window at George, who's in the garden. He's picking bees out of the fennel and holding them by their wings. He knows about bee stings. He's been stung in the past. Now I feel it's up to him. George likes insects, but I shouldn't think the feeling's mutual. The other day he came in with round green blotches all over his face, looking like a cartoon alien. He'd been stubbing out caterpillars on himself, like cigarettes. There's no malice involved; he doesn't set out to hurt caterpillars. It's just that he can't understand that squashing them causes them pain. His mentalizing powers don't extend even that far.

Now he's come in from the garden and into the room where I'm working. He's chewing a bit of paper towel. This is one of his most harmless habits, but for some reason it's one that particularly annoys me. He sorts through the pile of receipts I'd put out to send the tax man, and he's turning some of them into flappers. They're not much good. He's moved on to a Jiffy bag, and he's tearing a strip off it. It never crosses his mind that I might have a use for those receipts or that Jiffy bag, or that he's disturbing my work. He's not thinking about me at all. His entire mental energy is focused on finding something satisfying to flap.

Both boys leave a trail of minor destruction in their wake. Flower heads may be snapped off, especially juicy ones like tulips. Drinks may be spilled—one of the most irritating things George does is turn "empty" cups and beakers upside down when he's finished with them. Of course, there's always a drop left, so they leave a sticky ring. Sam tears the round bits off jigsaw pieces. They both snap sticks—I've just had to mend a broken flagpole brought to me by a distraught Jake. If there's a small hole in a sheet or a garment, Sam will enlarge it. He doesn't like buttons, and bites them off. As I write, he's come through the door, chewing the raised Harry Potter lettering off the front of his T-shirt. Sam's not destroying his T-shirt because he's angry. He's doing it because he is either annoyed or attracted by the rubberiness of the lettering, but he often does vent anger in physical ways, like tearing a book or breaking a toy. Despite George's apparently greater social awareness, it's more likely to be Sam who uses destructive behavior to express emotions. George is almost never defiant, but Sam will have one eye on me as he launches an assault on something he believes I value. I have to be quick off the mark to make sure that thing isn't Jake.

As I hope I will by now have made clear, the autist can have an abnormal response to absolutely anything, be it ever so mundane or apparently inoffensive. And the responses won't remain constant; the boys can change their minds and reverse their opinions. Take anything—take shoes. George was at one stage always barefoot; at another he would wear Wellingtons on the hottest day. He put his shoes on the wrong feet every day for a whole term, and it didn't make any difference my swapping them over, because as soon as I wasn't looking he'd swap them back. He wore slippers (huge, shaped like leopards) everywhere—in the snow, to the shops, on the train. Then he went off slippers completely. At one time only shoes with laces would do; at another laces were anathema. Whatever his preferred footwear at any time, his decision is absolute. This summer, the very hot summer of 2003, nothing would induce him to wear open sandals. Last year, they were all he would tolerate. I don't know what criteria George uses when fussing about his shoes. The one thing I'm sure of is that ideas about fashion or looking cool are never, ever an issue.

Autistic minds run along single tracks. This means that the mental force they bring to bear on achieving their goals is immense. At any time, my mind is trying to cope with hundreds of things at once; persuading George to wear sandals is only one of them. At the same moment, all George's mental energy is concentrated on avoiding sandals. It's easy to guess who wins.

Both boys have "issues" around nearly everything they eat, wear, sit on, watch, or touch. Pajamas are another case in point. When he was very young, George wanted to control the pajama wearing of the whole family. He would set his choices out on the bathroom radiators and become distressed if we didn't bend to his will. He still tries to control Sam's pajama wearing; it's not worth putting Sam to bed in pajamas that George deems "wrong," because in the middle of the night George will rip them off him. Sam used to find it immensely difficult to get out of his pajamas and into his clothes, so much so that I used to send him to school in his pajamas, and press a bagful of clothes into the hand of the waiting teacher. Then I changed tack, and put him to bed in his school uniform, minus the shoes. I just didn't have the two hours needed every morning to get him changed. This was one of the many "issues" that his home tutors have successfully addressed. He still takes a long time to dress in the morning, but it's half an hour now rather than two.

You need to be healthy in body and mind to deal with children like mine. You need energy, strength, and stamina; it's a hands-on job. Like many parents, I'm irritated by the overcautious attitude toward physical contact in schools insisted on by current legislation. I don't believe it's sensible or desirable to look after any young children without touching them, and for children with any sort of handicap it's impossible. There are times when George and Sam just have to be grabbed or restrained, for their own safety or the safety of other people. Any medical treatment will require a degree of physical coercion; the boys are impervious to reason, cajoling, or even bribes when it comes to taking medicine. All their normal, routine physical care is difficult—I still have to straddle Sam's chest if I want to brush his teeth properly. Hair washing and cutting, trimming finger and toenails, checking for head lice, foot measuring, the application of sunscreen, the dressing of wounds—the boys aren't going to submit willingly to any of it. You need speed, cunning, and, sometimes, moderate force. Thank goodness their adult teeth have come through reasonably straight and well spaced; orthodontic treatment is something I'm happy not to have to tackle. The ABA/VB therapy addresses these areas, and there has been progress. A few weeks ago Sam, accompanied by Delia and Ian, went to the barber's in Battle for a triumphantly successful haircut.

Touch wood, neither of them has been seriously ill. They don't complain about minor ailments, so these tend to go untreated, and I can't see that any harm has been done. They seem to have many fewer minor illnesses than most children, which suggests to me that the link between minor illness and thinking about illness is strong even in young children. It never occurs to George and Sam to be ill, so they're not.

Of course they do occasionally need treatment. Both have had general anesthetics to remove rotten teeth—dental work without a general anesthetic wouldn't be possible. Given their poor diet and the difficulty of inserting a toothbrush between their gritted lips, I'm surprised they haven't had more decay. The last extraction was about eighteen months ago. George was at the height of his food-refusing phase, and perhaps pain from the bad tooth contributed to it, though he never mentioned it. This was also a time at which he was reluctant to leave the house at all. I had to get him to the (unfamiliar) hospital for the operation. His quasi anorexia worked in my favor in carrying out the nil-by-mouth instructions, but coaxing him into the car was no easy matter. I allowed two hours for the twenty-minute journey, and we needed it. Once in the car, we drove around and around Bexhill listening to Bach. This had a soothing effect; eventually George, wearing Wellingtons, agreed to enter the hospital. He sat in the waiting room, shrieking and refusing to be weighed. In the end I had to stand on the scales with George in my arms and have my weight subtracted from the total. Again, his self-imposed starvation came in useful. It's not every mother who can easily scoop up her gangly twelve-year-old son.

He wouldn't tolerate the pre-med. I could see that no amount of plea bargaining was going to work; the gentle approach was only prolonging the agony. I asked the hospital staff to hold him down and administer the anesthetic by mask, not by needle. Brutal as that may look, it's quicker and therefore kinder. Six adults were needed. The struggle wasn't pleasant, but the tooth had to come out.

In the waiting room, the other parents and children had been staring at us, horrified. In the recovery room, roles were reversed. The other children moaned and groaned and extorted huge promises from their parents about game cubes and PlayStation Twos. George sat up, spat out some blood, drank some water, and said, "Let's go home now, Mum." No fuss, no whingeing. The only thing he insisted on was taking his bloodstained hospital blanket home. The nurse gave us his vast diseased molar, blackened and craggy like a citadel torched by barbarians. She presented it in a sweet little bag decorated with a pink fairy and blue elf, perched on a crescent moon.

The house is full of small signs of autism. The locked doors and cupboards are the obvious ones, but there are others, if you know what you're looking for. Any framed photographs have been placed facedown by George, who finds photographs of people too much for his nerves. A search through the kitchen bin will reveal evidence of Sam—a T-shirt he's ripped up, the chewed-up tires off one of Jake's toy lorries, a bowl and plate that he's thrown away along with their rejected contents. I usually give Sam plastic tableware, for this reason. Whenever I take the rubbish out, I have a quick check to make sure that Sam's definition of rubbish has coincided with my own.

Despite the mess he creates with food, paint, felt pens, and so on, Sam has a tidy mind. Boots and shoes will always be placed neatly in pairs. He stuffs his socks down into the toe of his shoes. He doesn't like to see coats or sweaters lying about and will always present them to their owners. He picks up stray toys and puts them away, though rarely in the right places. Sam's tidying-up techniques have refined themselves since the days when he used to throw everything out of the window.

A few months ago, George's main interest in life was sweet wrappers—only certain kinds, of course. He collected these and left them in little patterns around the house—seven yellow lollipop sticks in a fan shape, blue Softmint wrappers draped along the top of the radiator. It was quite hard to explain to helpful visitors why "having a bit of a tidy-up" would send George into a hysterical frenzy, just as it's hard to persuade people not to say to George, "Goodness, haven't you grown!" ("I won't! I won't! I'll stay little forever!") The mini-obsession with sweet wrappers disappeared as quickly and suddenly as it came on, to be replaced by a tiresome habit of throwing things down behind bookcases and radiators. Milk bills, bank statements, photographs, school reports, all disappear unless I whisk them quickly away. He'll give up on this soon, I expect. It's always been the pattern with both boys that one habit or fad disappears, to be replaced by another. It keeps me on my toes.

Autism directs the way I lead my life, in big things and in small. I say "directs" rather than "dictates"; I try to work around the obstacles that restrict my freedom, though I have to accept that many of them are unmovable. Unlike most parents, I can't foresee a time when my children will be independent of me. For the foreseeable future, their needs will come first in any plans I make. I'm fortunate in that, as a writer, I can work from home, and fit my working hours around their timetables. I'm also lucky in that I live in the place I like best. Moving house would, I imagine, be traumatic for most autists, change-resistant as they are, but I don't want to move, now or ever. My travel opportunities are limited, though I do get my breaks. I don't feel I can leave the boys for more than a week, more out of consideration for the exhausted babysitters than for any other reason. But I do manage to get away without them for a few days a couple of times a year, which is more than most parents of normal children manage. I can't travel much with George and Sam. It's the journey that's the most difficult thing. I did take them to France a couple of times when they were younger, but George really hated being on the plane (I think it was the noise) and the airport was not an ideal environment. "Whose child is that?" I heard someone say, as I struggled with the buckles on Sam's stroller. I felt I could guess whose child it was. I wheeled around, just in time to see George's feet disappearing through the curtain on the luggage carousel.

At the moment, foreign travel for them isn't worth the disruption and stress. We manage a few days with family in Dorset or Devon (long car rides aren't a problem), and then Jake and I go abroad for a week with friends, leaving the other two at home. They may dislike my absence, but they're not capable of feeling that Jake's being given preferential treatment, any more than they would notice or mind if Jake's Christmas present was more expensive than theirs. They can't imagine what it would be like to be in a place they've never visited, and if they could, that wouldn't make them curious to go there. East, west, home's best, as far as George and Sam are concerned.

So, I accommodate my life to theirs, but I still retain a good deal of scope within it. The petty restrictions are, if anything, harder to tolerate than the big limitations. At home, I can't have things just how I want them. I love the sight of a pretty china bowl piled with fruit, but if I leave such a thing unattended on the table, each piece of fruit will be bitten, and the bits spat out. Whether there are three apples in the bowl or thirty, they'll get the same treatment. I'd be happy if the fruit was eaten properly, actually digested, but it isn't. This annoys me, but I remind myself that it's only quite recently that I've been able to leave vases of flowers around the house. In the past, the water from the vases would have been tipped up or drunk, the flowers shredded. Now flowers are largely unmolested, so perhaps one day I'll be able to put the fruit bowls back out . . .

I'd like to be able to have a bath without anybody else joining me in it. I'd like to open my handbag without finding a bitten-off lipstick or a capless, leaking pen. I'd like to be able to leave a pot boiling on the stove while I answer the door, without finding that an ingredient I hadn't bargained for has been added in my absence. I'd like to be able to watch television; usually I can't, because the boys go to bed late, and while they're up, they often want a video. Buying a separate TV for myself wouldn't be an answer, because George and Sam still have to be supervised. I can't sit in a separate room and concentrate on something else while they're still rampant.

I'd love to be able to get on with anything—reading, writing, gardening—secure in the knowledge that my sons are all safely and constructively occupied without my constant vigilance. I'd like not to have to load the washing machine twice a day. I'd love to be able to do what my friends do—act spontaneously, pile their children into the car, and say, "It's a lovely day. Let's go to the beach" or "We're all going to spend the night with the so-and-sos." But this is just how life is, and I don't waste time or energy fretting about it. One good thing about having children like mine is that they don't leave you much spare time for gloomy ruminations.

EIGHTEEN

Compensations

Have I made life in an autistic family sound like hell? That hasn't been my intention. There are moments of extreme stress, but isn't that the case in most families? Our tensions, our flash points, are different from those of your average family, but who's to say they're more intolerable?

Perhaps this life would be hellish if I riled against it. Hell—my definition, anyway—is a place where you don't want to be, and from which you can't get out. When you have autistic children, there is no respite, either for them or for you. When they were younger, I used to watch them sometimes, and ask them, silently, look, couldn't you stop being autistic for a bit? Just for one day? I mean, a joke's a joke, lads, but this one's gone far enough. But I've long since settled into a fairly calm acceptance. They are what they are. That's all there is to it.

Our family life has its own rhythms, its own compensations. Every day, the boys make me feel bored and irritated; equally, every day they provide me with delight, amusement, and joy. The sight of them at supper last night, for instance. They all sat down at the table together: good. Time was when that would have been an impossibility. But I still can't serve them with the same meal. Last night, Jake had pizza, carrots, sugar snap peas, grapes, a plum, and a mug of milk. Sam had a bowl of Day-Glo-colored cereal called Rainbow Drops, most of which lived up to their name and dropped to the floor. George had the carcass of Sunday's roast duck. He hauled this out of the pantry himself, and tore at it with his teeth, like Obelix devouring a wild boar. The duck was still on its serving dish. George chomped on the skin and licked up the fat. To many, this would not have been a pretty sight, but I found it funny. Of course, on one level I wish that George and Sam would eat the carrots and the sugar snaps, but I can't worry about that all the time. What makes me smile is the way that every single thing they do is so utterly characteristic. Never imagine that a child who doesn't talk or play much lacks character. "Autism" is an umbrella term; the condition in no way reduces individuality. The boys express their characters in their every tiny action, and individuality is something I'm inclined to celebrate. When George had finished slavering over his dead duck, he said to me, "Thanks, mademoiselle." A little later, he asked, "Can you get spaghetti from an owl?"

As a rule of thumb, as long as the boys are happy, I'm happy. There have been times—there still are times, perhaps always will be times—when they are far from happy. Sam, in particular, has frequent periods of distress, though these are not as prolonged or as intense as they once were. His agitation, his tearless crying, the noise that Clara Claiborne Park calls the "banshee wail," still cuts me to the quick, every time. It's difficult to be the mother of a child who can't explain what's bothering him. It's as if I'm fighting an unseen enemy. Is he in pain? Is it something he's eaten? Is he frightened? Has he misunderstood something he's heard us discussing? Sam's shrieks could mean anything, from appendicitis to the fact that I've put his biscuits on a green plate instead of a blue one. The field of possibilities is dauntingly wide. It goes against the basic instincts of motherhood to raise children who can't be calmed, or comforted, or even properly fed. But the bad periods do seem to be growing shorter. The smiles, the social overtures, are becoming more frequent.

I learned, long ago, that loving children like these had to be unconditional. That's true of loving all children, actually, but with autism you quickly learn that you can't look for gratitude or reciprocity. You can't expect them to consider your feelings or share your interests. This wasn't a hard lesson to master. Loving them is the easy part. They're very loveable. Luckily, I'm not the only person who feels this. Some people may be alarmed or repelled by them, but others are attracted; both George and Sam have always had a secure fan base. Why should this be? As children go, they're unfriendly, indifferent, aloof. When Granny Eva fell downstairs and hurt her hand quite badly, she called out, "George, can you help me?" George trilled, "No, I can't," as he ran gaily past. How loveable is that? Part of their charm lies in their incorruptible innocence, which underlies even George's apparently callous response to his stricken grandmother. She asked a question; he supplied an answer. He doesn't mind what she thinks of his response. He doesn't mind what anyone thinks. It's not, exactly, that he doesn't care, it's that he hasn't got the capacity to consider the issue. The inability to think about the feelings of others has a positive side—George and Sam can never exploit or deceive. Soon after George was diagnosed, I described his condition to a friend. "Well," he said, "at least he won't be a nasty child. It would be

worse to be the parent of a bully, wouldn't it?" I think he was
probably right.

It takes a while to understand just how deep that innocence is,
to accept that autists don't mean anything personally. In *My Family and Autism,* the BBC documentary about the Jackson family,
Luke Jackson's nonautistic sisters try to explain to him why a
question like "Does my bum look big in this?" should not be an-
swered truthfully, or at least that the truth should be softened.
Luke, articulate speaker at conferences and author of two published books before the age of fourteen, just doesn't get it. He's
literal-minded; surely you should just tell the truth? It's unnerving
when an intelligent, verbally able person makes a personal remark
unmodified by social awareness. This hasn't yet arisen as a major
problem with George and Sam because they don't often make any
kind of comment about people. But George often tells visitors,
"Time for you to go now." I would never be able to persuade him
that this is rude. For him, it's just a statement of fact. Sam's equivalent is a simple "Go a-way."

The people who get on best with autists are those who can
put their own ego to one side. Once you get used to it, and
stop worrying about what the autist thinks of you (which is probably hardly anything at all), it's actually quite relaxing to be
around people who ask so little socially, whatever they demand of
you physically. I'm writing this in the garden. George is by my
side. He's completely happy with the September sunshine on his
back and an empty Minstrels packet to flap. He doesn't require
that I chat. Every now and then he makes a statement, which he
wants me to corroborate or refute: "Wolves are usually black";
"Helicopters have fires inside them"; "There's nothing in the
oven"—that kind of thing. As long as I supply the right answer,
I can go on writing. I couldn't possibly do this if Jake was around,

with his unquenchable thirst for interaction, but Jake has gone into Hastings with Ian to buy his first-ever pair of shin pads. Sam's safely in therapy. Sam demands no more than George in terms of conversational effort, but a great deal more in terms of supervision.

The Curious Incident of the Dog in the Night-Time, by Mark Haddon, is a novel about a fifteen-year-old called Christopher who has Asperger's syndrome. There's a scene when Christopher's father has to break bad news to him:

> Father said, "I'm afraid you won't be seeing your mother for a while."
>
> He didn't look at me when he said this. He kept on looking through the window . . . this was nice, having Father speak to me but not look at me.

This is the classic autistic reaction. What's important to Christopher is not the mood or the content of his father's doom-laden pronouncement, but the fact that, for once, he's not being looked at. Christopher doesn't immediately, intuitively ask himself why his father's looking out of the window, but no neurotypical person would be able to suppress such a question. The scene struck a chord with me. Both boys, but most particularly George, are far more comfortable with oblique contact. They're like wild deer in the way they cautiously approach, make contact, dart away again. And this can be more restful than the constant invasive chatter of normal children.

Many of the most aggravating habits of normal children are refreshingly absent. The boys have plenty of aggravating habits of their own, of course, but they don't whine, compete, squabble, or blame other people for their own shortcomings. They don't exaggerate minor injuries or try to get someone else into trouble. From George and Sam I never hear those tiresome phrases like "It's not fair" or "He started it" or "It wasn't me" or "Are we nearly there?" (which Jake's asking before we've pulled out of the drive). They may get cross with me when I thwart their desires, but they never criticize me, or anyone else. They never clamor for expensive treats or insist upon their rights; they are unmoved by crazes and playground fashions. They haven't the least notion of "cool." They are immune to peer pressure. They are always completely themselves.

And besides, they're very beautiful. There's an autistic "look," which Asperger noted in his original papers. "Elfin," "ethereal," and "dreamy" are the adjectives that come up most often. There are many exceptions to the rule, and some autistic children can be very plain indeed, but often they are outstandingly good-looking— much better-looking than one would expect from observing their parents. They have symmetrical faces, with dainty, regular features and large, bright eyes. They often look younger than they are; perhaps their faces, never distorted by the base emotions such as selfishness, malice, and guile, retain that unclouded purity that is so attractive in babies. I've yet to come across a scientific explanation for the look, but it seems to me to be just as likely a part of the syndrome as an excellent rote memory or advanced spatial abilities.

Sam is a handsome, well-knit boy, with glossy dark hair, an elegant neck, and a rather haughty expression, almost like an Indian brave. His ceaseless motion keeps his muscles toned; his lack of self-awareness gives his movements an unconscious grace. George is a high-cheekboned beauty, with luminous eyes, like a supermodel on drugs. The boys have no opinions about their looks, which only enhances the effect. I have never seen Sam look in a mirror. George sometimes does, but only to pull faces. When they show preferences for certain clothes, they're guided by comfort or color, or by some weird criteria of their own. I don't think they ever dress to improve their appearance, or to impress anybody else. The only awareness either of them has ever expressed to me is when George asks me to cut his hair "like a mushroom," in other words, with a straight pudding-bowl fringe. Similarly, I've never noticed the boys judging anyone else according to how they look, with the exception of George's taste for little girls with long blond hair, and his dislike of men with big black beards.

Whether we admit it or not, we are hugely affected by physical appearances. Despite plenty of evidence to the contrary, we associate good looks with intelligence. At one end of the scale, people with cerebral palsy, whose condition has affected their control of their facial muscles, have a hard job convincing the able-bodied that they are of normal intelligence. At the other extreme, beautiful, serene, autistic faces, with "speaking eyes," give an unshakable impression of hidden ability, of a normal child locked up. Autistic beauty augments the fairy-tale feeling that the child is in suspended animation, enclosed just out of reach in glass or ice, or that the child is a changeling, a being from another world somehow left in our charge.

The beauty of autistic children does them a service and a disservice. It's good, because people are attracted to them; they want to work with such a lovely child—they want to help. But it's bad, because people find it hard to believe that their handicap is as profound as it really is. Many parents find it stressful to go about in public with their good-looking, anarchic child. One glance at a Down's child and people know they may have to make certain allowances. One glance at an autistic child will not explain nearly so much. I carry a printed card in my wallet that reads, "This young person has autism," followed by a brief explanation. The idea is that you present this card to soothe an irate shopkeeper or café owner, but I must admit I've never yet had the presence of mind to do so.

It's hard to observe a handsome, physically fit child behaving strangely without feeling that they're "putting it on," that the child could control himself if he really wanted to. No one looks at a child in a wheelchair and thinks, "Oh, for goodness' sake, of course you can walk! Why don't you just pull yourself together?" No one looks at a child in a wheelchair and blames his parents for his immobility: "Why on earth haven't you taught him to walk yet?" But people do look at autistic children charging through crowds or throwing food about or (George's specialty) taking things out of litter bins, and they think—or sometimes say—"Why don't you keep your children under control?" George and I had to queue in the building society, not so long ago, and George was in a panic. "Don't touch me! Don't speak to me! Don't look at me!" he shrieked. A whiskery old lady in a head scarf bravely approached him—she was considerably shorter than he was—and admonished him. "Young man! Don't be so darned rude to your mother." George opened his mouth as wide as it would go and screamed in her face. I did my best to explain, but she wasn't having any truck with this autism malarkey. Nothing would dissuade her from the belief that what was needed was a jolly good hiding. Most people find it hard to grasp that it's just as impossible for an autist to "behave" in public as it is for a child with paralyzed legs to get up and walk. Autistic good looks distract from the severity of the condition. I know a mother who took her little boy to hospital for his diagnosis and was told, "He's beautiful. What are you worrying about?"

I suppose some people find it sad that a child with a perfect face is not "normal." I don't; for me, their angelic faces perfectly express their innocence and strange integrity. I find the boys' looks a huge compensation and solace. I never tire of gazing at them.

Though, of course, as their mother I would find them exquisite even if they looked like gargoyles, I'm always pleased when other people comment favorably on their appearance, as they very often do. It's something positive that can always be said because it's always true. Their behavior often leaves much to be desired; their appearance never does. And I can be as vain as I like on their behalf because there's no danger of swelling their heads. Vanity and autism are mutually exclusive.

The boys are disconcerting, messy, destructive, asocial, and unpredictable, unless you know them well. They are also non-malevolent, unworldly, handsome, and intriguing. Autism is a fascinating subject. Books or programs about savants with extraordinary "islands of ability" always attract public attention. My sons are very far from being savants, but still, it's interesting—if frustrating—to try and work out the reasons behind their oddities. Why does Sam take the stairs in a series of jumps, both feet together? Why, when George fell into a river, did he lie on his back, supported by his billowing anorak, and say, "That's our stew and dumplings gone west"? Jessy Park used to fill her glass with juice to a level determined by that day's weather and phase of the moon. Luke Jackson had to carry a Lilliput Lane ceramic house, a carriage clock, a soup ladle, and a "circle yellow pacifier." Donna Williams could hear a snake slither past the house when she was indoors. If you have to have a child with a disability, at least autism's an interesting one. On good days—on *very* good days—autism is its own compensation.

NINETEEN

What Next?

This book is about autistic childhood. George and Sam are both emphatically still children; George has some physical signs of puberty, but emotionally and socially the changes have not yet been dramatic. His quasi anorexia is connected with a fear of growing up, but this was bound in with anxieties about changing schools; now that he has settled happily into his new school, his eating is improving, thank goodness. His refusal of food wasn't connected with worries about body image in the normal sense. He is, perhaps, a little more rebellious than he once was, but his assertion of independence extends no further than an insistence on misaligning his shirt buttons and having double knots in his shoelaces. There's very little sexual awareness, and no more romantic interest than there's ever been—rather less, indeed, because when he was six or seven he used to single out certain little girls for special attention, and he doesn't do this now. He shows no desire for an independent social life. He doesn't want a mobile phone, a skateboard, designer clothes—he doesn't know that other people his age do want such things. I imagine that Sam, who is even less socially aware than George, will show still fewer of the expected characteristics of adolescence.

So, I can't attempt to deal with the autistic experience in adolescence or adulthood within the scope of this book. Change of some kind must surely be in store for my sons, but I can't predict the form it will take. Asking the parents of older autists doesn't clarify the picture, because experiences vary so widely. Some autists, usually the more able, are tormented by the longing for a love life and a group of friends without knowing how to achieve these. In others, such desires seem absent. Saskia Baron, director of *The Autism Puzzle,* says that her brother, Timothy, now forty-seven, has never shown any interest in making sexual contact with anybody at all. "We've been lucky, really, in that respect. If anything, Timothy seemed to find life easier as he grew older." I don't wish to imply that no one on the autistic spectrum can form a mutually satisfactory relationship with another person; it does happen. But autistic sexuality is an underresearched subject, and one that I don't feel qualified to say very much about.

Several older parents have explained that there is no cutoff point in the autist's ability to learn. Childhood goes on longer; great strides in understanding can be made into middle age and beyond. This is cheering news for me. I'm convinced that early diagnosis is very important, that the sooner you get to work on intervening between the child and the rigidities of autism, the better, but it's comforting to know that if you haven't achieved this, you haven't missed the boat—or rather, you may have missed that boat, but there'll be another one along in a while. Clara Park emphasizes that, while Jessy is still autistic and always will be, she's still developing and refining her social and practical skills in her late forties. The Parks are now confident that after their deaths Jessy will be able to live independently—an outcome that must have seemed highly improbable during her mute, unreachable childhood.

I can't imagine an independent existence for George and Sam. This doesn't mean it won't happen; it means exactly what it says—that I am not able to imagine it. I also feel that there's little point in trying to imagine it. Autism follows an unpredictable trajectory. The question I'm most often asked is "What will happen to the boys in the future?," and the only truthful answer is "I don't know." Looking after Sam, in particular, reminds me of one of the creatures in Dr. Seuss's *One Fish, Two Fish, Red Fish, Blue Fish*. The Seuss children are carrying a large, tusked, whiskery creature in a glass jar. They say,

> *Look what we found in the park*
> *In the dark.*
> *We will take him home.*
> *We will call him Clark.*
> *He will live at our house.*
> *He will grow and grow.*
> *Will our mother like this?*
> *We don't know.*

Clark's expression is ambiguous, neither fierce nor wholly benign, just "other." As he grows, will he burst out of his jar, or will the jar grow with him? All I know is, I've got the boys for keeps. The best I can do is watch them, and try to understand their needs. The chances are that the boys will outlive me. I sincerely hope they do. The life expectancy of autists is no different from that of anybody else. The only health problem that seems specific to autism is epilepsy, which sometimes develops in adolescence.

There are other conditions where the sufferers display autistic-like symptoms, such as fragile X and syndrome tuberous sclerosis, but these come under a separate heading from the autism that my boys have. Epilepsy aside, autists have no reason not to be as healthy as the next person. Indeed, their asocial nature makes them less likely to smoke, drink, or take drugs, so they may even be healthier. Therefore, I have to accept that I cannot be my sons' main carer forever. Nor can I lay that burden directly on any other person, most especially not on Jake. Naturally, I hope that Jake will always care about his brothers, that he'll always have their best interests at heart. I hope he'll never lose touch with them. But when I made the decision to have another child, I also decided that it would be unfair to bring that child up as carer-in-waiting for his brothers.

Researching possible residential placements would be a waste of energy right now. I believe that the setup here is about as "appropriate" as I can make it. They go to a good, specialist school; they're taken there in a taxi with a caring, competent escort; they come home, have a break, and then have two hours of Verbal Behavior therapy from tutors who know them well. Sometimes, the tutors take them on specially orchestrated trips into the community. The rest of the time they are looked after by me, helped by Ian, their nanny, of whom they are very fond. In addition, Granny Eva stays here a couple of nights a week, and they are in frequent contact with other family members and friends. Their father spends time with them on weekends. They have a large garden and adjoining fields and woods in which to roam; they have as much freedom as is compatible with the hazards caused by their condition. Problems arise every single day, some big, some small, but each one has to be tackled as it arises—the problems can't be foreseen. The boys' therapy has brought their behavior under control, and as long as they're manageable, I want to manage them. All this may change. There have been dramatic, unexpected changes in the past, both for better and for worse. To make coherent plans for their future is impossible. The boys exist in the here and now; in relation to them, so do I.

Maintaining this status quo requires money. The school and the taxi are free; the nanny and the tutors are not. The need to generate considerable amounts of money is the biggest challenge I face. But more even than money, our setup depends on goodwill and interest. My children are supported by a raft made of man- and womanpower, both paid and unpaid. A common complaint among "autistic" parents is that their friends fall away, that their child's behavior makes it impossible to maintain any kind of social life. This saddens me, because I can't see that it needs to happen. Other people are our lifeline. George and Sam can't make friends in the conventional way, so I have to forge social links for them. I'm lucky in that my family and friends are broad-minded and flexible enough to accommodate the boys in one way or another.

What kind of help and support can you give, if a friend of yours has an autistic child? I hope I'm not stating the obvious by saying that you should offer only what you know you can deliver. Don't imagine that you can transform or cure the child, that you'll be the one to unlock the prison of autism and release the beautiful soul within. You won't be. Think small. Try to imagine what daily life is like for your friend. Is it difficult for her to get to the supermarket, especially over the school holidays? ("Especially over the school holidays" is a rider that applies to all possible situations.) Does her child suffer from sensory overload in Sainsbury's? Are the bright lights, the queues, the glittering aisles, likely to tip him over into a screaming fit? If so, can you look after him at home while your friend shops, or do her shopping for her? What if he enjoys shopping (mine do, at the moment) but is too big to be wedged into the trolley and is therefore likely to wander? Could you accompany them, as an extra pair of hands?

If you feel you know the child well, and are confident about controlling him, you could offer to take him to the zoo, the park, the swimming pool, or whatever. This would give his mother and any neurotypical siblings a welcome respite from his company. Not everyone feels they can cope to this extent—well, perhaps you could do it the other way around, and take the neurotypicals off her hands? I find it much easier to pay proper attention to George and Sam if Jake's away playing with a friend. Or could you go with the mother on a family outing? There aren't many public places where I can safely manage all three boys single-handed, but with another adult I can go almost anywhere. It's very hard for us "autistic" parents to find babysitters. Often, the two parents take it in turns, which isn't great for married social life. Now that I've got Ian I've got oodles of wonderful babysitting, but lots of people haven't any. We can't just call in a local teenager to sit and do her homework while our little angels slumber peacefully aloft. It just isn't like that. Our babysitters need to be resourceful, alert, and experienced; anything less isn't safe. Could you babysit occasionally, perhaps in tandem with another friend? It's so important for us to be able to get out.

It's difficult to offer direct financial assistance, but it may be that your friend's quality of life would be improved by something she can't afford—a trampoline, say, or a swing. Could several of you club together and offer such a thing as a present? Be bold; don't wait to be asked, because you won't be. Your friend is proud, and is unlikely to ask for help, especially since she feels she can't repay it in kind.

Inviting an "autistic family" into your house is an act of true friendship. I appreciate enormously the friends who have Sam-proofed their houses before our arrival, hiding medicines and banned substances, checking that doors and windows are locked.

Brace yourself for a bit of chaos and damage, and you may be pleasantly surprised—some visits pass off without incident. If, on the other hand, you simply can't face the possibility of having all your daffodil heads snapped off or finding a large turd on the lawn ("It wasn't me! It was a hen!" said George, and I was glad that he was capable of telling a lie), then visit your friend at home instead. Break down the isolation that autism can impose. Keep in touch.

Above all, appreciate her child. Mothers may moan about their own children, but they very rarely want to hear other people criticize them. Some people take the you-poor-thing-it-must-be-so-hard-for-you approach, and while I appreciate their concern, I respond much more favorably to those people who take an interest in George and Sam, who praise them, find them funny, interesting, and beautiful, as I do. Awareness of autism has increased exponentially over the last few years. The word has become so well known that it is going the way of "spastic," and becoming a term of abuse, or a label sloppily applied to anyone who is a little quirky or socially incompetent. I heard Will Self on television describe the queen as "an autistic mother." Will Self is a clever man, and words are his business; he should know better. Autism does not equal "cold and aloof," which is what he meant.

So, soon we'll have to find a new word. That won't be entirely bad; "autism" comes from the Greek word for "the self," and for autists the concept of the self is complex, as I hope this book's made clear. But whatever term we use, the condition won't go away. These mysterious, impossible, enchanting beings will always be among us, unwitting yardsticks for our own moral behavior, uncomprehending challengers of our definition of what it means to be human. The onus is on us to create a place for them in our world, a comfortable place where they are free to be whatever it is they are. Jake, in a maudlin mood after listening to Don McLean's "American Pie" ("this'll be the day that I die"), gave way to tears over the inevitability of death. He only began to cheer up when he remembered that somebody had told him about the theory of reincarnation. "Mum," he gasped, his sobs receding, "please tell God, that when I come back in my next life, I want exactly the same brothers I've got now." I hope he always feels like that.

Reading List

There are many excellent books about autism. This is a personal list; it is not meant to be exhaustive.

Tony Attwood. *Asperger Syndrome: A Guide for Parents and Professionals*. Jessica Kingsley, 1996.

Simon Baron-Cohen. *The Essential Difference*. Allen Lane, 2003. Fascinating theory of autism as the result of the "extreme male brain."

Jill Dawson. *Wild Boy*. Sceptre, 2003. Fictionalized account of the Wild Boy of Aveyron, possibly the earliest fully documented autistic child.

Uta Frith. *Autism: Explaining the Enigma*. 2d. ed. Blackwell, 2003. My favorite among the "textbooks." Recently revised and updated.

Temple Grandin. *Thinking in Pictures*. Vintage, 1996.

Temple Grandin and Margaret M. Scariano. *Emergence: Labeled Autistic*. Warner Books, 1996. Grandin, a high-functioning autistic woman, describes her experiences and mental processes with clarity and insight.

Mark Haddon. *The Curious Incident of the Dog in the Night-Time*. Jonathan Cape,

2003. A novel, told from the point of view of an Asperger's teenager. It deserves the hype.

Robert Hughes. *Running with Walker.* Jessica Kingsley, 2003. Life with an autistic son.

Jacqui Jackson. *Multicoloured Mayhem.* Jessica Kingsley, 2003. Life in a family of seven children, of whom four are on the autistic spectrum. The Jacksons were the subject of a recent TV documentary, *My Family and Autism.*

Luke Jackson. *Freaks, Geeks and Asperger Syndrome: A User's Guide to Adolescence.* Jessica Kingsley, 2002. An insider's account; clear, hard-hitting, and informative.

————. *A User Guide to the GF/CF Diet for Autism, Asperger Syndrome and AD/HD.* Jessica Kingsley, 2003.

Marilyn Le Breton. *Diet Intervention and Autism.* Jessica Kingsley, 2001. Useful recipes, tips, and addresses, all based on firsthand experience.

Clara Claiborne Park. *The Siege.* Little, Brown, 1982. A mother's story about bringing up her autistic daughter, Jessy, in 1960s America—the era of "the refrigerator mother."

————. *Exiting Nirvana.* Aurum Press, 2001. Takes up where *The Siege* leaves off. Highly recommended.

Oliver Sacks. *An Anthropologist on Mars.* Picador, 1996. Case histories of neurological disorders of many kinds, including autism. Sacks's writing is intelligent and humane.

Clare Sainsbury. *Martian in the Playground.* Lucky Duck Publishing, 2000. What it's like to be an Asperger's child in a mainstream school.

Donna Williams. *Nobody Nowhere.* Random House, 1992.

————. *Somebody, Somewhere.* Corgi, 1995. Williams's are probably the best-known autobiographical accounts.

Lorna Wing. *The Autistic Spectrum.* Constable, 2003. A handbook for parents and professionals.

Directory of Useful Addresses

National Autistic Society
The National Autistic Society
393 City Road, London EC1V 1NG
Phone: 020 7833 2299
Fax: 020 7833 9666
E-mail: nas@nas.org.uk
www.nas.org.uk

Applied Behavioral Analysis

PEACH
Parents for the Early Intervention of Autism in Children
The Brackens, London Road, Ascot, Berkshire SL5 8BE
Phone: 01344 882248
Fax: 01344 882391
E-mail: info@peach.org.uk
www.peach.org.uk/Home

The Lovaas Institute for Early Intervention
LIFE Administrative Headquarters
Lovaas Institute for Early Intervention
11500 West Olympic Boulevard, Suite 460

Los Angeles, CA 90064
Phone: 310-914-5433
Fax: 001 310-914-5463
E-mail: info@lovaas.com
www.lovaas.com

U.K. Young Autism Project
11a Marjorie Grove
Battersea
London SW11 5SH
Phone: 020-7652-7427
E-mail: diane.hayward@ukyap.org
www.ukyap.org

Auditory Integration Therapy
The Counseling Center
AIT Division
7 Tokeneke Road
Darien, CT 06820
Phone: 203-655-1091
Fax: 203-655-9175
E-mail: aithelps@aol.com
www.auditoryintegration.net

Dietary Intervention
www.autismmedical.com

Autism Network International (ANI)
www.ani.autistics.org

Autism Research Institute (ARI)
4182 Adams Avenue
San Diego, CA 92116
Phone: 619-281-7165
Fax: 619-563-6840
www.autismresearchinstitute.com

Autism Society of America (ASA)
7910 Woodmont Avenue, Suite 300

Bethesda, MD 20814-3067
Phone: 301-657-0881 or 800-3AUTISM (800-328-8476)
www.autism-society.org

Center for the Study of Autism (CSA)
P.O. Box 4538
Salem, OR 97302
www.autism.org

Cure Autism Now Foundation (CAN)
5455 Wilshire Boulevard, Suite 715
Los Angeles, CA
Phone: 323-549-0500 or 888-8AUTISM (888-828-8476)
Fax: 323-549-0547
www.canfoundation.org

Families for Early Autism Treatment (FEAT)
P.O. Box 255722
Sacramento, CA 95865-5722
Phone: 916-843-1536
www.feat.org

National Alliance for Autism Research (NAAR)
99 Wall Street, Research Park
Princeton, NJ 08540
Phone: 888-777-NAAR (888-777-6227)
Fax: 609-430-9163
www.naar.org

National Autism Organization (NAA)
P.O. Box 1547
Marion, SC 29571
Phone: 877-622-2884
www.nationalautismassociation.org

O.A.S.I.S. (Online Asperger Syndrome Information and Support)
www.udel.edu/bkirby/asperger

Organization for Autism Research (OAR)
2111 Wilson Boulevard, Suite 600
Arlington, VA 22201
Phone: 703-351-5031
www.researchautism.org

Safe Minds
www.safeminds.org

Schafer Autism Report
9629 Old Placerville Road
Sacramento, CA 95827
E-mail: schafer@sprynet.com
www.sarnet.org

Talk About Curing Autism (TACA)
www.tacanow.com

University Students with Autism and Asperger's Syndrome
www.users.dircon.co.uk/~cns

World Autism Organization (WAO)
www.worldautism.org